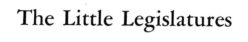

The Little Legislatures

The Little

Legislatures

COMMITTEES OF CONGRESS

GEORGE GOODWIN, JR.

THE UNIVERSITY OF MASSACHUSETTS PRESS 1970

Copyright © 1970 by the
University of Massachusetts Press
All rights reserved
Library of Congress Catalog Card Number 75-103477
Printed in the United States of America

For Ellen

Contents

Preface

THOUGH AMERICA is young, its democratic institutions of government have by now reached maturity. What more proof is needed than the fact that a foreigner seeking knowledge of these institutions would start by reading a constitution written in 1787? The authors of the Constitution created a complex system, parceling out some power to the national government where it was to be shared among legislative, executive, and judicial branches, while reserving some for the states. Relationships among the various units of government have changed throughout the years, but all have continued powerful and important. The national legislative branch has remained remarkably virile even in the middle of the twentieth century, a period that has not been kind to representative bodies. For all its faults, alleged and actual, the committee system has played a crucial role in the maintenance of the power of Congress.

Testimony as to the importance of committees is not lacking in the literature on American government. Woodrow Wilson wrote in 1885 that "Congressional government is Committee government." Not long afterwards Speaker Thomas B. Reed commented, "The Committee is the eye, the ear, the hand and very often the brains of the assembly." More recently, Senator Russell B. Long said, "Our whole parliamentary system is built on the investigations conducted by committees."[1]

1. Woodrow Wilson, *Congressional Government*, Meridian Paperback Edition (New York: Meridian Books, 1956), p. 102; Reed's statement cited in

The tremendous importance of committee work is clear. Virtually all legislation is referred to committee, with only a small fraction ever emerging from those "dim dungeons of silence," as Woodrow Wilson categorized them. Those bills that do emerge have been permanently shaped in committee, and the committee's will carries great weight in the floor struggle, in the eventual conference committee reconciliation between the two houses of Congress, and in the execution of the measure by the administration.

In spite of general recognition of the importance of the committeees of Congress, they have until recently received relatively little academic attention, much less than the administrative agencies of the executive branch. The present study, by concentrating on committees, allows a more thorough picture of this important aspect of Congress. It draws attention to the immense diversity found among these very human institutions. It tests the generalizations that have been made concerning the committee system, many of which, like Wilson's, have been highly critical of the institution. And it gives further insights into the viability of representative government in the middle of the twentieth century.

Students of Congress have widely differing views of what they want their national legislature to be. Since both their descriptions and prescriptions are shaped by these views, it seems advisable at the start of a study such as this, to be as explicit as possible concerning one's outlook. I find it useful to think in terms of four alternate models of how Congress might be organized, both internally and in its relations with the president. John Saloma, to whom I am indebted for the formulation, called these models presidential-responsible party, presidential-pluralist, constitutional balance, and congressional supremacy (see table 1).[2]

Clarence Cannon, *Procedure in the House of Representatives* (Washington, D.C.: Government Printing Office, 1959), p. 83; Long's statement in *Congressional Record*, 80th Cong., 1st sess., 1947, p. 5222.

2. John S. Saloma III, *Congress and the New Politics* (Boston: Little, Brown & Co., 1969), chap. 2. He develops four models of legislative-executive relations and four models of internal congressional organization, whereas I am handling congressional organization as part of each legislative-executive re-

TABLE I
Four Models of Congressional Organization in Summary Form

Model	Legislative-Executive Relations	Role of Political Party	Internal Organization of Congress
Presidential-responsible party	President dominates	Strong national party links president and Congress	Leadership from president-dominated national party
Presidential-pluralist	President can be strongest of parties-in-interest	One of many parties-in-interest	Both party and committee leaders play important roles
Constitutional balance	Branches coequal	Weak, since emphasis is on congressional majorities	Committee important in refining policies for decision by congressional majorities
Congressional supremacy	Congress dominates	Strong, but independent of president	Committee leaders subordinate to party leaders

According to the presidential-responsible party model, two national programmatic parties present clear alternatives to the voters. A majority electoral decision establishes the outline of national policy for the ensuing four years. The president and Congress work within that mandate, linked together by a strong party. Under such an alternative, committee leaders are responsive to party leaders, who are in turn responsive to the president and to whatever national party organization is established to interpret the will of the country between elections.

According to the presidential-pluralist model, public policy is the outcome of the bargaining that goes on among the many private and political groups. Both the president and Congress play important roles in the group arena, though the president can play a dominant role when he has the skill and the desire, because of his

---

lations model. He notes his indebtedness, as do I, to Roger H. Davidson, David M. Kovenock, and Michael K. O'Leary, *Congress in Crisis: Politics and Congressional Reform* (Belmont, Calif.: Wadsworth Publishing Co., 1966), pp. 15–37.

position and the fact that Congress is decentralized. Under such an alternative, party lines are not sharply drawn, and neither the parliamentary nor the national parties are particularly effective. Committees maintain a large measure of independence and play a role in the bargaining process at least as important as that of the interest groups involved.

According to the constitutional balance model, Congress maintains itself as a coequal of the president. It has the organization and procedures to enable bipartisan majorities to make decisions after careful analysis and rational debate. Under such an alternative, committees play an important role as rational decision-makers under the watchful eye of the full house.

Finally, according to the congressional supremacy model, Congress dominates the executive in the field of lawmaking. Internally, it is organized by strong party leaders who operate independently of the national parties. Under such a system, committee leaders are powerful, but they are closely tied in with the congressional party leaders.

The four models are arranged in a spectrum that moves from one in which the president dominates as he operates through a strong national party to one in which the Congress dominates as it operates through a strong parliamentary party. I believe that the two models that fall between these two extremes—the presidential-pluralist and the constitutional balance—are the most useful. Congress as we know it today comes closest to the presidential-pluralist model, though it has many of the attributes of the constitutional balance model as well. An assessment of the difficulties of drastic change in the American constitutional and political system leads me to favor reforms that would move Congress further in the direction of the constitutional balance model.

The opening chapters of the book are introductory. The first chapter deals with the development of the committee system, from the early days of ad hoc committees under strict congressional control to modern independent standing committees. Chapter 2 concentrates on the postwar period. It starts by discussing the eleven Congresses with which this book is primarily concerned, then it discusses congressional attempts at reform that opened and closed the period.

These are followed by a series of chapters that are primarily concerned with the organization and make-up of committees. Chapter 3, on committee organization, looks first at rivalries among committees, then at formal subdivisions within committees. Chapters 4 and 5 are concerned with the "giant jigsaw puzzle" of making committee assignments, first for the House, then for the Senate. Chapter 6 is concerned with the differences among standing committees as they have been developed by rule, custom, the decisions of congressional leaders, and the preferences of individual legislators. Chapter 7 stresses the fact that committees are made up of people—senior and junior members, and staff.

The next group of chapters is concerned with the part committees play in the legislative process. Chapter 8 discusses the procedures under which committees operate, and then the work of committees in the preparation of legislative proposals during public hearings and executive sessions. Chapters 9 and 10 are concerned with relationships between committees and the floor, first for the House and then for the Senate. This is largely a study of the relations between seniority leaders and party leaders. Chapter 11 discusses the work of committees after legislative proposals reach the floor: in managing floor action, in conference, and in supervision of the execution of legislative policy.

The concluding chapter assesses the committee system and the possibilities for reform.

Table 2 lists the standing committees of Congress, the main concern of this book, as they existed at the end of the eleven postwar Congresses that make up the time span on which this study concentrates.

One of the problems of writing on committees is the sheer volume of research material—millions of pages of congressional hearings, thousands of pages of committee reports, hundreds of volumes of the *Congressional Record*—all increasing at a rate that

TABLE 2
Committees at the Close of the 90th Congress

HOUSE COMMITTEES	SENATE COMMITTEES
Agriculture	Aeronautical & Space Sciences
Appropriations	Agriculture & Forestry
Armed Services	Appropriations
Banking & Currency	Armed Services
District of Columbia	Banking & Currency
Education & Labor	Commerce
Foreign Affairs	District of Columbia
Government Operations	Finance
House Administration	Foreign Relations
Interior & Insular Affairs	Government Operations
Interstate & Foreign Commerce	Interior & Insular Affairs
Judiciary	Judiciary
Merchant Marine & Fisheries	Labor & Public Welfare
Post Office & Civil Service	Post Office & Civil Service
Public Works	Public Works
Rules	Rules & Administration
Science & Astronautics	
Standards of Official Conduct	* The name of this committee was
Un-American Activities*	changed to Internal Security in
Veterans' Affairs	1968.
Ways and Means	

leaves the researcher breathless. These written sources can provide answers to many questions but they leave some of the more
important ones tantalizingly unanswered. Some, such as how committee members reach their decisions in executive session, cannot
be answered, in detail at least, for congressmen insist that there
must be times when they can speak without the public listening.
Yet extended observation of committee people and committee activities is absolutely necessary in a study such as this.

During my visits to Washington while working on this book,
I attended hearings of nearly every committee, and I talked with
members of each committee and of each committee staff. I never
cease to be surprised and grateful for the amount of time and very
real assistance offered me by almost all of these people. Many commented that committees had been too much neglected in the litera-

ture on Congress, and that when committees had been discussed at all, it was by "ivory tower people" who were not sure enough of the facts of committee life, or by "plumbers" so interested in details that they never got beyond them. I wish that more were written about committees by insiders; yet congressmen and staff people lack the time to do this. (Some committee regulations specifically prohibit staff members from writing about their committee experiences.) Lacking such commentaries, this outsider has had the temerity to tackle the subject, knowing that it will satisfy no one familiar with Congress, but hoping that its approach falls somewhere between that of the plumber and the resident of the ivory tower.

The Eagleton Institute at Rutgers University generously made it possible for me to take a semester's leave of absence to work on the book. Both the University of Massachusetts and the University of Rhode Island have given invaluable help in financing the costs of the research. And the Jones Library in Amherst provided a necessary ingredient, a quiet place to work.

I have tried to mention in the footnotes the many people, both congressional and academic, who helped me. If I single out only three here—Earle C. Clements, former Senate whip; Richard Fenno Jr. of the University of Rochester; and the late George B. Galloway of the Legislative Reference Service—it is because they gave generously of their time on many different occasions. My students have been of great assistance. Those who best combined imagination and a willingness to do hard, careful research were Ernest Chaples Jr., William J. Crotty Jr., Stuart MacKown, Wayne Swanson, and Harold Sullivan. Skillful editorial assistance was supplied by my sister, Mary Goodwin. And my wife, Ellen Safford Goodwin, has provided a magic combination of constructive criticism and encouragement.

Mrs. Charles Hoffman, Mrs. Andrea Bassignani, Mrs. Joyce Emerle, and Miss Judi O'Donnell deserve great credit for their skillful typing.

I
Introduction

1.

The Life & Death of
Standing Committees

EACH HOUSE of Congress is in a position to determine its own rules, and as one house often finds itself reading public opinion in a different manner than the other, it is not surprising that each should show marked differences in organization. In spite of this, they show some striking similarities. A chronological listing of the dates of creation of the present committees of Congress, as given in table 1:1, makes this clear. It is evident that external factors create considerable uniformity.

Our national expansion, the world situation, and the development of our economy and our technology have each been reflected in the growth of committees. Congress reacted to scientific advance, for example, by creating space committees in 1958, just as it reacted to the Industrial Revolution by forming labor committees shortly after the Civil War.

The committee system also reflects the organization of the executive branch. The two houses have tended to create committees that parallel the administrative agencies in jurisdiction—foreign affairs committees to oversee the work of the State Department and judiciary committees to oversee the work of the Department of Justice, for example.[1] The correlation is not so clear in all cases, however. The lines of supervision of the admin-

1. Though the judiciary committees are concerned with crimes and criminal procedure, and it would seem that criminal legislation controlling narcotics would fall within their jurisdiction, it is referred to the Finance Committee in the Senate and Ways and Means in the House, for these committees have jurisdiction over the Treasury Department, the agency that handles narcotics control.

TABLE I:I

*Dates of Creation of Present Standing Committees**

HOUSE	SENATE
1789 Enrolled Bills (House Administration)	1789 Enrolled Bills (Rules & Administration)
1795 Commerce & Manufacturers (Interstate & Foreign Commerce)	
1795 Ways & Means	
1805 Public Lands (Interior & Insular Affairs)	
1808 Post Office & Post Roads (Post Office & Civil Service)	
1808 District of Columbia	
1813 Judiciary	
1813 Pensions & Revolutionary Claims (Veterans' Affairs)	
1816 Expenditures in Executive Departments (Government Operations)	1816 Commerce & Manufactures (Commerce)
	1816 District of Columbia
	1816 Finance
	1816 Foreign Relations
	1816 Judiciary
	1816 Military Affairs (Armed Services)
	1816 Naval Affairs (Armed Services)
	1816 Post Office & Post Roads (Post Office & Civil Service)
	1816 Public Lands & Survey (Interior & Insular Affairs)
1820 Agriculture	
1822 Foreign Affairs	
1822 Military Affairs (Armed Services)	
1822 Naval Affairs (Armed Services)	
	1825 Agriculture (Agriculture & Forestry)
1837 Public Buildings & Gnds. (Public Works)	1837 Public Buildings and Grounds (Public Works)

1865 Appropriations
1865 Banking & Currency
1867 Education & Labor

1880 Rules
1887 Merchant Marine & Fisheries

1945 Un-American Activities
1958 Science & Astronautics
1967 Standards of Official Conduct

1842 Expenditures in Executive Departments (Government Operations)

1867 Appropriations
1869 Education & Labor
(Labor & Public Welfare)

1913 Banking & Currency

1958 Aeronautical & Space Sciences

* Only committees in existence today are listed. Where committees have been consolidated, the date cited is that of the component committee that was established first. Names in parentheses are of present committees where they differ from the original name.

istrative agencies concerned with promotion and regulation of business are somewhat confused. Further, committee organization has not been changed to centralize the supervision of the new departments: Health, Education, and Welfare (1953), Housing and Urban Development (1966), and Transportation (1966).

In each case, the organization of the other house of Congress has also had its effect on committee structure, never more deliberately so than with the 1946 reorganization. Eight committees now have identical jurisdiction (these are committees on Agriculture, Appropriations, Banking, the District of Columbia, Government Operations, Interior, Post Office, and Public Works), and four have nearly identical jurisdiction (committees on Armed Services, Foreign Affairs, House Administration, and Judiciary). The greatest departures from parallel organization are in areas of social welfare and economic activities. Health matters, for example, come under the jurisdiction of the Labor and the Public Welfare Committee in the Senate and the Commerce Committee in the House. That the House has more committees than the Senate and that some are oriented toward clearly defined clienteles are complicating factors. (Evidently, members of the House feel that their greater size and their different constituencies justify a greater number of standing committees, though this tendency, if carried to extremes, could seriously reduce the possibility of House-Senate cooperation.) The House, for example, has a Committee on Veterans' Affairs that has disproportionate power because the Senate divides veterans' matters between its Finance and Labor Committees. The House also has a separate Merchant Marine Committee, though these matters are handled by the Commerce Committee in the Senate.

Early Development of Committees

Congress did not at first commit itself to government by standing committees. Federalists looked upon them as dangerous rivals to department heads, and some Republicans believed that the major work of Congress should be performed by the entire membership of each house. Gradually, however, Congress turned its back on a system of automatic reference of legislative proposals to the appropriate executive agencies; it abandoned its early custom of establishing guiding principles in the Committee of the Whole before referring proposals to committees; and it determined to assign most of its legislative work to standing rather than ad hoc committees. Though the following description refers specifically to the House of Representatives, very similar developments took place in the Senate.[2]

Secretary of the Treasury, Alexander Hamilton, nearly succeeded in establishing a system whereby legislative proposals were first referred to an executive agency. Federalists tended to place great "reliance on the information, initiative and planning of the

2. This section draws heavily on Joseph Cooper, "Congress and Its Committees" (Ph.D. diss., Harvard University, 1961), chap. 1. See also Ralph V. Harlow, *The History of Legislative Methods in the Period before 1825* (New Haven: Yale University Press, 1917), chap. 12; Nelson W. Polsby, "The Institutionalization of the U.S. House of Representatives," *American Political Science Review* (March 1968): 144; and Roy Swanstrom, *The United States Senate: 1787–1801*, Senate Document 64, 87th Cong., 1st sess., 1962.

executive."[3] In the 3rd Congress (1793–95), however, they temporarily lost control of the House to the Republicans who favored an independent legislature. In 1794 they succeeded in blocking the reference of a revenue measure to Secretary of the Treasury Hamilton. In the following year, Hamilton resigned and the House established a standing committee on ways and means. These steps put an end to a tendency that could have moved the country in the direction of British cabinet government.

In the early Congresses, both Federalists and Republicans agreed that committees should be controlled by legislative majorities. Thomas Jefferson's *Manual of Parliamentary Practice* states in part:

> Matters of great concernment are usually referred to a Committee of the Whole House, where general principles are digested in the form of resolutions, which are debated and amended until they get into the shape which meets the approbation of a majority. These being reported and confirmed by the House are then referred to one or more select committees. . . .[4]

At various other points in the *Manual*, it is made clear that committees were to follow majority rule, that they were not to change any principles that had been settled previously in the Committee of the Whole, and that no bill was to be reported back save by specific permission of the House.

The Jeffersonian Period (1801–29) saw the committee provisions of the *Manual* become "largely obsolete," according to the House Parliamentarian. Matters came to be referred to committees before the Committee of the Whole had made broad determinations as to principles. Originally just routine matters went directly to committees in order to save the time of the House.

3. Leonard D. White, *The Federalists* (New York: Macmillan Co., 1948), p. 72.
4. Section 12. Vice President Jefferson, as president of the Senate from 1797 to 1801, prepared this manual for his guidance. It may now be found in the *Rules and Manuals of the U.S. House of Representatives*.

Later, more complex bills were referred because a smaller, specialized body was more able to gather and systematize facts. Cooper found that this began to take place as early as 1795. In the first fifty days of the 8th Congress (1803), ten measures were discussed in the Committee of the Whole prior to reference to committee; in the same period in the 20th Congress (1827), none were.[5] Committees were allowed to report bills to Congress without permission as a routine matter as early as the 9th Congress (1805–07).

The early Congresses referred measures to select committees that, by their very nature, were subservient to the Committee of the Whole. No member who had spoken in opposition to a measure on the floor was to be appointed to one of these ad hoc committees, for "the child is not to be put to the nurse that cares not for it."[6]

As a final step toward committee independence, the House largely replaced this system of select committees with one of standing committees. The resulting continuity of membership, it was argued, would lead to more expeditious, wiser, and more uniform committee decisions. Only six standing committees had been created under the Federalists (1789–1801), and all but two of these were for the performance of housekeeping functions. In the Jeffersonian Period, twenty-six committees were created, many of major importance. (Only nine more had been created by the time of the Civil War.) Permanence of committee membership meant that now legislation could be given to unfriendly "nurses." The principle of seniority as a means of gaining and maintaining committee positions, which is in conflict with control by either bipartisan or party majorities, was followed to an increasing extent.[7] As a result, the powers of committees to block and change legislation increased at the expense of the full House; the powers

---

5. Cooper, "Congress and Its Committees," p. 56.
6. Jefferson, *Manual of Parliamentary Practice*, sec. 26.
7. Joseph Cooper found that in the 11th and 12th Congresses (1809–12), 25 percent of the members who could have been reappointed to the Foreign Affairs Committee were reappointed; in the 17th, 18th, and 19th Congresses (1821–26), 75 percent were. Cooper, "Congress and Its Committees," p. 62.

of seniority-chosen chairmen increased at the expense of majority rule within committees.

Each model of congressional organization discussed in the preface has its distinctive means of controlling the legislative program. Decisions may be made largely by the president as the national party leader (presidential-responsible party), by specialized committees (presidential-pluralist), by shifting majorities of the full membership (constitutional balance), or by the congressional party (congressional supremacy). The early Congresses vested control in legislative majorities. When members found that they lacked the time and the detailed knowledge to make many decisions, they placed great powers in the hands of their standing committees.

The alternatives that would give control to political parties have been tried only sporadically. They require the members to submit to strong discipline, something that a constituency-oriented legislature is reluctant to do. The House did so under Henry Clay in the 1820s, Thomas B. Reed in the 1890s and Joseph G. Cannon in the early twentieth century; the Senate did so under Nelson W. Aldrich's informal leadership in the early 1900s, under Majority Leader Joseph W. Kern from 1911 to 1917, and during the first four years of the New Deal. It is, of course, entirely possible that the congressional party leaders are attempting to operate under the congressional supremacy model rather than the presidential-responsible party model. In order that the branches work together in effective majority party control of legislative policy-making, a fortuitous combination of circumstances is required—one that is not encouraged by our constitutional separation of powers or by the individualist, antimajoritarian folkways of the American people. At a minimum, both legislative houses and the executive must be controlled by the same party, yet during the one hundred and eight years from the 1861 start of our present two-party system until 1868, thirty years have been under divided party control. The leaders of both houses must be both strong and willing to cooperate with one another and with the president. Most important, the president must have both the desire to exert strong leadership and the ability to do so. The magic combination allowing control by the majority party has arisen most clearly under the the presidencies of Thomas Jefferson, Woodrow Wilson, Franklin D. Roosevelt, and Lyndon B. Johnson, and then only for limited periods of time.

Development of Committees in the House

A brief history of the creation of standing committees shows both the diversity of House and Senate organization and the underlying pattern of similarity.[8] These committees developed somewhat more rapidly in the House than in the Senate, as may be seen from table 1:1. The first ten years saw the creation of six House standing committees. Not surprisingly, the first were for housekeeping purposes (Elections, Enrolled Bills, Claims, Revisal, Unfinished Business). The important committees of Ways and Means and Commerce and Manufactures were created in 1795. By 1825, the end of Henry Clay's last term as Speaker, committees of the House had gained most of the power they hold today and the committee pattern was largely set. The following present-day committees trace their inception to this period: Interior, Post Office, District of Columbia, Judiciary, Veterans' Affairs, Government Operations, Agriculture, Foreign Affairs, Armed Services, and Public Works.

Between the Civil War and 1900, the number of standing committees jumped from thirty-four to fifty-eight. The appropriations function was taken from an overburdened and lax Ways and Means Committee in 1865. Beginning in 1877, however, the Appropriations Committee lost much of its power when functional committees were allowed to recommend appropriations for the

8. Except where noted, information in this section came from "Records of the House of Representatives," Preliminary Inventories no. 113 (Washington, D.C.: National Archives, 1959); George B. Galloway, "Development of the Committee System in the House of Representatives," *American Historical Review* (Oct. 1959): 17; and George B. Galloway, *Congress at the Crossroads* (New York: Thomas Y. Crowell Co., 1946), chap. 5.

departments with which they were concerned, and it did not win back its power until 1920.[9] Banking and Currency was created in 1865, Education and Labor in 1867, Rules in 1880, and Merchant Marine and Fisheries in 1887.

Relatively few new committees have been created in the twentieth century. Un-American Activities (1945), Science and Astronautics (1958), and Standards of Official Conduct (1968), all postwar, are the only ones that continued in existence at the end of the period under consideration. Most congressional effort has been devoted to abolishing obsolete committees or consolidating similar committees. In 1909 six minor committees were dropped. This change was facilitated by the opening of the House Office Building, making it possible for members to have offices of their own without being committee chairmen. Six more committees were abolished in a 1911 shift of control to the Democrats, and in 1927 a Republican reorganization abolished sixteen.

Notable consolidations also took place. In 1920 the Appropriations Committee was given the functions previously divided among nine committees. The eleven expenditure committees were merged into one in 1927. The Legislative Reorganization Act reduced the total number of House committees from forty-eight to nineteen, dropping two entirely and consolidating the rest.[10]

Development of Committees in the Senate

The Senate, in its first years, showed greater reluctance than the larger House to delegate power to committees, very probably because of its smaller size.[11] Until 1816 only committees of a house-

9. Richard F. Fenno Jr., *The Power of the Purse* (Boston: Little, Brown & Co., 1966), pp. 43–51.
10. The proposal of the Joint Committee on the Organization of Congress was for eighteen committees, the work of the District of Columbia Committee to be absorbed by the Civil Service Committee.
11. George H. Haynes, *The Senate of the United States* (Boston: Houghton Mifflin Co., 1938), chap. 6; and George B. Galloway, *Legislative Process in Congress* (New York: Thomas Y. Crowell Co., 1953), pp. 274–78.

keeping nature were formed—Enrolled Bills (1789), Engrossed Bills (1806), and Contingent Expenses (1807). Much use was made of small, select committees that came to handle not just a specific assignment but a number of related matters. A move was made in 1816 to reduce the necessity of frequent choice of select committees. Twelve standing committees were created, eight of which are still organized, though some under different names: Armed Services, Commerce, District of Columbia, Finance, Foreign Relations, Interior, Judiciary, and Post Office. Agriculture was formed in 1825, Public Buildings and Grounds (now part of Public Works) in 1837, and Expenditures in Executive Departments (now Government Operations) in 1842. By the time of the Civil War the Senate had over twenty-five committees.

After the war, several new committees were formed, closely paralleling the developments in the House. Appropriations was set off from Finance in 1867, and in 1899, twenty-two years after the House took such action, its powers were severely limited when other committees were allowed to pass on the appropriations of the administrative agencies with which they were concerned. Education and Labor (now Labor and Public Welfare) was formed in 1869. There was also a proliferation of committees concerned with commerce, with public works, and with housekeeping affairs. By 1900 the Senate had fifty committees, the House fifty-eight.

Although minor committees were created in the early part of the twentieth century, the only important one was Banking and Currency. As in the House, however, much effective consolidating and dropping of committees was carried on. In 1922 the Appropriations Committee regained its control over appropriations legislation, as a result of the Budgeting and Accounting Act. (As part of the bargain, a unique provision was made for ex officio members of the Appropriations Committee chosen by the legislative committees that had taken over appropriations power during the period between 1899 and 1922. These members from other committees were to have full privileges, including the power to vote, on appropriations subcommittees when the budget of the executive agency with which they were concerned was being considered.) In the same year the number of Senate committees was reduced from seventy-four to thirty-four. Again, in 1947, as a result of the Legislative Reorganization Act, the number was reduced to fifteen. Out of this reorganization came a new committee, Rules and Administration, a consolidation of six previously existing housekeeping committees. The only new standing committee to have been created since 1947 is Aeronautical and Space Sciences, formed in 1958.

In the history of Congress, it has been easier for the House and the Senate to create than to kill off committees. The reasons for this are not hard to find. The loss of a chairmanship meant a loss of prestige, staff, and often office space. The loss of a committee meant the loss of specialized treatment of particular problems, often desired by different interest groups. It is interesting that the smaller Senate showed a greater tendency to spawn committees than the House. It reached a peak of seventy-four in 1913. The House never seems to have exceeded a total of sixty-one committees, the peak it reached in 1925.

2.

Congress Since World War II

THIS BOOK is primarily concerned with congressional committees in the eleven postwar Congresses, the 80th through the 90th, which covered the years 1947 to 1968.[1] Before focusing on committees, however, it will be useful, by way of introduction, to describe congressional developments in the postwar period and the reform proposals of the two Joint Committees on the Organization of Congress that opened and closed the period under consideration.

The Postwar Congresses

The period was one of continuity as well as change for the United States Congress. Probably few legislatures in democratic countries underwent as few changes in operating rules, served under such unchanging legislative leadership, and had greater continuity in membership. The senior members of the House and Senate in the 90th Congress, for example, were Senator Carl Hayden and Representative Emanuel Celler. Hayden had been elected to the House in 1912 and had moved to the Senate in 1927; Celler had been elected to the House in 1923. Sixteen senators and fifty-three representatives who had been members of the 80th Congress re-

[1]. A single Congress actually overlaps into an odd-numbered year by a few days. For the sake of clarity, in all cases the years given for a Congress are the two important ones, starting with the odd number and ending with the even number.

mained in their respective houses at the commencement of the 90th Congress.[2] Over two-thirds of the standing committees in 1968 had members who had been with them continuously since at least 1947.

Nevertheless, it was a period of great, if sometimes slow-moving change. A chart would show peaks of legislative activity during Harry S. Truman's 81st Congress and Lyndon B. Johnson's 89th. Between them stretches the valley of the Eisenhower years, though his last Congress, the 86th, as well as John F. Kennedy's, would clearly be foothill years on the chart. One cannot isolate the exact combination that produced these mountain tops. Certainly it would include an active and skillful president, large Democratic majorities in Congress, and widely held agreement as to the need for reform. In the valley years, many felt that the American system of government could not survive without radical change. They found, however, that relatively minor incremental changes brought a remarkably efficient system in the peak years.

This section discusses the incremental changes that took place during the eleven Congresses. The political context can be seen in broad outline in table 2:1.

The portion of the period under study when Democrat Harry S. Truman was president (1947–52) started with the 80th Congress, the first Republican Congress in fifteen years, and one that had been somewhat restructured by the Legislative Reorganization Act of 1946. Speaker Joseph W. Martin Jr. vowed that he would "start each day with a prayer and end it with an investigation." The Congress did not give Truman much that he wanted in the domestic area, though it passed important presidential proposals in the foreign field. In the 81st Congress, the Democrats picked up strength in the Senate, though not enough to stop the passage of a conservative amendment to the rules concerning cloture. The

2. Twelve of these senators were Democrats and four were Republicans. Nine came from the South, three from the West, and two each from the East and the Midwest. Forty-seven of the representatives were Democrats, six were Republicans. Twenty-four came from the South, fourteen from the Midwest, twelve from the East, and three from the West.

TABLE 2:1

The Postwar Congresses, 1947–68

Congress	President	President's Percent of Two-Party Vote		Percent of Majority Party Control of Senate		Percent of Majority Party Control of House	
80 (1947–48)	(Truman)			(R)	53.2	(R)	56.6
81 (1949–50)	Truman	(D)	52.3	(D)	56.3	(D)	60.6
82 (1951–52)				(D)	51.0	(D)	54.0
83 (1953–54)	Eisenhower	(R)	55.8	(R)	50.6	(R)	51.2
84 (1955–56)				(D)	50.6	(D)	53.3
85 (1957–58)	Eisenhower	(R)	57.8	(D)	51.0	(D)	53.8
86 (1959–60)				(D)	66.0	(D)	64.8
87 (1961–62)	Kennedy	(D)	50.1	(D)	64.0	(D)	60.0
88 (1963–64)				(D)	67.0	(D)	59.3
89 (1965–66)	Johnson	(D)	61.3	(D)	68.0	(D)	67.8
90 (1967–68)				(D)	64.0	(D)	57.0

House, which had a Democratic majority of greater than 60 percent, however, passed the 21-Day Rule which enabled committee chairmen to by-pass the conservative Rules Committee and have their measures brought up on the floor. A greater number of important measures, many of them bringing about a liberalization of our domestic policies, were passed in this Congress than any other until the epochal 89th Congress (1965–66). The 82nd Congress saw the decline of Democratic majorities in both houses. The 21-Day Rule was abandoned, and there was a decrease in the amount of important legislation passed.

Republican Dwight D. Eisenhower was president from 1953 to 1960, during the 83rd through the 86th Congresses. The Republicans controlled only the 83rd Congress, and that by narrow margins. Eisenhower asked less of this Congress than any other, and the output was moderate in both size and tenor. Lyndon Johnson became Senate minority leader and started what became an important modification of the seniority system as it applied to initial assignments and transfers to committees. The Democrats took over control of Congress by a slight margin in 1955. Texans Sam Rayburn and Lyndon Johnson coordinated their skilled political leadership of the two houses. While they rarely opposed the president's requests, they generally asked that Congress give Eisenhower a little more than he asked. The House adopted a moderate committee "bill of rights" in the 84th Congress in reaction to the excesses of investigation committees. Much the same pattern continued in the 85th Congress. New space committees were created in 1958. In that fall's elections Democrats won wide margins in both houses. At least partly as a result, Republican Charles A. Halleck unseated Minority Leader Joseph W. Martin Jr. In the Senate, Johnson adjusted committee size drastically in order to accommodate the host of new Democrats, and he brought about a mild liberalization of the cloture rule.

Much of the social energy of the Truman era was revived with the election of John F. Kennedy in 1960, though he won by a more narrow margin than any other president since 1888. Democratic majorities in Congress dropped somewhat, but they were greater than 60 percent. In the Senate, Majority Leader Mike Mansfield proved to be less powerful than Lyndon Johnson, and an attempt to ease the cloture rule failed. In the House, Speaker Rayburn was successful in partially harnessing the Rules Committee by increasing its size and by seeing that two new and loyal members were appointed. He died at the end of the first session of the 87th Congress and was succeeded by John McCormack. The 88th Congress, which President Johnson inherited at the halfway point, though it saw no major organization changes, proved to be liberal in legislative output. Cloture, for example, was successfully applied to the civil rights bill for the first time in history.

By this time the Supreme Court's "one man–one vote" decisions were bringing about the creation of larger, more heterogeneous congressional districts; and the Court's desegregation decisions, followed by Congress's civil rights legislation, were increasing Negro voting strength so that the southern grip on Congress was beginning to be challenged. Senator Barry Goldwater's candidacy clearly helped swell President Johnson's electoral margin to the highest since the one earned by Franklin D. Roosevelt in his second election, and pushed the Democratic margin in both houses of Congress to above the two-thirds mark.

At the commencement of the 89th Congress, House Republicans changed their minority leader, this time deserting Charles A. Halleck for Gerald R. Ford. The House adopted a 21-Day Rule, though this time the Speaker was given discretion as to whether to recognize chairmen, a choice he did not have in the 81st Congress. Cloture was invoked successfully in the Senate to bring about the passage of new civil rights legislation primarily concerned with Negro voting. A new Joint Committee on the Organization of Congress was established, similar to the one that had produced the 1946 Legislative Reorganization Act. Such major new legislation was passed as federal aid to education and a medical care program for the elderly. And Congress turned its sights to the problems of the environment, the city, and the poor as it never had before.

The 90th Congress, in sharp contrast, saw a decline in Democratic strength, the abandonment of the 21-Day Rule, and the virtual end of the domestic Great Society program, as the divided country turned its attention to the Vietnam war. Even a relatively mild Legislative Reorganization Act failed of passage at the end of the second session. George Mahon, chairman of the House Appropriations Committee, explained the change in part with his comment: "We certainly can't have an 89th Congress every two years. Once is enough for a decade."[3]

The Two Joint Committees on the Organization of Congress

The period under consideration in this study commenced with a reorganization authorized by the passage of the Legislative Reorganization Act of 1946, and closed with an unsuccessful attempt

3. *Nation's Business*, Feb. 1968, p. 53.

at further reform by the second Joint Committee on the Organization of Congress. Both committees were greatly concerned with the committee system.

The Legislative Reorganization Act of 1946, often referred to as the LaFollette-Monroney Act, brought about the greatest consolidation of committees that had ever taken place and made numerous important changes in committee organization and procedure.[4] It made no basic changes, however, in the relationship between committees and the legislature, or between committees and the executive branch.

Senator Francis Maloney proposed that a reorganization survey be undertaken, though he did not live to see its adoption. The idea caught on in the period of congressional and public interest in reform immediately following World War II. Republican Senator Robert M. LaFollette Jr. had chosen to chair the Joint Committee on the Organization of Congress, and Democratic Representative A. S. Mike Monroney was designated as vice chairman of the committee, which was made up of six Senate and six House members, evenly divided between the two parties.[5] The committee held extensive hearings in the spring of 1945 under the supervision of its staff director, political scientist George Galloway. The report, which was issued in March of 1946, clearly bore the Galloway imprint. It noted that the members of the committee were unable to reach agreement on the seniority system, the role of the House

4. Major sources of information on the act were: interview with Senator A. S. Mike Monroney, Aug. 7, 1961; interview with Dr. George B. Galloway, Aug. 10, 1961; George B. Galloway, *Congress at the Crossroads* (New York: Thomas Y. Crowell Co., 1946), pp. 240–356; Joint Committee on the Organization of Congress, Hearings, *The Organization of Congress,* pursuant to H. Con. Res. 18, 79th Cong., 1st sess., 1945; Joint Committee on the Organization of Congress, *Organization of Congress,* Senate Report 1011, pursuant to H. Con. Res. 18, 79th Cong., 2nd sess., 1946; *Congressional Record,* 79th Cong., 2nd sess., 1946, pp. 6365–98,.6439–70, 6517–78, 10037–10104.

5. The six Senate members were Claude D. Pepper (D., Fla.), Richard B. Russell (D., Ga.), Elbert D. Thomas (D., Utah), C. Wayland Brooks (R., Ill.), Robert M. LaFollette Jr. (R., Wis.), and Wallace H. White Jr. (R., Maine); House members were E. E. Cox (D., Ga.), Thomas J. Lane (D., Mass.), A. S. Mike Monroney (D., Okla.), Everett M. Dirksen (R., Ill.), Earl C. Michener (R., Mich.), and Charles A. Plumley (R., Vt.).

Committee on Rules, or the advisability of broadcasting legislative proceedings. Beyond this, the report was supported by all members, with the exception of four dissents on specific items.[6] The report made recommendations concerning committee structure and operation, policy committees, staff, fiscal procedures, more efficient use of congressional time, pay and retirement benefits, and lobby registration. The theme of the report was the necessity for the strengthening of Congress in a time of crisis. Clearly favoring the constitutional balance model, it stated that to all proposals made in the hearings, the committee "applied the simple test: will they strengthen Congress and enable it to do a better job?" Not surprisingly, many proposals sought to strengthen Congress vis-a-vis the executive—proposals for better bill-drafting service and for professional staffs for committees and members so that less reliance would have to be placed on the executive, as well as proposals for better legislative oversight of the executive.

Senator LaFollette was largely responsible for the passage of the Legislative Reorganization Act in the Senate. During four days of debate relatively little opposition developed, except toward the proposal for a director of congressional personnel (a "Director-Generalissimo," according to Senator Kenneth McKellar), a provision that was dropped from the bill. Senator Walter George, chairman of the Committee on Finance, successfully objected to the creation of a new committee on veterans' affairs, on the grounds that it would be unfortunate to lose the accumulated experience of the Finance Committee which had traditionally handled these matters. Other objections to the loss of specialized committee experience or to the hardship of being confined to only two committees fell on deaf ears, however. A proposed committee of interior, natural resources, and public works was divided in two —a Committee on Interior and Insular Affairs, and a Committee on Public Works. Provision was dropped for a monthly commit-

6. Representative Cox objected to the proposed House committee reorganization and to the idea of policy committees; Representative Lane objected to the salary increase; Senator Russell opposed self-rule of the District of Columbia.

tee "docket day" on which members who had bills pending before a committee could appear to state their cases. With these minor changes, the bill was passed by a nonpartisan vote of 49 to 16 on June 10, 1946.

For the next six weeks negotiations were carried on in the House with Speaker Rayburn,[7] Majority Leader McCormack, and Minority Leader Martin. The provisions relevant to committee organization that were deleted as the price of admission to the floor reveal the differences between the House and the Senate. The proposed Republican and Democratic policy committees were dropped, for the House party leaders, who enjoy more power than those in the Senate, suspected a resulting decrease in their power. The Speaker feared a loss of control over committee investigations. As a result he insisted that the provision automatically granting all committees the subpoena power be deleted, thus enabling him to keep a greater check on "runaway" inquiries. He also opposed a prohibition against investigations by select committees. Since he has the power to appoint members of select committees, this can occasionally be a useful device for circumventing the effects of the seniority system. The House leaders showed their fear that senators would dominate joint committee hearings by taking out the section calling for more bicameral committee cooperation. They showed a greater hesitation to court unfavorable public opinion than senators, who have the safety factor of a six-year term. They deleted the provision calling for highly paid administrative assistants, fearing the traditional public charge of payroll-padding, and they turned down the requirement of public reporting of committee attendance, knowing that this would provide easy ammunition to be used against members running for

7. Speaking on the floor of the House in 1954, Rayburn said, "there were two matters in [the Reorganization Act] that I tried to look after. One was the matter of the increase in salary. I was for that. Then I followed the Committee as far as I could to prevent the taking away from the Speakership of any more powers. I think those two purposes were accomplished, but, to be frank, they were the only provisions in the reorganization bill about which I was very enthusiastic" (*Congressional Record*, 83rd Cong., 2nd sess., 1954, p. 2296).

reelection. Other provisions to fall were those calling for staff preparation of bill digests, and for alternating days spent in committee hearings and days of floor debate. With these deletions, and after eight hours of debate led by Representatives Monroney and Everett Dirksen, the bill was passed on July 25, by a vote of 229 to 61, in substantially the same form in which it was presented to the House.

Congress finds it difficult to reform itself. That the Joint Committee on the Organization of Congress was as successful as it was is a tribute to the leadership that showed both an ability to arouse broad public support for reform and a tactical skill in handling the bill in Congress. Care was taken to consult all interested congressmen. Compromises, such as the decision not to propose abolition of the House Committee on the Merchant Marine over the dogged opposition of its chairman, were made whenever it was felt that the overall program would not suffer. Ample sugar coating was supplied in the form of substantial House and Senate pay increases and greatly improved retirement benefits. As it worked out, the six weeks delay on the Speaker's Table in the House was helpful to eventual passage. The bill did not come up in the House until the last two weeks of the session and its acceptance proved to be the means by which members could increase their inadequate salaries. Because of the lateness of House passage, the Senate agreed to the House changes and the bill became law without going to conference.

In spite of changes and deletions, the Legislative Reorganization Act of 1946 has had an extremely important effect on the committee system of Congress, as can be seen from a summary of the relevant provisions of the act. The number of standing committees was reduced from thirty-three to fifteen in the Senate, and from forty-eight to nineteen in the House, undoubtedly the most difficult accomplishment of the act. With minor exceptions, senators were limited to service on no more than two committees, representatives to one. Committee jurisdiction was more clearly defined than it had been. Provision was made for professional and clerical staff for all committees. A joint committee on the budget was proposed, which would consist of the members of the Appropriations and Revenue committees of the two houses.

As to committee procedure, committees were directed to establish regular meeting days. Witnesses were to be requested to submit written statements in advance of hearings. Staff members were to digest these statements and to draw up suggested questions to be asked by members of the committees. Chairmen were directed to report all bills approved by their committees and to seek rapid floor consideration. Conference committees were limited to actual differences in bills as passed by both houses and were prohibited from changing matters on which there was agreement. Complete records were to be kept of all committee proceedings, save those in executive session, and old committee records were to be transferred to the National Archives.

The shift in party control of Congress that took place after the passage of the act undoubtedly helped to put it into successful operation. The task of shuffling committee assignments, which is difficult at best, was incredibly complex in 1947, and there was talk of ignoring the part of the act that reduced the number of committees. The change in party control no doubt helped hold the line. If the Democrats had retained their control of Congress, seventeen of their members in the Senate and thirty in the House would have lost chairmanships through the reduction in the number of committees. Instead, Republicans organized the committees for the first time since 1929 in the House, and 1931 in the Senate. Because the same Republican senator was often ranking member of a number of committees, only eighteen individual Republicans could lay claim to a chairmanship at the close of the 79th Congress. Of these, four did not return to Congress. As a result only three lost positions that would clearly have been theirs had there been no reorganization, and they were carefully placed on committees of greater importance.[8] On the House side, there were thirty-six different ranking Republicans on the forty-eight committees.

8. Senator Daniel Brewster went from Libraries to Finance and Commerce, Harlan J. Bushfield from Canals to Agriculture and Finance, Clyde M. Reed from Mines and Post Office to Appropriations and Commerce.

Five of these did not return to the 80th Congress. The fifteen who lost chairmanships were given important committee assignments, as in the Senate.

The change in party control also had an important effect on the development of committee staffs. George Smith, a staff member of the Senate Republican Policy Committee, was influential in setting standards and acting as a clearing house for the hiring of competent personnel on both sides of Congress. Even more important, however, if the Democrats had retained control, they would undoubtedly have continued to call on the executive branch for most of their staff work. Republicans, however, found it to their advantage to hire an independent staff rather than to rely on administrators responsible to the opposite party. It is, in fact, generally the case that congressional staff plays a more important role when the two branches of government are controlled by different parties.

The Legislative Reorganization Act has continued to have an important effect on the committee system. Only two of the act's major provisions have not been given at least lip service. The proposed joint committee on the budget has not developed. It proved an awkward arrangement and there has not been the will to devise more workable machinery. In response to the demands of members for better committee assignments and the desire of party leaders to increase their bargaining power, another provision that has fallen by the wayside is the limitation on the number of a member's committee assignments.

Committee staffs have increased in size and, in most cases, in professional competence. Most committees abide by the directive that they hold regular meeting days. Committee procedure has been regularized. Not the least remarkable is the fact that the pattern of standing committees as established in 1946 has remained essentially unchanged, though with some name changes,[9] in spite

9. There have been several changes in committee names during this period. In the Senate, the Committee on Civil Service became the Committee on Post Office and Civil Service in 1947; the Committee on Public Lands became the Committee on Interior and Insular Affairs in 1948; the Committee on Ex-

of many proposals calling for the creation of new committees.[10]

The party leadership and the oligarchy of committee chairmen have guarded the 1946 "treaty" so that there have been fewer changes than in any similar period since the system of standing committees was firmly established. The only new committees to be created have been House and Senate space committees (1958) and the House Committee on Standards of Official Conduct (1968). The new space committees reflected technological advance and the cold war situation. They were given the function of overseeing the National Aeronautics and Space Administration. The House Committee on Standards of Official Conduct was created in somewhat halfhearted reaction to public concern over legislative conduct.[11]

Some twenty years after the Legislative Reorganization Act of 1946, pressures for another thorough look at Congress began building among journalists, political scientists, and legislators themselves. A new Joint Committee on the Organization of Congress was created,[12] which held lengthy hearings and drew up a mea-

---

penditures in Executive Departments became Government Operations in 1952; the Committee on Interstate and Foreign Commerce became the Committee on Commerce in 1961. In the House, the name of Public Lands was changed to Interior and Insular Affairs in 1951, that of Expenditures in Executive Departments to Government Operations in 1952, and that of Un-American Activities to Internal Security in 1969.

10. The most persistent proposal in the Senate has been for the creation of a veterans' affairs committee. In the House frequent suggestions have been made to split Education and Labor in two.

11. This was established first as a select committee in 1966. The Senate Select Committee on Standards of Conduct was created in 1964.

12. Major sources of information about the second Joint Committee on the Organization of Congress were: interview with Walter Kravitz of the Legislative Reference Service, July 11, 1968; interviews with committee staff members Nicholas A. Masters (July 11 and Sept. 5, 1968), George Meader (May 22, 1967), and W. DeVier Pierson (Jan. 1, 1967); Joint Committee on the Organization of Congress, Hearings, *The Organization of Congress,* pursuant to S. Con. Res. 2, 89th Cong., 1st sess., 1965; Senate Report 426 (1965); Senate Report 948 (1966); Senate Report 1414 (1966); Special Committee on the Organization of Congress, Hearings, *Organization of Congress,* pursuant to S. Res. 293, 89th Cong., 2nd sess., 1966; *Congressional Record,* 90th Cong., 1st sess., 1967, pp. S251–3294, daily edition.

sure that was complex in the variety of reforms proposed, but moderate in the direction of its reforms, all fitting neatly within the constitutional balance model. The measure passed the Senate in 1967, but failed to reach the floor of the House by the end of the 90th Congress. Perhaps neither that Congress nor its predecessor was very receptive to such a measure. The 89th saw so many legislative achievements under the unreformed system that the need for change seemed less evident, and the attention of the 90th Congress was turned to the divisive Vietnam war.

Senator A. S. Mike Monroney, who had been the House chairman of the earlier Joint Committee, took the lead in sponsoring the creation of the new committee. His cochairman was House Democrat Ray J. Madden. The twelve-member committee was established in March 1965, and it had the same membership pattern as its predecessor—three Democratic and three Republican Senators appointed by the vice president, and three Democratic and three Republican Representatives appointed by the Speaker.[13] Instead of a single staff director, each of the four delegations chose a staff member, with the one chosen by the Senate Democrats designated as the chief counsel. The hearings were held between May 10 and September 23, 1965, and they produced over two thousand pages of testimony. A final report was issued on July 21, 1966, and proposed legislation was sent to the Senate Committee on Rules and Administration and to the House Committee on Rules shortly thereafter.

The report did not have as unified a point of view as its predecessor, which showed the hand of its staff director, George Galloway. There was somewhat less emphasis on strengthening the Congress in its relations with the executive, and no suggestion that party mechanisms should be strengthened. The proposed legisla-

13. The six Senate members were A. S. Mike Monroney (D. Okla.), John J. Sparkman (D., Ala.), Lee Metcalf (D., Mont.), Karl E. Mundt (R., S. Dak.), Clifford P. Case (R., N.J.), J. Caleb Boggs (R., Del.); House members were Ray J. Madden (D., Ind.), Jack Brooks (D., Tex.), Ken Hechler (D., W. Va.), Thomas B. Curtis (R., Mo.), Robert P. Griffin (R., Mich.), Durward G. Hall (R., Mo.) James C. Cleveland (R., N.H.) was appointed on May 18, 1966, to succeed Griffin who resigned to accept appointment to the Senate.

tion, patterned along the lines of the 1946 act, was divided into five titles that dealt with the committee system, fiscal controls, sources of information, Congress as an institution, and regulation of lobbying. The provisions that most closely concern the committee system are outlined below.

COMMITTEE STRUCTURE

The following new committees were proposed: a Senate Committee on Veterans' Affairs to parallel the existing House committee, a House Committee on Standards of Conduct to parallel the existing Senate select committee, and a new Joint Committee on Congressional Operations. The education functions were to be split off from the Labor committees in both houses and given separate committee status. The Senate Committee on Aeronautical and Space Sciences was to be given the name and the broader jurisdiction of the House Committee of Science and Astronautics. Banking and Currency committees were to be redesignated as Banking, Housing, and Urban Affairs committees to more accurately reflect their activities.

COMMITTEE ASSIGNMENTS

Senators were to serve on not more than one of the four top committees: Appropriations, Armed Services, Finance, and Foreign Relations. They were to serve on two major and one minor committee. (A minor committee assignment was designated as District of Columbia, Post Office and Civil Service, Rules and Administration, Science and Astronautics, Veterans' Affairs, a joint committee, or a special or select committee.) Members were to be limited to one committee chairmanship and one subcommittee chairmanship on a major committee.

COMMITTEE PROCEDURE

Each committee was to have a "bill of rights" that would eliminate proxy voting and give a committee majority the right to call meetings and to require a chairman to report legislation. Subcommittees were to follow the rules of the parent committee, and their budget was to be voted on by the entire committee in a single annual resolution. Committee hearings were to be announced two weeks in advance, and witnesses were to submit their statements two days prior to a hearing. The minority was to have a day to call witnesses of its choice. Hearings, including those of the Appropriations committees, were to be open and to be broadcast, unless they involved matters concerning the national security. Committees were to be allowed to meet during floor sessions of the full house with the permission of the majority and minority leaders. Daily summaries of testimony were to be prepared by committee staff. Committee meetings, as distinguished from hearings, were also to be open except when a majority vote determined otherwise, and the results of all roll-call votes were to be made public daily. Majority committee reports were to be circulated two days before filing, in order to give the minority time to write its reports, and they were to be available to house members three days before consideration.

COMMITTEE STAFF

The professional staff available to each committee was to be increased from four to six, with an additional staff member employed to review the work of the administrative agencies with which each committee is primarily concerned. Two professional and one clerical positions were to be assigned to the committee minority if it so requested.

CONFERENCE COMMITTEES

Senate conferees were to prepare an explanatory statement to accompany their reports, as House conferees do now. The minority was to have equal time during the debate over a conference report.

The Senate Committee on Rules and Administration directed the Senate members of the Joint Committee to seek testimony concerning their proposals from all chairmen and ranking members, and, as a result, several of the original items were eliminated before the measure was brought to the Senate floor in 1967. Specifically, the Appropriations Committee was exempted from the application of the committee "bill of rights," the separate Committee on Education was abandoned and the limited jurisdiction of the Committee on Aeronautical and Space Sciences remained untouched. Senate debate lasted for seventeen days, and it was clearly dominated by Senator Monroney, who had won Senator Karl E. Mundt to his side and had placated veteran Senator Hayden, chairman of the Appropriations Committee. Amendments were proposed both by those who, like Senator Joseph S. Clark, wanted greater democratization of Senate rules and by those who, like Senator Russell B. Long, felt that the proposals seriously limited chairmen's prerogatives and allowed too much opportunity for delaying actions on the part of the minority. Some thirty of the more than one hundred amendments were accepted, most of them concerned with committee procedure. Perhaps the most important were the provision that committee actions could not be challenged from the floor for not having followed the exact procedures prescribed by the act, the elimination of the prohibition on proxies except on the final committee vote, and the allowing of the majority and minority leadership to waive the requirement that a committee report must lie before the house for three days before it could be acted on.

The measure passed the Senate on March 7, 1968, by a vote of 75 to 9. The nine opponents included five chairmen, one ranking committee Democrat, and one ranking committee Republican.

On the House side there were more opponents and fewer proponents. Lewis Deschler, the powerful parliamentarian, and a number of committee chairmen had strong reservations. In general, there was concern for the provisions that would allow committee minorities to delay action and committee majorities to reduce the powers of chairmen and the leadership. The original measure went against the well-established House custom of closed meetings of the Appropriations Committee and a prohibition of broadcasting hearings. Perhaps most important, Cochairman Madden, who was ranking Democrat on the Rules Committee, did not give the same sort of leadership that Monroney had on the Senate side. One day's hearings were held by the Rules Committee on

April 11, 1967, and there was no further action taken. Only after the Speaker let it be known that he wanted some reform measure passed did second ranking Democrat, Jack Brooks, assume some leadership and push a measure that deleted most of the procedural changes and stressed sources of information and regulation of lobbying. It was evidently too late, for the Rules Committee voted not to send the measure to the floor late in 1968. By the end of the 90th Congress, the only committee change proposed by the Joint Committee that was adopted on the House side was the creation of a Committee on Standards of Official Conduct, though a number of other provisions had been adopted on a piecemeal basis.[14]

Congress has had proposals for party-oriented, president-centered reform before it for a long time, from Woodrow Wilson's academic treatise to Joseph Clark's tract, written from the vantage point of a senator.[15] It is quite obviously not going to accede to this type of reform of its own accord.

The type of reform it has proposed has tended to strengthen committees and bipartisan majorities and not party mechanisms. Even such moderate suggestions as those of the second Joint Committee failed of passage, primarily because of weak leadership, the covert opposition of party leaders who feared a weakening of their powers, and the lack of feeling a pressing need for change.

---

14. "Congressional Reform Actions Attributable to the Joint Committee on the Organization of Congress, as of June 24, 1968," *Congressional Record,* 90th Cong., 2nd sess., Oct. 11, 1968, pp. H9881–83, daily edition.
15. Joseph S. Clark, *Congress: The Sapless Branch* (New York: Harper and Row, 1964), chaps. 8, 9.

II

Committees & the Structure of Congress

3.

Committee Organization

THIS CHAPTER, which is concerned with certain aspects of committee organization, first discusses committee jurisdiction as an example of the problems of the relations among committees, and then turns to subcommittees as an example of the problems of the relations within committees.

War and Peace Among Committees[1]

Even with the stable pattern that has been in effect since 1947, the committees have not existed in a state of harmony. Committee members show human tendencies of wanting to broaden their areas of operations. Groups outside Congress are likely to seek to have favored legislation steered to friendly committees and bills

1. For valuable discussions of jurisdictional problems, see Wallace Judson Parks, "Realigning the Congressional Committee Structure," in U.S. Senate, Committee on Government Operations, *Organization and Operation of Congress*, Hearings, 82nd Cong., 1st sess. (Washington, D.C.: Government Printing Office, 1951), p. 622; and various articles in U.S. Senate, Committee on Government Operations, *The Organization of Congress: Some Problems of Committee Jurisdiction*, Senate Doc. 51, 82nd Cong., 1st sess. (Washington, D.C.: Government Printing Office, 1951). Insights concerning common types of conflicts can be gleaned from Senate disputes over committee reference summarized at the back of the *Senate Journal*, and from the section entitled "Jurisdiction of Committees" in Clarence Cannon, *Procedure in the House of Representatives* (Washington, D.C.: Government Printing Office, 1959), pp. 344–409. Lewis Deschler, parliamentarian of the House, and Floyd M. Riddick, assistant parliamentarian of the Senate, gave helpful suggestions for this section.

they oppose sent to committees that will be hostile. Yet, even in a never-never land lacking in such rivalry, there would be committee disputes, for the issues handled by Congress are too complex to allow for easy and objective decisions as to each committee's jurisdiction.

One type of conflict arises among committees that look at government problems from different points of view. Some committees concentrate on the carrying out of a broad function of government for the public, while others cut across a number of different functions.[2] Some of these nonfunction-oriented committees may be concerned with money (House and Senate Appropriations, Ways and Means, and Finance), with personnel (House and Senate Post Office and Civil Service), or with government organization (House and Senate Government Operations and Judiciary committees, House Administration, House Rules, Senate Rules and Administration), and this specialization may bring them in conflict with function-oriented committees.[3] In concentrating on expenditures, for example, they may raise such questions as: should Appropriations or Foreign Relations have jurisdiction over the budget of the Department of State?[4] In concentrating on revenue, they may raise such questions as: should Finance or Agricul-

2. Some authors write of committees as being organized on the basis of function, clientele, geographical area, and process. It becomes so difficult, however, to distinguish among these four that less precise terms are intentionally being used here.

3. For the sake of simplicity, the revenue and Judiciary committees are listed as nonfunction-oriented, though they fit into the function-oriented category for some of their work—social security and tariff measures for the revenue committees, civil liberties and antitrust matters for the Judiciary committees.

4. An idea of the depth of resentment that function-oriented committees are likely to feel towards the "interference" of the Appropriations committees can be seen from the fact that in 1885 the House and in 1899 the Senate stripped them of the power of approving departmental appropriations. De Alva Stanwood Alexander, writing in 1916, was critical of this but he doubted that the functional committees could ever be persuaded to give up their right to appropriate. See his *History and Procedures of the House of Representatives* (Boston: Houghton Mifflin Co., 1916), p. 254.

ture have control over a proposal to repeal a tax on oleomargarine? In concentrating on government personnel they may raise such questions as: should Post Office and Civil Service or Judiciary handle conflict-of-interest bills? In concentrating on some phase of government organization they may raise a number of questions such as: should Government Operations or Armed Services consider the unification of the armed forces? Should Rules and Administration or Interior handle the creation of a select committee to study petroleum reserves? Should Judiciary or Commerce handle an interstate compact on petroleum production?

These nonfunction-oriented committees may cut across the functional committees in a different manner. They may concentrate on a specific clientele, becoming interested in the effect of a number of different functions upon the specific group with which they are concerned. The District of Columbia committees are concerned with the performance of many governmental functions as they affect the capital city. The Veterans' Committee is concerned with the health and welfare of its particular constituents, while other committees concern themselves with general health and welfare matters. An increase of this type of clientele organization, while it may be beneficial to the groups involved, can increase the chance of jurisdictional conflict.

Even if all committees were function-oriented, it is not likely that Congress could so organize its work that no conflicts would develop. In a complex world a number of questions are bound to arise. Should Armed Services or Foreign Relations handle foreign military assistance? Should Foreign Relations be given sole jurisdiction over foreign economic matters when committees concerned with revenue, agriculture, and commerce are also vitally involved? Should a proposed Missouri Valley Authority be consigned to Interior or Public Works?

The House and the Senate handle the problem of jurisdictional conflicts in characteristically different ways. In the House, the Speaker has the formal power of reference, but it is actually carried out by the parliamentarian. (The incumbent during the entire period under consideration was Lewis Deschler, who had been appointed by Republican Speaker Nicholas Longworth in 1928.) The Speaker will rarely discuss the matter of reference with the parliamentarian. Where there is leeway as to reference, however, Deschler may well represent his unspoken will. An appeal may be taken from his decision, but the parliamentarian can recall only one instance in which this was done during his long tour of duty. Actually, in the House, the struggle for jurisdiction may come at an earlier stage, when a bill is still being drafted. A measure concerning water resources, for example, could be sent to Interior, Public Works, Agriculture, or Commerce. A title such as "Matters of concern of the Department of Interior and related agencies" and friendly support of party leaders would increase the chances that it would end up in the Interior Committee, though in most cases jurisdictional lines are so clear that this type of slanted drafting is fruitless.[5]

In the Senate, a less disciplined body, there has been somewhat more latitude in assigning measures to committees. The first Joint Committee on the Organization of Congress, which sought to allocate committee jurisdiction logically and to spell it out in such detail that few questions could arise, singled out the Senate for special criticism and recommended "the exercise of more care in the reference of Senate bills."[6] Some flexibility still exists, how-

5. One of the rare public charges that this sort of thing was taking place appeared in the *Congressional Record* in 1949: "It is evident that those who drafted HR 4312 which is the bill which has been referred to the Committee on Interstate and Foreign Commerce, intended to draft it so as to enable it to detour the Ways and Means Committee and land in the Committee on Interstate and Foreign Commerce. . . . [Their purpose was one of] artfully trying to write language into the bill that will make it appear that the method by which the money is to be secured for financing this program is not taxation" (*Congressional Record*, 81st Cong., 1st sess., 1949, appendix, p. 2532; cited in George B. Galloway, *Legislative Process in Congress* [New York: Thomas Y. Crowell Co., 1953], p. 597).

6. Joint Committee on the Organization of Congress, *Organization of Congress*, Senate Report 1011, pursuant to H. Con. Res. 18, 79th Cong., 2nd sess., 1946, p. 5.

ever. Examples are the sending of a carefully tailored Kennedy civil rights bill concerning public accommodations to a friendly Commerce Committee, and a Johnson civil rights measure concerning open housing to a friendly Banking and Currency Committee. As in the House, the parliamentarian makes reference in all but a small percentage of cases, using various rules of thumb worked out over the years. (Charles L. Watkins served as parliamentarian from 1937 until 1965 when the man who had been his assistant since 1952, Floyd M. Riddick, succeeded him.) While disputes about reference are probably no more common in the Senate than in the House, they are certainly more openly discussed. It is not only procedurally easier to challenge a reference on the floor but, in the freer Senate ethos, it is less politically unwise. An 80th Congress example in which a reference by the presiding officer was overruled will serve as an illustration of the complex problems involved.

There has been a long history of disputes over the reference of measures that would tax oleomargine. In 1886 the House had overruled the Speaker when he referred an oleo tax measure to Ways and Means. Since that time, according to precedent, all oleo tax measures had been referred to House Agriculture. In the 80th Congress, after repeated attempts, a tax repeal bill was forced out of the prodairy Agriculture Committee under discharge procedure. When the measure came to the Senate, it was referred by President Pro Tem Arthur H. Vandenberg to the Senate Agriculture Committee, though most previous measures had gone to the Senate Finance Committee which had no majority interested in supporting the dairy interests. Vandenberg, from a dairy state, ruled that though the tax was mentioned in the title, the measure was of primary concern to the agricultural economy. He noted that, though some similar measures had been handled by Finance, the original 1886 measure had been brought out by Senate Agriculture and that the House Agriculture Committee had handled the present bill. J. W. Fulbright was successful in appealing the decision and having the measure sent to Finance, which gave it a favorable report. Dairy interests, however, were successful in blocking its passage and the repeal did not come until the 81st Congress.[7]

By reducing the number of standing committees and hardening their jurisdictional lines, the Legislative Reorganization Act tended to strengthen committee autonomy and in so doing it deprived party leaders of some flexibility—flexibility that could be used for either conservative or liberal ends, but that gave the leadership greater leverage. The post-1946 experience concerning intercommittee cooperation and the creation of special committees within a single house, as well as intercommittee cooperation between the House and the Senate and the creation of joint committees has been affected by this increased autonomy of standing committees.

The Senate, for example, which has had more open jurisdictional disputes among committees than the House, has shown somewhat greater ingenuity in working out cooperative arrangements among committees with overlapping interests. One approach to the problem is to devise some means for bringing together the interested committees. This can be done by having joint meetings of committees such as were held by the Senate Foreign Relations and Armed Services committees with some fre-

---

7. Another interesting dispute over committee reference in the 80th Congress concerned rival claims for use of water from the Colorado River and involved seven western states. Although an interstate compact had been agreed to in 1922, a dispute arose over distribution of the water in the lower basin. California and Nevada proposed that the issue be settled by arbitration or by a Supreme Court decision. Arizona and the other states refused, whereupon the senators from California and Nevada introduced S.J. Res. 145 that would direct the Attorney General to start proceedings against the other states in order that water rights might be determined. The measure was referred by the presiding officer to the Judiciary Committee, since it involved action by the Department of Justice. The only member on this committee from any of the states involved was Senator Pat McCarran of Nevada, one of the sponsors of the resolution and the ranking Democrat on the committee. Senator Carl Hayden of Arizona successfully appealed the reference, asking that it be referred to Interior. He argued that it involved an interstate compact, but it might be noted as well that the Interior committee had members sympathetic to Arizona's water needs.

quency when Tom Connally was Foreign Relations chairman during the 81st and 82nd Congresses (1949–52).[8] Most of these concerned our military assistance program and they were dominated by Connally, though Armed Services Chairman Richard B. Russell presided at the MacArthur removal hearings in 1951. From time to time since then, Armed Services has met jointly with the Foreign Relations and the Appropriations committees. Hearings of this sort create some ticklish problems such as who should preside and in what order should members ask questions. Where Foreign Relations people seemed to dominate the hearings, Armed Services attendance dropped noticeably in successive days. Perhaps the most serious drawback to this procedure is the fact that combined committees are generally too large for effective questioning by all the members.

A way around this has been to get together smaller groups of interested committee members. One approach has been to hold joint meetings of interested subcommittees such as the hearing on universal copyrights held in 1954 by subcommittees of Foreign Relations and Judiciary. The Senate Appropriations Committtee has, since 1922, made provision that three representatives of key committees (two of the majority and one of the minority party) sit in with subcommittees when the budget of the executive agency with which each is concerned is being considered.[9] Members of the Appropriations Committee feel that this arrangement has been successful. Attendance of ex officio members, who bring

8. See hearings on military assistance programs for 1949, 1950, 1951, and 1952. See also 1951 hearings on assignment of ground forces to Europe. A further joint hearing with Armed Services was held in 1957, Foreign Relations Chairman Theodore Francis Green presiding, to consider the Eisenhower Middle Eastern Doctrine. Two other recent examples are the joint hearings between Foreign Relations and the Senate members of the Joint Atomic Energy Committee on an international atomic energy treaty in 1957, and between Armed Services and Aeronautical and Space Sciences on missile matters in 1958.

9. These committees are Aeronautical and Space Sciences, Agriculture and Forestry, Armed Services, District of Columbia, Foreign Relations, Post Office and Civil Service, Public Works, and the Joint Committee on Atomic Energy.

a valuable subject-matter knowledge to the discussion, has been good. The 90th Congress saw the creation of an intercommittee group, under the leadership of Senator Richard B. Russell, to oversee the activities of the Central Intelligence Agency. It consisted of members of the Armed Services, Appropriations, and Foreign Relations committees and was an informal settlement of a dispute that had reached the floor the previous year when Armed Services Chairman Russell accused the Foreign Relations Committee of trying to muscle in on his authority. In the Senate, further, a bill has occasionally been referred to two or more committees simultaneously or consecutively, as has been the case of several military assistance bills in recent years. Joint committee or subcommittee meetings, the use of ex officio membership, and multiple reference have each been tried occasionally in the Senate. No serious attempt has been made, however, to create greater intercommittee cooperation by the creation of a policy committee consisting of all committee chairmen, as has sometimes been suggested.[10]

The House Committee on Foreign Affairs voted in 1947 to invite interested subcommittees to sit with it whenever the subject of a hearing was of common interest, but little or nothing ever came of this gesture. There seem to have been almost no examples during the years since 1947 of joint meetings of House committees beyond Armed Services meetings with Foreign Affairs and Appropriations on the Cuban and Vietnam crises. The House Appropriations Committee has no interest in following the Senate's example of ex officio committee membership. This type of solution is more difficult in the House, which is too large to afford membership on two committees to all of its members, though it is not inconceivable that cross membership on some committees with interests in common would be possible.

All in all, there has been little imaginative intrahouse committee cooperation on either side of Congress, in large part because of the century-old tradition of committee autonomy that was bolstered even more by the Legislative Reorganization Act. Some flexibility

10. Galloway, *Legislative Process in Congress*, p. 598.

can be brought into the picture by the creation of special (or select) committees. V. Stanley Vardys, in a review of the House select committees created between 1947 and 1958, found that these had been created for one of a combination of four reasons, all of which relate to problems created by standing committee boundaries:

> (1) to accommodate interest groups that do not feel they have access to the standing committees; (2) to help solve problems of a personal nature that arise in the House, e.g., to compensate and reward individual congressmen or to make use of their experience and expertise; (3) to evade or circumvent standing committees when these are considered 'inadequate' for particular tasks; and (4) to perform specific duties in areas of overlapping jurisdiction.[11]

According to Senator Robert M. LaFollette Jr., the members of the Joint Committee on the Organization of Congress had hoped to abolish all select or special committees, "because we felt that if a special investigation were necessary, it ought to be made in an orderly procedure by the committee which ultimately would have to consider any legislative remedies necessary to meet any situations which developed as a result of these inquiries."[12] The prohibition was deleted from the act in the House, however, probably because Speaker Sam Rayburn could conceive of instances when there would be great value to a committee whose chairman he would choose, appointed for a special purpose and with a staff of its own. However, the manner in which the act carved out clearly defined jurisdictions for each standing committee did serve the purpose of limiting the creation of special committees, for existing committees did not welcome legislative rivals, except under special circumstances.

11. V. Stanley Vardys, "Select Committee of the House of Representatives," *Midwest Journal of Political Science* (Aug. 1962): 251–52.
12. U.S. Senate, Committee on Expenditures in Executive Departments, *Legislative Reorganization Act of 1946*, Hearings, 80th Cong., 2nd sess., 1948, p. 77.

A perusal of the index of the *Congressional Record* shows that the device has not been abandoned, though there have been noticeably fewer select committees created since 1946. Senate party policy committees and the House and Senate small business committees have been in existence in each of the Congresses under consideration.[13] Since 1960 the Senate has had a Special Committee on the Aging, and since 1964 a Committee on Standards and Conduct. Not counting these, the Senate has established at least ten committees for one or more Congresses, the House eleven. A number of these were for minor housekeeping activities but about one-half grappled with major domestic and foreign problems. The recital of their names brings back important memories—Senator Daniel B. Brewster's Committee to Investigate the National Defense Program, Senator Estes Kefauver's Committee to Investigate Crime, Senator John L. McClellan's Committee on Improper Activities in the Labor or Management Field, and Representative Christian A. Herter's Committee to Investigate Tax-Exempt Foundations.

If the Legislative Reorganization Act sought to discourage the creation of select committees, it sought to encourage the creation of joint committees and greater House-Senate cooperation. Little new has developed in this field since 1946, however, again partly because of the clarification of committee jurisdiction brought about by the act.

The *Congressional Directory* for the 90th Congress lists thirty-eight joint committees, commissions, and boards, but a perusal of the titles shows that, with a few exceptions, this is not where legislative power lies. Their functions are, generally, either ceremonial or housekeeping in nature. Roughly a third will be disbanded when their specific duties have been performed.

Some of the more important of these committees were created to tie together the activities of already existing House and Senate

13. The policy committees were created by statute, as was the Senate small business committee in 1950. The House committee on small business must be created anew in each Congress. No one of these committees has permission to report legislation.

committees. The Joint Committee on the Library and the Joint Committee on Printing, for example, are made up of the members of the subcommittees of House Administration and Senate Rules and Administration concerned with these subjects. The Joint Committee on Defense Production is made up of the senior members of the two Banking and Currency committees; the Joint Committee on Immigration and Nationality Policy (which, incidentally, never met during the period under study because of House-Senate rivalries) is made up of the senior members of the two Judiciary committees; the Joint Committee on Internal Revenue Taxation, of senior members of House Ways and Means and Senate Finance.

Two committees of particular importance, however, have no direct relations to already existing House and Senate committees. The Joint Economic Committee has served as a vehicle for the expression of more liberal views than those that have predominated on the two revenue committees. Because of the quality of its membership and its staff, it has played an important nonlegislative role. The Joint Committee on Atomic Energy is the only one of these committees authorized to report legislation. It was established in 1946 by the Atomic Energy Act, a fact that has contributed to its remaining a joint committee, despite the traditional House antipathy to this method of organization. Its initial creation can probably be attributed to the newness of the field. Interest groups were not clearly established and jurisdictional committee jealousies came into less play. Also, the fact that strictest security was necessary contributed to the decision to establish a single joint committee. Our World War II atomic development was not known to Congress in general, but only to the chairmen of the Senate and House Appropriations and Military Affairs committees who acted somewhat as a joint committee in the early stages.[14]

Unsuccessful attempts to form joint committees on the budget and on space illustrate the difficulties in this type of cooperation.

14. See Morgan Thomas, *Atomic Energy and Congress* (Ann Arbor: University of Michigan Press, 1956); Harold P. Green and Alan Rosenthal, *Government of the Atom* (New York: Atherton Press, 1963).

The Legislative Reorganization Act of 1946 (in section 138) asked that the four money committees meet jointly, as the Joint Committee on the Budget, to review the president's budget, estimate total receipts and expenditures for the coming year, and, by February 15, set a ceiling on appropriations and expenditures and designate the means for raising the needed money. In 1947 the House and Senate could not agree on a ceiling; they were able to agree in 1948 but eventually surpassed it by six billion dollars; since that time the provisions have been ignored.

The plan had some obvious problems—the necessity for early action, for one, and the unwieldiness of the joint committee, for another (in the 80th Congress the four committees had a total membership of one hundred and one). Further, there was never a will to comply on the part of the committee leaders or, indeed, by the members of Congress, for Congress is not organized for this kind of self-discipline. Most important, House leaders felt that the provision gave the Senate too much equality in a field where the House guarded its preeminence carefully. This is borne out by the fact that the perennial proposal for a new Joint Committee on the Budget, which has been sponsored by Senator John L. McClellan, has been passed by the Senate in nearly every Congress since 1946 but has never been brought to the floor of the House.[15]

The Senate's proposal for a joint committee to oversee the space agencies, patterned after the Atomic Energy Committee, was turned down, partly because of the usual interhouse jealousies but partly for more personal reasons. The House leadership was worried about the succession of ranking Democrat, Overton Brooks, to the chairmanship of the important Armed Services Committee and it saw one of those rare chances to thwart the seniority system by persuading Brooks to move to the chairmanship of the newly created Science and Astronautics Committee.[16]

15. Richard F. Fenno Jr., *The Power of the Purse* (Boston: Little, Brown & Co., 1966), pp. 122, 521.
16. Allison Griffith, "The Genesis of the National Aeronautics and Space Act of 1958" (masters thesis, Columbia University, n.d.).

As suggested above, joint committees are likely to run into institutional committee jealousies, House-Senate rivalries, and fears on the part of outside groups. How large will the new committee be? If there is to be one vote per member, rather than unit rule as in conference committtees, will the committee be even-numbered and therefore susceptible to tie votes? Should the committee meet on the Senate or on the House side of the Capitol? Shall the chairman be a representative or a senator?[17] Would a single bicameral hearing tend to deprive certain groups of their prized access to Congress?

A survey of testimony before the Joint Committee on the Organization of Congress taken in 1965 turns up very few examples of Senate-House cooperation of even a less dramatic nature than the establishment of joint committees. Joint hearings are extremely rare and difficult to arrange. Staff members of parallel committees do cooperate but, on their own evidence, on a far less regular basis than might be expected.

The Miniature Legislatures of Congress[18]

The autonomy of the standing committees is jealously guarded. Within these standing committees a great variety of relationships exist. At one end of the spectrum there is no subcommittee organization at all, at the other end is a pattern of almost autonomous subcommittees. As one staff member described the latter extreme, "Given an active subcommittee chairman, working in a specialized field with a staff of his own, the parent committee can do no more than change the grammar of a subcommittee report."

17. Most committees have solved the chairmanship problem by rotating it annually between House and Senate members. In the 83rd Congress when both Speaker Joseph Martin and Sam Rayburn demanded that the House be given the chairmanship of the Atomic Energy Committee in even numbered years, they spoke in terms of institutional, not personal, prestige.
18. Much of the information in this section was gathered from interviews with members and staff connected with each of the House and Senate committees in 1960 and 1961.

Observers have often deplored the proliferation of subcommittees. Their persistence, however, testifies to their convenience and their congeniality to the working habits and purposes of members. When the Legislative Reorganization Act reduced the number and consolidated and rationalized jurisdictions of the standing committees, the average number of subcommittees per committee increased—as might be expected; and the trend has continued upward. In 1945 the total was 180; of these, 106 were in the House, 68 in the Senate, and 6 from joint committees.[19] By 1968 the number had grown by more than one-third to a total of 258, of which 139 were in the House, 104 in the Senate and 15 from joint committees.[20] Senator Everett M. Dirksen said in describing the problem this increase has caused for some congressmen:

> I would not dare to say to the people of Illinois that I knew all the things that go on, when I serve on five subcommittees of the Committee on the Judiciary, and on three subcommittees of the Committee on Government Operations. To do so I would really need roller skates to get from one subcommittee to another, without even then knowing entirely everything about every subject matter which is considered by the various committees.[21]

A blanket condemnation of the growth of subcommittees, however, is likely to ignore their uses in a complex world. The cold war and the industrial expansion of the country since the end of World War II have created new problems. National expenditures have doubled and the executive branch has added new departments of Health, Education, and Welfare (1953), Housing and Urban Development (1966), and Transportation (1966), as well as many other agencies. Congress, too, has reacted to these changes, most visibly by adjusting its subcommittee structure.

19. Joint Committee on the Organization of Congress, Hearings, *The Organization of Congress,* pursuant to H. Con. Res. 18, 79th Cong., 1st sess., 1945, p. 1039.
20. *Congressional Quarterly Weekly Report,* April 12, 1968, pp. 754–81.
21. *Congressional Record,* 83rd Cong., 2nd sess., 1954, p. 1417.

Senate Banking and Currency, for example, dropped a subcommittee concerned with rent control and created a new one in international finance. House Foreign Affairs divided its subcommittee on the Near East and Africa in two, and Senate Foreign Relations added one on disarmament. Senate Judiciary has added a subcommittee on juvenile delinquency.

Again, some division of committee functions helps solve the ever-present problem of securing a quorum. By dividing up the work, a wisely worked out subcommittee system can also cut down the total amout of time each member is required to spend with the affairs of a given committee, and at the same time allow for a greater degree of specialization. Senator LaFollette commented in 1948: "The essential and important difference between a hodge-podge committee system and an integrated scheme is not in the relative number of subcommittees, but rather in the formalization of fixed and definite jurisdictions so that each new piece of legislation in a given field can have the benefit of the staff work and specialized experience of members of Congress."[22]

Further, subcommittees have often "been an outgrowth of internal friction and resentment generated by one-man rule."[23] They can, within limits, allow less senior legislators to gain prestige, to follow their interests, and to exploit their abilities as they could not in a seniority-governed committee system that tolerated no subcommittees. It is significant, for example, that Albert Rains was able to establish a subcommittee on housing of the House Banking and Currency Committee, under the chairmanship of Brent Spence, when all other subcommittees were designated by number and given no clear jurisdiction. Other examples are John E. Moss Jr.'s subcommittee on governmental information (Government Operations, House) and Henry M. Jackson's policy machinery subcommittee (Government Operations, Senate).

Whether committees are adapting to increasingly difficult times, providing for greater specialization, or giving less senior men a

22. *Legislative Reorganization Act of 1946*, Hearings, 1948, p. 63.
23. Stewart L. Udall, "A Defense of the Seniority System," *New York Times Magazine*, Jan. 13, 1957, p. 64.

position of greater importance, there comes a point of no return, and it would seem that Senator Dirksen had passed this point when he confessed his inability to keep up with his work load. This is largely a problem of the Senate and not of the House, for there are roughly one-quarter as many members to share in a task equal to that of the House of Representatives. An analysis of the number of subcommittee assignments per member in both houses shows that a representative is likely to have two subcommittee assignments at the most, while a senator is likely to have at least six.

There is a startling variety in the pattern of subcommittee organization. Some committees have no subcommittees at all; others a few, perhaps designated by number only and without clear jurisdiction; and some perform most of their important work in full committee, even though they have a well-defined subcommittee system. In the 90th Congress there were eight House and seven Senate committees that fitted into these categories (see table 3:1). These committees include some of the most important ones of Congress. Five of the eight House and four of the seven Senate committees fall in the top half of the most coveted committees (see table 6:5).

Other committees establish a large number of subcommittees with clear jurisdiction and grant them great autonomy. In its relatively short lifetime, the House Committee on Science and Astronautics has passed through all of these stages. What determines whether or not a committee will subdivide its work?

There is a tendency to form subcommittees when committee work involves a great deal of detail or when it includes a number of distinct subject-matter areas, the more so if the work is technical and noncontroversial, so that it matters less who handles which assignment—no one wants to be left out of a fight that matters to him. The business of the Appropriations and Judiciary committees involves so much burdensome detail that subcommittees are inevitable, even though some of the work is controversial. The relatively noncontroversial Administration, Interior, and Public

TABLE 3:1
Committees That Have Resisted Subcommittee Autonomy, 90th Congress

HOUSE	SENATE

There are no standing subcommittees
    Rules*   Aeronautical & Space Sciences
    Un-American Activities*   Finance*
    Ways & Means*

Subcommittees are not given clearly defined jurisdictions
    Armed Services*
    District of Columbia
    Judiciary*

More than half of the committee's meetings are for the full committee†

HOUSE		SENATE	
House Administration	(70.4%)	Rules and Administration	(88.0%)
Banking & Currency	(54.6%)	Foreign Relations*	(85.6%)
		Agriculture & Forestry*	(75.5%)
		Post Office & Civil Service	(69.3%)
		Commerce*	(52.3%)

* Committee falls in the top half of the most coveted committees as indexed in table 6:5.
† Percentages are from page 65 of the *Final Report* of the Joint Committee on the Organization of Congress (1966), They apply to the 88th Congress but are roughly similar for the 90th.

Works committees (each a consolidation of a number of different committees brought together under the Legislative Reorganization Act) have such varied tasks to perform that they inevitably work through subcommittees. On the other hand, committees are less likely to subdivide their work if it involves broad policy rather than great detail, or if it does not fall easily into categories that can be assigned to regular subcommittees. The more controversial the work, the less likely there is to be subcommittee autonomy. The activities of the House Committee on Rules (which determines the conditions under which most major legislation reaches the floor) and Un-American Activities (which is primarily an investigating committee) do not lend themselves to subcommittee organization. A somewhat better case could be made for the use of subcommittees on the two revenue-raising committees, yet they generally handle important matters that senior members are reluctant to turn over to subcommittees.[24] Even though the foreign relations committees have carefully organized subcommittee systems for study purposes, the major share of the work is done by the full committee, because of the broad nature of their work.

Beyond limits derived from the character of a committee's assigned tasks, organization reflects to a great extent the nature of the chairman—his personality, his political ideology, and his concept of his role. No recent change of chairmen has illustrated this better than the succession of Adam Clayton Powell of Harlem to the top position on the House Committee on Education and Labor in the 87th Congress. His conservative predecessor, Graham Barden of North Carolina, had succeeded in bottling up many liberal proposals in the eight years of his chairmanship. He formed only those subcommittees made necessary by the varied jurisdiction of this committee, and he saw that they were headed by trusted conservatives, passing over second-ranking Powell in the process. In 1961 Powell brought a burst of activity to the committee that was not expected by some observers, since he had not previously taken his committee work seriously. He followed a novel approach of creating three subcommittees on education and three on labor. Two of these six subcommittees were called "general," two "special," and two "select," but these titles meant nothing. By increasing the number of subcommittees he was able, without depriving existing subcommittee chairmen of their positions, to reach lower down the seniority ladder and provide chairmanships for liberals such as Edith Green, James Roosevelt, and Frank Thompson Jr., and he channeled controversial social measures to their subcommittees. Carl D. Perkins, who succeeded Powell as chairman in 1967, continued the same pattern.

24. The House Ways and Means Committee has made use of ad hoc subcommittees but has not given them power to recommend legislation to the full committee. Senator Joseph S. Clark has called for the creation of subcommittees on social security and on tax measures within the Finance Committee, claiming that it has "perhaps the most extended and complicated jurisdiction of any of the committees of the Senate" *Congressional Record*, 88th Cong., 1st sess., 1963, p. 2664).

A conservative chairman usually will not want to see much development of subcommittees, especially if he heads one of the important control committees of Congress. It is significant that neither Senate Finance nor House Ways and Means has subcommittees, though there are logical subdivisions into which the work could be divided.[25] For a conservative chairman, perhaps the next best thing to having no subcommittees is to have numbered subcommittees without specified jurisdiction and to assign bills to them according to their responsiveness to his desires. The subcommittees with vague jurisdictions are all in the House. All have had chairmen of great seniority and two have had predominately conservative chairmen—the Armed Services Committee with Carl Vinson of Georgia and L. Mendel Rivers of South Carolina, and the District of Columbia Committee with John L. MacMillan of South Carolina. Judiciary has maintained numbered subcommittees, though their jurisdictions are fairly clear, out of deference to its chairman, Emanuel Celler, the senior member of the House in the 90th Congress.

Not all chairmen resist the development of subcommittees. Some may subdivide committee work from a desire for greater committee democracy. Clare Engle, when he was chairman of the House Committee on Interior and Insular Affairs, deliberately held his committee with a loose rein. He took a hand in the drawing up of rules that provided for a unique degree of democratic participation in committee activities and a large measure of subcommitte autonomy. Or some chairmen may create subcommittees for some strategic reason. It may be a move to prevent a rebellion on the part of the members, which seems to have been the reason for the creation of some subcommittees on House Education and Labor by Chairman Barden; or it may be a desire to maintain

25. During the period under consideration in this book the chairmen of the Finance Committee have been: Eugene D. Milliken (R., Colo., 1947–48, 1953–54), Walter F. George (D., Ga., 1949–52), Harry F. Byrd (D., Va., 1955–65), and Russell B. Long (D., La., 1965–68). Ways and Means chairmen have been: Harold Knudsen (R., Minn., 1947–48), Robert L. Doughton (D., N.C., 1949–52), Daniel A. Reed (R., N.Y., 1953–54), Jere Cooper (D., Tenn., 1955–56), and Wilbur D. Mills (D., Ark., 1958–68).

friendly relations with outside groups. Lister Hill, when chairman of the Senate Committee on Labor and Public Welfare, reportedly found it advisable to divest himself of direct contact with the problems of the aging, for he wanted to remain on good terms with the American Medical Association. A subcommittee was created in the 86th Congress to handle this subject and it was given great autonomy. In the 87th Congress it was made a select committee of the Senate and thus divorced entirely from the Labor Committee.

Two other factors play a part in encouraging the creation of subcommittees: the large size of the House, and the desire of outside groups for points of contact in Congress. There is certainly pressure for the establishment of subcommittees in the House, which acts as a counterbalance to the tendency of House chairmen to maintain more centralized control. There are more members looking for something to do and more demands from them for some means of achieving public recognition. Secondly, both nongovernmental pressure groups and government agencies find it to their advantage to have subcommittees, preferably with permanent staffs, with which they can work. As an example, both Judiciary subcommittees on immigration have provided a point of contact for interests believing in a restrictive immigration policy. Liberal interests in the field have given strong support to the special Senate Judiciary subcommittee to investigate problems connected with refugees and escapees.

Most subcommittees are organized to handle a specific functional problem of government such as agricultural production, Indian affairs, education, flood control, or disarmament. Some committees, however, have experimented with different types of organization. The House Agriculture Committee, for example, has two sets of subcommittees, one concerned with broad agricultural problems such as farm production, and another with specific agricultural commodities. Some staff members prefer the former as a means of getting committee members to take a broader view of agricultural policy. Committee members themselves seem to prefer the commodity organization as a means of better representing their specific clientele interests.[26] It is significant that the commodity subcommittees usually win when there is a jurisdictional dispute between them and the functional subcommittees.

Both House and Senate Foreign Affairs committees have subcommittees organized on a geographical basis (Europe, Africa, etc.) as well as those organized to handle such problems as disarmament and national security. They are all called consultative subcommittees and they are used primarily as a means of liaison with the Department of State.[27] Legislative proposals are handled by the full committee or by ad hoc subcommittees, though recently the House committee has begun to assign some bills to the consultative subcommittees. This practice may lead to jurisdictional disputes as to whether a matter should be referred to a geographical or a problem subcommittee.

Subcommitte organization in the Senate is rarely identical with that of the parallel House committee. Where their jurisdiction falls into natural subdivisions, subcommittee organization is more likely to be similar. The Interior committees are examples. They are, incidentally, the only committees to have maintained almost the same subcommittee organization since the 80th Congress. The two committees on Government Operations, on the other hand, have a far more vague jurisdiction, encompassing the entire field of government. Their subcommittees tend to reflect the interests of the chairmen and individual members.[28]

26. Jones found that, with three execptions, members of the House Agriculture Committee in the 85th Congress served on subcommittees that dealt with commodities produced in their districts. See Charles O. Jones, "Representation in Congress: The Case of the House Agriculture Committee," *American Political Science Review* (June 1961): 358.

27. The activity of these consultative subcommittees varies greatly with each chairman. Senator John F. Kennedy's African affairs subcommittee, for example, was largely inactive in 1959 and 1960 because its chairman had more pressing demands on his time.

28. In the 90th Congress, the House Committee on Government Operations had these subcommittees: executive and legislative reorganization, foreign operations and government information, government activities, intergovern-

Even though the House and Senate Interior committees have almost identical subcommittee pattern, this fact does not seem to lend impetus to bicameral subcommittee cooperation. In fact, there is very little cooperation between House and Senate subcommittees. A questionnaire sent to all committees produced only four examples of joint subcommittee hearings held in recent years: The District of Columbia committees on tax problems, Government Operations committees on intergovernmental relations, the Judiciary committees on the Immigration Act of 1952, and the Public Works committees on Niagara power. But six sets of parallel committees reported fairly close staff cooperation along subcommittee lines.[29]

Neither the House nor the Senate maintains any kind of detailed control over subcommittee organization. This may seem surprising, for subcommittee recommendations often become the law of the land without suffering major changes in the full committee or in the entire Congress. It is in keeping, however, with the general pattern of committee autonomy and the lack of any very effective party discipline.

The rules of the House and Senate do specify certain procedures that must be followed by subcommittees. For example, all subcommittee hearings, with certain stated exceptions, are to be open, and a subcommittee quorum may not be less than one-third of the membership except at a meeting for the purpose of taking testimony.[30]

The parent house has occasionally called for the establishment of specific subcommittees or instructed certain subcommittees

---

mental relations, legal and monetary affairs, military operations, natural resources and power, research and technical programs, special studies, and donable property. The Senate committee had: executive reorganization, foreign aid expenditures, government research, intergovernmental relations, national security and international operations, and permanent investigations.

29. Committees on Appropriations, Armed Services, District of Columbia, Foreign Affairs, Judiciary, and Labor.

30. See section 133 of the Legislative Reorganization Act (Public Law 601, 79th Cong., 2nd sess.); House Rule XI; Senate Rule XXV.

to carry out a designated task, but the overwhelming practice is to leave these decisions to the committees.[31] The parent house may also specifically call for a report to be made directly to the floor without the intervening approval of the full committee.[32] Again, however, the overwhelming practice is for the full committee to approve and submit subcommittee reports. The major house control is that of granting additional funds for subcommittee staff and expenses beyond the ten positions (four professional and six clerical) automatically granted each committee by the Legislative Reorganization Act. Committees, however, are rarely denied their requested budgets.

The most effective controls over subcommittees lie clearly in the hands of the individual committees. Whether these controls are exercised by a dominant senior minority of the membership or by a majority of the full committee varies from one committee to the next. There is likely to be a tug of war between the chairman (often joined by other senior members) and the junior members. These newer members may attempt to win greater control because they do not agree with the policies of the senior members, because they are impatient with committee inactivity on a particular topic, or because they seek the publicity that can come from a skillfully timed subcommittee investigation. Chairmen are generally fearful of letting too much power slip into the hands of members. Once a system of subdivision has been established or a subcommittee chairman appointed, a chairman can rarely undo the action, though he may occasionally reorganize subcommittees as a means of decreasing the powers of particular subcommittee chairmen. Many chairmen are painfully aware of the fact that a subcommittee, especially an investigating subcommittee, can capture the limelight and severely limit the freedom of action of the

31. Charles L. Watkins and Floyd M. Riddick, *Senate Procedure* (Washington, D.C.: Government Printing Office, 1958), p. 156; and Asher Hinds and Clarence Cannon, *Precedents of the House*, 11 vols. (Washington, D.C.: Government Printing Office, 1907), 3: sec. 1754.
32. Watkins and Riddick, *Senate Procedure*, p. 529; and Hinds and Cannon, *Precedents of the House*, 4: sec. 4551.

parent committee.[33] Often, but by no means always, chairmen are conservatives, fearful of sharing power with the more liberal junior colleagues. Again, a chairman may hold out against delegating subcommittee powers to individual committee members because he lacks confidence in their competence or readiness to discharge committee duties adequately.

In this struggle, the chairman deals from a stacked deck of cards. He should be able to maintain control even against rank-and-file rebellion, unless he is politically inept. A strong chairman can, in most cases, establish subcommittees, determine their size, appoint the members, establish party ratios, maintain ex officio membership, control the referral of bills, and either assign or hold back staff money for subcommittee operations. In recent years, however, committee members have developed a number of limits on these powers of chairmen.

Common practice allows the chairman primary control over subcommittee structure,[34] though he may well find it advisable to consult with other committee members. As has been pointed out, he may allow no subcommittees, work primarily by means of ad hoc subcommittees, create standing subcommittees but give them numbers and assign them no continuing jurisdiction, or he may establish standing subcommittees with clearly outlined jurisdiction and some degree of autonomy.

Subcommittee members are most commonly designated by the chairman alone, or in consultation with the ranking minority member. Appointments may be designed to punish slackers and enemies and to reward friends. Often senior members will be appointed to more subcommittees than junior members as a

---

33. For a fascinating example of such a situation, see Bernard Schwartz, *The Professor and the Commission* (New York: Alfred A. Knopf, 1959).
34. The power of a chairman to establish subcommittees has been challenged in the courts on the grounds that a competent tribunal must be created by resolution of the full committee. A Federal Court of Appeals, however, stated that "it is the unvarying practice of the Senate to follow the method of creating and appointing subcommittees which was employed in this instance." See *Meyers v. United States*, 171 Federal Reporter (Second Series) 800 (1948).

means of preventing the newer men from gaining too much control. Membership approval of appointments is not required on a majority of committees. Those interested in limiting the powers of committee chairmen often advocate rules that subcommittee chairmen be chosen on the basis of seniority, thus removing an element of discretion, and hence influence, on the part of chairmen. The House committees on Education and Labor, Interior and Insular Affairs, and Post Office and Civil Service are the only ones with such provisions written into their rules, but the pattern is evidently widely followed. One of the major reasons for this is that senior members are often unwilling to sit under junior subcommittee chairmen in the seniority-concious Congress. In the 90th Congress there were seventeen House committees which had subcommittees, and in nine of these no senior member of the majority party had been by-passed in the choice of subcommittee chairmen. In the Senate, eight of the fourteen subdivided committees followed seniority. Interestingly, in the less party-oriented Senate, two Republicans were allowed subcommittee chairmanships in the Democratically controlled 90th Congress. George D. Aiken was chairman of the Canadian affairs subcommittee of the Committee on Foreign Relations, and Everett M. Dirksen of the federal charters, holidays, and celebrations subcommittee of the Judiciary Committee.[35]

Party ratios on subcommittees may also be controlled by the chairmen, since the full house exercises no control here. The full committee is less likely to reverse the decisions of large subcommittees, especially with a safe majority party margin. Yet under certain circumstances, a small subcommittee can serve a chairman's needs, for he may be helped by absenteeism in the minority party. The ranking Republican member of the House Committee

35. Prior to the 84th Congress, the Judiciary Committee had a custom, after a change in party control, of giving the previous chairman of the full committee a subcommittee chairmanship. Senator Alexander Wiley was chairman of patents in the 81st and 82nd Congresses. Senator Pat McCarran was chairman of judicial machinery in the 83rd Congress. Republican J. Glenn Beall served as chairman of the business and commerce subcommittee of District of Columbia from the 84th through the 87th Congresses.

on Armed Services asked, unsuccessfully, at its organization meet-ing in 1961 that the party ratio on the special investigations sub-committee be raised from 3 to 2 to 4 to 3, so that "at least two members could be present most of the time."[36] Occasional com-plaints reach the stage of floor debate, as in 1951 when Clare E. Hoffman called for a resolution instructing the chairman of the House Committee on Appropriations to divide subcommittee membership between Democrats and Republicans "in as near as possible the same ratio that exists in the House" instead of using this device to "punish members who voted against his pet idea of the way appropriations bill should be handled."[37] A survey of subcommittee ratios during the 89th Congress when both houses had roughly 2 to 1 party ratios shows little uniformity. Few had ratios less favorable to the minority party than 2 to 1, and the great majority were more favorably divided.

Chairmen and ranking minority members often retain ex officio membership on all subcommittees. While this may not mean that these committee leaders attend regularly, it is another means of exerting control if a need is felt. The rules of ten of the twenty House committees give ex officio membership to both chairmen and ranking minority member, while in the case of Armed Services and Judiciary, only the chairman is made a member. There is no provision for ex officio membership by ranking minority members in the Senate, but the chairman is made a member in five of the sixteen committees.

The less automatic the referral of legislative matters to subcom-mittees is, the greater are the chairmen's powers. In two House committees in the 90th Congress, for example (Armed Services and District of Columbia), subcommittees had no clear field of jurisdiction and referral was made entirely at the discretion of the chairman. Other committee chairmen have used this device from time to time in the past. Charles Wolverton, Republican chairman

36. U.S. House of Representatives, Committee on Armed Services, "The Organization of the House Committee on Armed Services," committee print, Feb. 16, 1961, p. 9.
37. *Congressional Record*, 82nd Cong., 1st sess., 1951, p. 1174.

of the House Committee on Interstate and Foreign Commerce during the 80th Congress (1947–48) reportedly abolished sub-committee specialization because he was in basic disagreement with some of his senior Republican colleagues. Even the timing of referral can increase the chairman's power. Lister Hill of the Senate Labor and Public Welfare Committee did not refer important legislative matters until he had done careful preparatory groundwork, whereas in many committees, referral is handled by the clerk in routine fashion.

On the other hand, the Education and Labor, Post Office and Civil Service, and Public Works committees have placed limitations on committee chairmen by spelling out subcommittee jurisdiction in detail and making referral as automatic as possible. Education and Labor's rules are the most detailed, since they were adopted to limit former chairman Powell's ability to delay committee action. The chairman is to notify all subcommittee chairmen of proposed referrals, which are to be made according to defined subcommittee jurisdictions and without regard for the desires of the authors of the measures involved. If, after three days, there are no objections, final referral is made, though this must be done within a week from the day on which the measure was first received. A committee majority has the power to refer a measure at any time.

Chairmen are also in a position to control committee staff assignments. Most prefer to rotate staff members and not have them permanently assigned to a subcommittee. If a subcommittee can obtain its own permanent staff it has taken a major step towards independence from the full committee. In the 90th Congress, seven House and seven Senate committees had assigned permanent staff to at least a majority of their standing committees.

Chairmen can make skillful use of the allocation of funds to subcommittees. A subcommittee appropriation with few strings attached allows great freedom in the hiring of staff and other subcommittee activities. Also, the allocation of travel funds can be used effectively to reward and punish members. At the other extreme, subcommittee chairmen of the Education and Labor

Committee won complete control over these funds in the 89th Congress.

Finally, a chairman may, in the case of investigating subcommittees, withhold the subpoena power. Bernard Schwartz, recounting his experiences as staff man for the legislative oversight subcommittee of the House Committee on Interstate and Foreign Commerce, spoke to this point: "If Moulder [the subcommittee chairman] and I were given the subpoena power and the authority to secure a competent loyal staff, we would have obtained the very tools we needed to undertake a thorough probe which no one could control."[38]

Taking all these factors into consideration, which committees are the most centralized and which the least? The Finance Committee is clearly the most centralized committee in the Senate. Its chairmen have fought successfully against expansion of the size and liberalization of the membership of this important committee. Although its jurisdiction is easily divisible into such subject-matter areas as taxation, foreign trade, social security, and veterans' benefits, the committee's chairmen, not wanting to give its members "public forums for the expression of discontent," have never allowed the formation of subcommittees. Its budget has been kept low and its staff limited. Chairman Harry F. Byrd (1955–66) hired only one professional and supplemented his services with the staffs of the Legislative Reference Service and of the Joint Committee on Internal Revenue Taxation, a committee made up of the three top majority and the two top minority members of the Senate Finance and House Ways and Means committees. When Russell B. Long became chairman, he received permission to hire an additional six professional and six clerical staff people, but he had not filled all of these positions by the end of the 90th Congress. Though committee proceedings became more open and more informal under Long, the chairman continued to hold tight reigns on the committee.

By most tests, Judiciary Committee Chairman James O. East-

38. Schwartz, *The Professor and the Commission*, p. 102.

land of Mississippi has run as decentralized a committee as any in the Senate. He has given his senior members great freedom to develop subcommittee autonomy, with the tacit understanding that they would not be too aggressively pro civil rights. Testimony as to this autonomy may be gathered from a comparison of the size of Senate committee staffs. In 1965, when the total staff for each Senate committee averaged 28, Judiciary had 137, with all but 14 employed by twelve subcommittees.[39]

On the House side there have been more examples of chairmen who keep a great deal of power in their own hands, and also more examples of committees that have revolted against the powers of their chairmen. Probably the most centralized committee is Ways and Means, the opposite number of the Senate Finance Committee. Like Finance, the work of Ways and Means lends itself to subcommittee organization, and it was organized along these lines until 1961. Wilbur D. Mills made his reputation as chairman of a subcommittee on internal revenue, but he abolished all subcommittees a short time after he succeeded to the chairmanship of the full committee. The fact that the Democrats on the Ways and Means Committee also act as a committee-on-committees for their party gives the chairman, when Democrats control the House, unique added powers.

At least two House committees, at different times, have experienced extreme decentralization. During Clare Hoffman's chairmanship of Government Operations in the Republican 83rd Congress, committee members not only mutinied, but even more unusual, the whole affair was discussed at some length on the floor of the House.[40] Hoffman was a lone operator who had few legislative friends and who had alienated President Dwight D. Eisenhower by refusing for a long time to refer to subcommittee executive proposals to establish the Second Hoover Commission

39. Joint Committee on the Organization of Congress, Hearings, *The Organization of Congress*, pursuant to S. Con. Res. 2, 89th Cong., 1st sess., 1965, p. 206.
40. *Congressional Record*, 83rd Cong., 1st sess., 1953, pp. 9092–97, 9103–07, 9242–54, 10352–82.

and the Commission on Intergovernmental Relations. He made great use of ad hoc subcommittees consisting of two Republicans and one Democrat, appointed minority members without consulting the ranking Democrat on the committee, and evidently, in at least one instance, failed to notify the ranking Democrat of such a subcommittee's creation. Rebellion took place on July 15, 1953, when members voted 23 to 1 (six members abstaining) to prohibit further creation of ad hoc subcommittees save by resolution of the full committee. They further voted to grant virtual autonomy to the five existing standing subcommittees, giving each the power to appoint staff members and to fix their pay, to subpoena witnesses and to hold hearings outside Washington. Throughout that Congress subcommittee chairmen signed their own expense vouchers. Even in defeat, however, Hoffman did maintain his power to refer bills to subcommittees, and to approve the printing of subcommittee hearings and reports, and he used these to harass the rest of the committee members.[41] The Democratic chairman of Government Operations, William L. Dawson, has encountered no rebellion of this sort. His subcommittees have large permanent staffs and sizeable budgets; they issue their own press releases and carry on their own mailing operations. The chairman, however, does maintain considerable quiet control over the creation, assignment of members, and reference of measures to subcommittees. He also maintains a degree of control over committee budget and staff.

In 1965 there was a rebellion against Tom Murray of Tennessee who had served as the chairman of the Post Office and Civil Service Committee since 1949, with the exception of the Republican 83rd Congress. In that liberal 89th Congress, committee members reacted against their chairman's conservative attitude toward government salaries. They adopted committee rules that severely limited his choice of subcommittee chairmen and members, his freedom of referring matters to them, and his control over budget

41. It took great pressure from President Eisenhower to get Chairman Hoffman to refer to subcommittee proposals to establish the Second Hoover Commission and the Commission on Intergovernmental Relations.

and staff. In the 90th Congress, the rules were modified to give somewhat greater power to the new chairman, Thaddeus J. Dulski, but the committee remained one of the most decentralized in the House.

Conflicting drives for authority between chairmen and less senior members will continue to appear in the subcommittee structure. Subcommittees allow greater specialization in the legislative branch in an era that puts a premium on specialization. They also give a flexibility to the seniority system, by allowing less senior committee members to play effective legislative roles. These facts and the gradual coming to power of younger, more organization-minded chairmen must inevitably cut into the degree of centralized control that was once maintained by such chairmen as Harry Byrd and Carl Vinson.

4.

The Giant Jigsaw Puzzle:
Assigning Members of the House

"A new Congressman's first thought," said Representative D. S. Saund, "is to obtain an appointment on a good committee."[1] If he fails to receive a good initial appointment, he will seek to transfer to one that suits his experience and the interests of his constituency as soon as an opening is available. Once he finds what he wants, he will be tempted to settle in so that he can reap the rewards of the seniority system. By his committee work he will establish his reputation with his colleagues, leave his mark on legislation, and help his reputation in his home district.. The greater part of his legislative time, with the exception of errand running for his constituents, will be spent on committee work. As a result, members will "fight tooth and nail" for favorable assignments,[2] though the struggle rarely receives public attention.

The task of assigning members to committees is a complex one, and perhaps it is best to discuss House and Senate practices separately. Before doing so, however, a few general comments are in order concerning committee size and representation of the minor party on committees.

Concerning the problem of committee size, Robert Luce has said:

> The committee has three functions: first, the acquiring of information and opinion from outside; next, the forming

1. D. S. Saund, *Congressman from India* (New York: E. P. Dutton, 1960), p. 117.
2. Champ Clark, *My Quarter Century of American Politics*, 2 vols. (New York: Harpers, 1920), I: 205.

and formulation of judgment from within; thirdly, the persuading of the House to adopt the conclusions reached. For the first and third of these, the committee can hardly be too large. . . .

On the other hand, the forming and formulating of preliminary judgment call for a membership small enough to permit the desirable interplay of ideas which is found to be most effective when but a few men sit around a table. . . . A larger number invites for formalities of oratory; . . . and weakens personal interest by diminishing personal sense of responsibility.[3]

Here, of course, the Senate with its 100 members and sixteen committees has the advantage over the House with its 435 members and twenty-one committees. The average Senate committee in the 90th Congress had 16 members while the average House committee had 30. Even with this favorable differential, some senators complain about the size of their committees. When Majority Leader Lyndon B. Johnson proposed increasing the membership of the more important committees in 1959, Senator Russell B. Long commented:

> I have served on some of the larger committees. I say, as a junior member on some of them, that if an important witness comes before some of them it takes the witness all day before he can get back to his office dowtown to do his work. If a junior Senator wishes to ask a question, he must often wait until the Senate has been in session two hours before he can ask the question. Simply as a matter of seniority, the usual result is that a junior Senator on the major committees is foreclosed from asking a question, as a practical matter, if an important executive department witness is before the committee.[4]

3. Robert Luce, *Legislative Procedure* (Boston: Houghton Mifflin Co., 1922), pp. 129–30.
4. *Congressional Record*, 86th Cong., 1st sess., 1959, p. 652.

Some few voices have been raised against the representation of the members of the minority party on committees. Though he was speaking of ad hoc and not of standing committees, Thomas Jefferson's statement has been used as an argument against such representation. He said, ". . . the child is not to be put to the nurse that cares not for it. . . . It is therefore a constant rule 'that no man is to be employed in any matter who has declared himself against it.' "[5] Woodrow Wilson also opposed the practice, claiming that "it is plainly the representation of both parties on the Committees that makes party responsibility indistinct and organized party action almost impossible."[6]

In justifying the practice of seating all members on committees, Robert Luce has said,

> Every member of Congress has the chance to contribute towards good legislation. If he belongs to the majority party, he is not necessarily a voting dummy as in Parliament: If he belongs to the minority, he is not restricted to mere fault finding, as Mr. Wilson wanted him to be, but in the committee room may play a most useful part in constructive effort for the public good.[7]

Committee Size

In making committee assignments one of the basic considerations is the size of committees as fixed by the rules of the House, a factor that determines the total number of committee positions available. In the 79th Congress, prior to the Legislative Reorganization Act, over one-half of the representatives had single committee assignments, though one member had nine. This was

5. Thomas Jefferson, *Manual of Parliamentary Practice*, sec. 26, *Rules of the U.S. House of Representatives.*
6. Woodrow Wilson, *Congressional Government*, Meridian Paperback Edition (New York: Meridian Books, 1956), p. 81.
7. Robert Luce, *Congress: An Evaluation* (Cambridge: Harvard University Press, 1926), p. 107.

changed by the Reorganization Act so that all but fifty members had single assignments and none had more than two.[8] (The act's promise of more equitable distribution of committee positions probably appealed to less-senior House members, just as its promise of fewer committees and therefore a greater assurance of control by those with seniority had appeal to members with longevity.) The number of committees was reduced by over one-half, from forty-eight to nineteen, with a resulting increase in the average committee size from nineteen to twenty-five. The maximum number of berths was fixed at 484. The House since has changed committee sizes from those fixed by the Reorganization Act more freely than in the Senate. In the 90th Congress, House committees had an average of five more members than they were originally allotted.[9]

Second committee assignments have never been restricted as severely in the House and third assignments in the Senate. The Legislative Reorganization Act provided that members of District of Columbia and Un-American Activities and majority members of Government Operations and House Administration could serve on two committees, with the rest to serve on only one. In July 1952, this rule was changed to allow both majority and minority members of the four named committees to have second assignments. In 1953, however, the rule was abandoned entirely, because of the close party balance in the House. Instead, certain informal understandings have been followed. Appropriations, Rules, and Ways and Means are considered exclusive assignments. Nine committees are considered semiexclusive in that a member may serve

8. There has been a steady increase in the number of double committee assignments since the Legislative Reorganization Act, from 50 in 1947 to 188 in 1967. See Louis C. Gawthrop, "Changing Membership Patterns in House Committees," *American Political Science Review* (June 1966): 366.

9. House Administration, Un-American Activities, and Ways and Means had the same size in the 90th Congress that they had in the 80th; the District of Columbia and Veterans' Affairs committees had been reduced in size; and the remaining fourteen committees had been increased by between one and eleven members. Science and Astronautics has also been increased since it was created in 1958.

on any one of them and on any one of the eight nonexclusive committees. The so-called semiexclusive committees are Agriculture, Armed Services, Banking and Currency, Education and Labor, Foreign Affairs, Interstate and Foreign Commerce, Judiciary, Public Works, and Science and Astronautics. The nonexclusive committees are District of Columbia, Government Operations, House Administration, Interior and Insular Affairs, Merchant Marine and Fisheries, Post Office and Civil Service, Un-American Activities, and Veterans' Affairs. Republicans do not follow exactly the same grouping of committees, although only rarely will a member of Appropriations, Rules, or Ways and Means receive a second committee assignment.

Matters of party ratios on committees, as well as decisions as to size, are worked out by the majority and minority party leaders of the House. For the period under consideration, party strength on committees has closely reflected party strength in the House. The majority party was most overrepresented during the 83rd Congress, when the two parties in the House were most evenly divided. This was necessary in order to give the majority party a margin of control of committees, and even then the Veterans' Affairs Committee was evenly divided between Republicans and Democrats. The majority party was least overrepresented in Congresses when it had a wide margin of control. Looking at specific committees rather than at specific Congresses, the three control committees have had fixed party ratios that give the majority party an advantage in numbers, regardless of the party ratio in the House. Rules was set at 8 to 4 (this ratio was changed to 10 to 5 in the 87th Congress); Ways and Means was set at 15 to 10 (this ratio was changed to 17 to 8 in the 89th Congress only); and, from the 82nd through the 88th Congresses, Appropriations was kept at a ratio of 30 to 20, in the 89th Congress it was set at 34 to 16, and in the 90th, 30 to 21; Un-American Activities, on the other hand, has been kept as nearly even balanced as possible, with a 5 to 4 ratio, as is often the case with investigating committees.[10] The

10. The only exception to this was the 6 to 3 ratio in the 89th Congress.

other committees fall into place between these two extremes, with Armed Services and Foreign Affairs actually giving some overrepresentation to the minority party.

Assigning Members[11]

In the struggle within the House of Representatives over where the power of making committee appointments should lie, it was inevitable that the full membership of the House should lose. The task was too complex to allow for individual balloting on each committee position. The Speaker won the power, only to have some portions of it taken away in the revolt against Speaker Joseph Cannon in 1910. He can no longer by-pass the seniority system in making promotions within committee and in designating chairmen. He can no longer control committee assignments of the minority party. He and the majority leader, in cooperation with his party's committee-on-committees, can, however, usually control initial appointments of committee members of the majority party.

In the 1st Congress, the Speaker made assignments to committees with three or fewer members. Members of larger committees were chosen by the awkward process of balloting. The next year, however, the Speaker took over the task of making assignments unless the House determined otherwise. For more than a century, members attempted, unsuccessfully, to take this power away from the Speaker, with the struggle increasing during the forceful regimes of Speakers Thomas B. Reed and Joseph Cannon.[12] In-

11. Much of the information in this section is based on Nicholas A. Masters, "House Committee Assignments," *American Political Science Review* (June 1961): 353; and Charles L. Clapp, *The Congressman: His Work as He Sees It* (Washington D.C.: The Brookings Institution, 1963), chap. 5. Leo H. Irwin, chief counsel of the Ways and Means Committee, and several members of both Democratic and Republican committees-on-committees have been helpful to the author in his research.

12. Even when he completely dominated committee assignments, the Speaker tended to follow seniority as a means of regularizing his task. One study of

surgent Republican George Norris, the leader of the anti-Cannon revolt, felt that "committee assignments were the rawhide used to promote party subserviency and to crush any spirit of independence," and he wanted the task of making assignments given to a newly constituted Rules Committee which would represent the entire country and every interest in the country but which would not include the Speaker.[13] The Democrats and insurgent Republicans could only agree on weakening the Speaker's powers, however, not on this method of making assignments. Beginning with the 62nd Congress (1911–13), the appointment power was taken from the Speaker and nominally given to the full House. Since the parties immediately agreed to leave each other the task of designating their own members according to an agreement worked out between their leaders as to size and party ratios, floor election became a fiction.[14] Appointments have been made by each party's committee-on-committees. The party caucuses ratify the appointments and the full House elects them on separate motions from the floor made by the party leaders. These motions are privileged (and, therefore, they may be brought up at any time), they are not divisible (and, therefore, cannot be amended), and it is in order to move and second a previous question (and, therefore, there is not likely to be any debate on the lists presented).[15]

---

the Speakership notes that seniority prevailed in four-fifths of Cannon's appointments during the 58th through the 61st Congresses. See Chang Wei Chiu, *The Speaker of the House of Representatives* (New York: Columbia University Press, 1928), p. 71.

13. George W. Norris, *Fighting Liberal* (New York: Macmillan Co., 1945), p. 132.

14. Luce, *Legislative Procedure*, pp. 106–109.

15. See the note on Rule X in *Rules of the U.S. House of Representatives*. The Speaker has continually held the power to appoint members of conference committees, and he has usually held the power to appoint members of select committees, though prior to 1880, the House occasionally deprived him of this right.

Delegates from Puerto Rico and, prior to 1959, Alaska and Hawaii, have been assigned, according to the rules, to Agriculture, Armed Services, Interior, and Merchant Marine. Delegates may make motions in committees but they may not vote.

In 1911 the Democrats decided to give the task of making committee assignments to their members on the Ways and Means
Committee. At this time, and until 1923, the ranking Democrat on
that committee was the floor leader, and the choice was made so
as not to weaken his control over the appointments. Nominations
for new members of Ways and Means are made in the Democratic
caucus, and they almost invariably follow the wishes of the party
leaders. The detailed paper work of making assignments is performed by the staff of the committee.

The Democratic members of Ways and Means, who compose
the Democratic committee-on-committees as it has been constituted from the 80th through the 90th Congress, have reflected the
regional strength of the Democratic party fairly accurately, as
may be seen from the table 4:1. The committee has had a relatively high percentage of liberal and moderate members: 60.3 percent fell into the liberal category on the basis of their floor voting
record, 31.4 percent in the moderate category, and only 8.3 percent were classified as conservatives (see chapter 6 for a discussion
of the terms liberal, moderate, and conservative). A glance at the
constituencies of the members during the 90th Congress shows
that all but George M. Rhodes of Pennsylvania and Dan Rosten-
kowski of Illinois had won the last election by greater than 60
percent of the vote.

Nicholas Masters, in his study of House committee assignments,
concludes that the committee is "ill-designed for flexibility and
responsiveness to electoral changes and public opinion trends.

TABLE 4:1
Regional Representation of Democrats on the Ways and Means
Committee and in the House, 80th through 90th Congresses

	EAST	MIDWEST	SOUTH	WEST
Percentage of Ways and Means Democrats by region	20.6	20.6	47.8	11.0
Percentage of House Democrats by region	24.7	19.1	44.3	11.9
Disproportion in committee representation	−4.1	+1.5	+3.5	−.9

Rather, it is analogous to a firmly entrenched bureaucracy, not completely immune, but well insulated, and capable of resistance to pressures placed upon it." In performing its tasks, the committee shows moderation and detachment, in keeping with House norms. Senior members are not likely to favor giving the delicate task of assigning members to committees to those with less legislative experience. Junior members realize that they might hurt their legislative future if they were given the task of deciding on transfer requests of senior members.[16]

New members of Congress and those who want to change their assignments state their preferences in writing, usually after having discussed the matter with the dean of their state delegation and the member of Ways and Means from their zone. They may also speak with their party leaders and the committee chairmen. Their requests are tempered by their assessment of chances of winning appointment to the more popular committees. Members generally point out how their request can best allow them to serve their constituents and assist them in reelection.

Committee-on-committees members are each assigned to a zone, that is a number of states, generally contiguous, including the member's own district, and made up of a roughly equal number of Democratic congressmen. At a committee meeting, members, speaking in the order of seniority, nominate candidates from their zones to fill the openings. The committee votes separately on each assignment and the nominee with the highest vote wins. Masters notes that the fact that committee-on-committee members are also members of a standing committee militates against this being a meeting of equals. The chairman and those who have won respect for their work on Ways and Means are more likely to be successful in their nominations.

While the Democratic Speaker and floor leader are not members of this committee their presence is felt in the deliberations, as the following ditty notes:

16. Masters, "House Committee Assignments," pp. 348, 350.

> I love Speaker Rayburn, his heart is so warm,
> And if I love him he'll do me no harm.
> So I shan't sass the Speaker one little bitty,
> And then I'll wind up on a major committee.[17]

Speaker Sam Rayburn left his imprint on many House committees, though evidence of this rarely appears in the *Congressional Record* as clearly as in the following statement addressed by Floor Leader John W. McCormack to Howard Smith in the course of the 1961 debate over the enlargement of the House Rules Committee:

> I might say that I was a member of the committee-on-committees, and my friend, the gentleman from Virginia, is the only Democratic member in my thirty-three years that was elected by the committee-on-committees to the Committee on Rules when he was not recommended by the Speaker and the Majority Leader. He was the choice of those of us who were defeated.[18]

McCormack was referring to the fact that, even though they had been defeated in their quest for the House leadership, Rayburn and he had succeeded in placing Smith on the Rules Committee. The newly elected Speaker, Henry T. Rainey, had neglected to exercise his traditional power over committee assignments. It is common knowledge that Rayburn showed a continuing interest in Democratic appointments to Ways and Means, making sure that members would favor reciprocal trade programs and would oppose any change in the depletion tax allowance granted the oil companies. Further, he is reported to have played a role in stacking the Appropriations Committee against its chairman, Clarence Cannon, and to have liberalized the membership of the Un-American Activities Committee and the Committee on Education and Labor.

17. Quoted by Arthur Krock, *New York Times,* April 8, 1958.
18. *Congressional Record,* 87th Cong., 1st sess., 1961, p. 1580.

Rayburn and McCormack were not always successful in having their choices named to committees, however. For example, Earle C. Clements of Kentucky, elected to the 79th Congress, was able to win the support of enough influential members of the committee-on-committees to defeat the choice of the party leaders for a position on Agriculture. In 1963 the Democratic caucus that chooses its Ways and Means delegation turned down Speaker McCormack's choice of Phil. W. Landrum of Georgia in favor of W. Pat Jennings of Virginia.[19] While such an occurrence is rare, it points up the fact that a wedge can sometimes be driven between the leaders and the committee or the caucus, and that the leader of the Democrats on Ways and Means has independent leverage.

After the Cannon revolt of 1910, Republicans gave the task of making assignments directly to their floor leader. But in 1919, when the party gained control of the House for the first time since 1910, the caucus established its own committee-on-committees that has as its sole purpose the making of assignments, unlike its Democratic counterpart. It consists of one member from each state, who has as many votes as there are Republicans in his delegation. The Republican Speaker, or floor leader when the party is not in control of Congress, has a more formal relationship to the committee than the Democratic party leader, for he presides without vote over its meeting. The method of weighted voting gives greater strength to the predominately Republican states than the Democratic method does for the states with large Democratic delegations. In the 90th Congress members from seven big states (California, Illinios, Michigan, New Jersey, New York, Ohio, and Pennsylvania) controlled 94 of the 187 votes, or just over 50 percent.[20] Masters concludes that the Republican committee is no

19. The belief at the time was that McCormack supported Landrum's candidacy for Ways and Means in return for the Georgia delegation's support for permanent enlargement of the Rules Committee in 1963. See Richard Bolling, *House Out Of Order* (New York: E. P. Dutton, 1965), p. 75.
20. No conservatism scores can be worked out for the members of the committee for the entire period, for the membership records were lost in the shift of control from Joseph Martin Jr. to Charles A. Halleck.

more sensitive to electoral change than that of the Democrats. He suggests that the major difference is

> that the Republicans have built into their system a voting formula that rewards heavy Republican areas; the Democrats offer no comparable leverage to the large delegations. Nor is it likely that Democrats would even consider such a plan as long as the seniority system prevails. For it would only lessen the power of Southern Democrats by putting more control over committee assignments into the hands of the larger northern, midwestern and western delegations, with their many different traditions and interests.[21]

The Republican committee is larger than the Democratic committee (forty-three in the 90th Congress, as compared with fifteen), and it varies with the number of states with Republican congressmen. Most of the detailed work is performed by a subcommittee that generally consists of members from the big Republican delegations. It is appointed by and works closely with the party leader, and its decisions are invariable accepted by the full committee. Joseph Martin, Republican floor leader from the 76th through the 85th Congresses, with the exceptions of the 80th and the 83rd when he was Speaker, tells of having made sure that only "mature men" received important committee positions:

> While the committee-on-committees may formally select members for committees, for example, the Speaker does in fact exercise a strong influence over these choices from among the ranks of his own party. Thus members must look to him for a chance of advancement. In the four years that I served as Speaker no Republican went on an important committee without my approval.[22]

The process of seeking favorable assignments and the decisions

21. Masters, "House Committee Assignments, p. 350.
22. Joseph Martin, *My First Fifty Years in Politics* (New York: McGraw-Hill, 1960), p. 181.

made by the committee-on-committees are essentially the same as those followed by the Democratic party. The routine work is performed by the staff of the party leader's office. The major differences between the two parties are somewhat greater attempts on the part of Republicans to use assignments to reward or punish members according to their ideological support, and to spread out leadership and ranking standing committee positions. (Since 1965, no Republican has been allowed to serve as both party and committee leader.)[23]

In working out the "giant jigsaw puzzle" of committee appointments,[24] both committees-on-committees operate in a similar fashion. They must, of course, be guided by the number of committee positions agreed upon by the leaders of the two parties, by the number and place of the vacancies, and by the applications for transfers and for initial assignments. For members who seek to transfer, seniority in the House is an important but not a controlling factor. Representatives are ranked according to length of uninterrupted service, dating from the day on which they are sworn in. Credit is given for previous House service. Those with three nonconsecutive terms, for example, are ranked ahead of those with two consecutive terms, though below those with three consecutive terms. Previous experiences as an elected official are given some weight.

Masters found that somewhat different criteria are used in making assignments to the three all-important control committees—Appropriations, Rules, and Ways and Means—than to the other committees. Here party leaders play their most influential role. They use these assignments "to bargain with the leaders of party group or faction, in order to preserve and fortify their leadership positions and conciliate potential rivals, as well as to reward mem-

23. Randall B. Ripley, *Party Leaders in the House of Representatives* (Washington, D.C.: The Brookings Institution, 1967), pp. 190–92.
24. "It is a perfectly terrific headache for those who have the job of trying to make committee assignments" (Senator Wallace H. White in U.S. Congress, Joint Committee on the Organization of Congress, Hearings, *The Organization of Congress*, pursuant to H. Con. Res. 18, 79th Cong., 1st sess., 1945, p. 394.

bers who have cooperated."[25] These choice assignments usually go to members who have served two or more terms, who come from districts that will allow them to "make controversial decisions on major policy questions without constant fear of reprisals at the polls,"[26] and who have demonstrated their "legislative responsibility." Responsible members are those who show a respect for their colleagues and for the legislative process, a willingness to compromise, and a gradualist approach. "In short," Masters concludes, "a responsible legislator is politically pliant, but not without conviction."[27]

Assignments to the other committees are generally less carefully scrutinized by the party leaders. In making appointments to these, the most important consideration, according to Masters, "is to provide each member with an assignment which will help reinsure his reelection. . . . In distributing assignments the party acts as a mutual benefit and improvement society, and this for the obvious reason that control of the House depends on the reelection of party members."[28] This means, for example, that members from farm districts will be given preference on the Agricultural Committee, those from districts with union strength on Education and Labor, those from port districts on Merchant Marine and Fisheries, and those from districts including public land and power projects on Interior and Insular Affairs. The system by no means guarantees the representation of different points of view on committees,

25. Masters, "House Committee Assignments," p. 357. For example, Representative John Flynt of Georgia was told that he could not have a coveted position on Appropriations if he voted against Rayburn on enlargement of the Rules Committee in 1961. See *Congressional Quarterly Weekly Report*, Nov. 17, 1961, p. 1853. Flynt did not make it in that Congress, but he did in the next. He had voted for enlargement of the committee in 1963; he had not in 1961.

26. Masters, "House Committee Assignments," p. 353.

27. Ibid., p. 357. Richard Fenno has pointed out the similarity of legislative responsibility and "the folkways of the Senate," a phrase used by Donald R. Matthews in *U. S. Senators and Their World* (Chapel Hill: University of North Carolina Press, 1960), chap. 5. See Richard F. Fenno Jr., "The House Appropriations Committee," *American Political Science Review* (June 1962): 310.

28. Masters, "House Committee Assignments," p. 357.

but rather tends to increase committee support for a given function of government and for the executive agency that handles the function. Charles O. Jones tells of an interesting exception to the general pattern in his study of the House Agriculture Committee. Victor Anfuso of Brooklyn made some political hay as representative of consumer interests when he was a member during the 84th Congress. He was, however, transferred to Merchant Marine and to Science and Astronautics in the 86th Congress. "I didn't ask to be taken off the Committee," he stated, "but the committee-on-committees wanted to have more farm legislators on the committee and they told me I would be put on committees which would be of more interest to me."[29] The idea of an urban member of Agriculture evidently caught on, however, for Benjamin S. Rosenthal of Queens served in the 88th Congress and Frank J. Brasco of Brooklyn in the 90th.[30]

Generally, chairmen and the ranking members have the power to suggest and to veto nominations to their committees, unless they happen to be out of favor with the party leadership. This helps to explain the homogeneity and teamwork of some committee delegations. And chairmen may well be contacted by those who seek to get a member on a given committee. When President Franklin D. Roosevelt, for example, wanted to have freshman Congressman Lyndon B. Johnson assigned to the Naval Affairs Committee, he invited its chairman, Carl Vinson, to dinner at the White House.[31]

Interest groups are vitally concerned with the appointments to committees that concern them. A Brookings Institution round-

29. Charles O. Jones, "The Relationship of Congressional Committee Action to a Theory of Representation" (Ph.D. diss., University of Wisconsin, 1960).

30. When Shirley Chisholm, the first Negro woman to be elected to the House, learned at the opening of the 91st Congress that she had been assigned to the Agriculture Committee, she commented: "Apparently all they know in Washington about Brooklyn is that a tree grew there. I can think of no other reason for assigning me to the House Agriculture Committee" (*Washington Post*, Jan. 30, 1969).

31. William S. White, *The Professional* (Boston: Houghton Mifflin Co., 1964), p. 139.

table discussion among members of the House noted particularly the activities of business, labor, and agricultural groups.[32] Rather than attempting to influence the committee-on-committees or the chairmen, however, they are more likely to encourage a member who is known to be sympathetic to apply for membership, or to remain on a particular committee when he is considering transferring. It is not unusual for interest groups to contribute to the campaign fund of such a member.

Masters notes a number of factors that play a role in committee assignments beyond the consideration of a member's constituency and the influences of interest groups. A member's section, his professional background, his religion and race, and his ideological position receive some attention. In general, only large states have more than one member on a party committee delegation, but the goal of balanced geographical representation is given low priority except on Appropriations and Ways and Means. Professional background is noted at least to the extent that positions on Judiciary and Un-American Activities are reserved for lawyers, and those with previous experience in international relations are often given preference on Foreign Affairs and on Armed Services. Democrats feel that it is important to have a Roman Catholic on such committees as Ways and Means and Education and Labor. Charles Diggs was helped in his quest for an assignment to Foreign Affairs by the fact that he was a Negro.[33] A member's ideological position is often noted, not so much with an eye to giving balance to committees as to keeping extremists off the most important committees. Finally, some assignments are made totally at random, usually for freshmen who fail to make their desires known or to win support for their applications.

32. Clapp, *The Congressman*, p. 205.
33. The six Negroes elected to the 90th Congress had the following committee assignments: John Conyers Jr. (D., Mich., 1965–   ), Judiciary; William L. Dawson (D., Ill., 1943–   ), chairman of Government Operations, District of Columbia; Charles C. Diggs Jr. (D., Mich., 1955–   ), District of Columbia, Foreign Affairs; Augustus F. Hawkins (D., Calif., 1963–   ), Education and Labor; Robert P. Nix (D., Pa., 1958–   ), Foreign Affairs, Post Office; Adam Clayton Powell (D., N.Y., 1945–   ), removed from chairmanship of Education and Labor.

5.

The Giant Jigsaw Puzzle: Assigning Members of the Senate

SIMPLE MATHEMATICS would lead one to conclude that the struggle for favorable committee assignments is less serious in the Senate than in the House, for there are approximately one-quarter as many people competing. A reading of the *Congressional Record*, however, turns up ample evidence that members are greatly concerned and some highly dissatisfied with the "jigsaw puzzle" as it has been worked out in the Senate.

Committee Size

Persuasive arguments can be made, especially in the smaller Senate, for placing a strict limitation on the total number of committee positions, and thus on the number of assignments for each Senator: it makes for a more equitable distribution of committee seats between the two parties; it decreases the work load of each senator and thus allows for greater specialization; and it makes for less formalized, more democratic committee procedure.[1] These arguments were accepted by the framers of the Legislative Reorganization Act. The act reduced the average number of assignments per senator from five to two. The number of committees was halved, their size was reduced, and a maximum of 203 stand-

1. See testimony of the former chairman of the Joint Committee on the Organization of Congress, Robert LaFollette, in U.S. Senate, Committee on Expenditures in Executive Departments, *The Organization of Congress*, Hearings, 1948, p. 64.

ing committee openings was fixed—two for each of the 96 members plus eleven third committee assignments for members of the majority party on District of Columbia and Government Operations.

There are also persuasive arguments for increasing the number of committee positions and not submitting to "the tyranny of numbers."[2] If more members are allowed third committee assignments, it is possible to keep more experienced senators on the less important committees.[3] It allows greater flexibility in placing members where they are best fitted by interest and skills.[4] It gives the party leaders more favors in the form of choice committee posts to distribute as a means of encouraging their loyalty. The arguments for flexibility and party power have evidently been more persuasive than those for specialization, for the number of positions has been increased in each Congress since the 83rd. The average Senate committee had two more members in the 90th Congress than it had under the provisions of the Legislative Reorganization Act, and the total number of committee positions had been increased by forty-nine.[5]

With a desire not to overload individual senators, third committee assignments were strictly limited by the Legislative Reorganization Act, and they were meant primarily as a means of allowing the majority party to have a favorable margin in all committees. Third assignments were allowed to only eleven members

2. This phrase was used by Senator Francis Case in discussing committee assignments, *Congressional Record*, 83rd Cong., 1st sess., 1953, p. 334.
3. Senator Robert Taft noted that the District of Columbia Committee lost Senators George Aiken and Homer Ferguson, who had long contributed to the work of that committee, because of the strict two-assignment rule for minority party members (*Congressional Record*, 80th Cong., 2nd. sess., 1948, p. 131).
4. Senator Elmer Thomas objected to the cut in his committee assignments in the 80th Congress. He said that he should look after the needs of the Indians and the farmers in his state and he deserved a position on Appropriations because of his seniority. See *Congressional Record*, 80th Cong., 1st sess., 1947, p. 6455.
5. This figure reflects the creation of a new fifteen-member committee, Aeronautical and Space Sciences, and the additon of four new senators from Alaska and Hawaii.

of the majority party, on District of Columbia and Government Operations. In the 90th Congress, third committee assignments were allowed to nineteen majority and ten minority party members on District of Columbia, Post Office, and Rules and Administration.

According to the Legislative Reorganization Act, all committees were to have thirteen members, except for Appropriations which was fixed at twenty-one, and this arrangement held until the 83rd Congress, though there were rumblings of discontent from the minority party. The changes made, beginning in 1953, have brought about an increase in the membership of the more popular committees and a decrease in those that are less sought after. By the 90th Congress, twelve committees had increased in size and three, all housekeeping committees, had decreased.[6] In presenting his proposal for a general increase in committee sizes in the 86th Congress, Majority Leader Lyndon B. Johnson, with the agreement of Minority Leader Everett M. Dirksen, stated that the goal was to suit the background and interests of the members, to distribute the work load, and "to combine youth and vigor with experience and years of service."[7] Senator Russell B. Long voiced a lone criticism, complaining that larger committees give less chance for junior members to participate meaningfully in committee proceedings. Increasing the size of a committee is also a means of changing its ideological complexion. Senator Joseph S. Clark made this very clear when, at the start of the 88th Congress, he made an unsuccessful motion that the seventeen-member Finance Committee (eleven Democrats, six Republicans) be increased to twenty-one (fourteen Democrats, seven Republicans), so that the liberal faction could become more effective in responding to President John F. Kennedy's program.[8]

6. Foreign Relations increased by six members; Appropriations, Armed Services, and Commerce, by five; Finance and Interior, by four; Judiciary, Labor, and Public Works, by three; Agriculture and Government Operations, by two; and Banking and Currency, by one. Aeronautical and Space Sciences has remained at fifteen. Rules and Administration has been reduced by six, District of Columbia by five, and Post Office by one.

7. *Congressional Record*, 86th Cong., 1st sess., 1949, p. 650.

8. *Congressional Record*, 88th Cong., 1st sess., 1963, p. 2564.

Unlike the House, no Senate committees have an agreed-upon party ratio that holds over from one Congress to the next, regardless of the relative size of the two parties in the Senate. Committee ratios have fairly accurately reflected changes of party strength, though some distortion is inevitable when the two parties are nearly evenly divided, in order to give the majority at least nominal control of committees.[9]

Assigning Members[10]

The Senate, being a smaller body than the House, and not having its party leader as presiding officer, has never concentrated in one person the power of making committee assignments, as the House did with its Speaker for a long period in its history. The first method used in the Senate was that of election of members from the floor, and it kept returning to this procedure after experimenting with giving the power to the presiding officer from 1822 to 1826, and more specifically, to the president pro tem from 1828 to 1833.[11] Election from the floor was time-consuming and contained a large element of chance, however. In 1846 the present method, essentially the same as that used by the House since 1911, was adopted. Committees-on-committees, working closely with party leaders, fill vacancies; their decisions are ratified by the party

9. For illustration, see the colloquy between Alben W. Barkley and Robert A. Taft in the 80th Congress concerning the Republican decision to have a two-man margin on Interior, Labor, and Rules rather than the one-man margin of the rest of the committees (*Congressional Record*, 80th Cong., 1st sess., 1947, pp. 115–18). In the 81st Congress, Senator Arthur H. Vandenberg objected to the decrease in minority representation on Foreign Relations, claiming it to be a blow to a bipartisan foreign policy (*Congressional Record*, 81st Cong., 1st sess., 1949, p. 61).

10. Assistance in the preparation of this section was given by Senator Earl C. Clements (former whip), Robert G. Baker (former secretary for the majority), and J. Mark Trice (secretary for the minority).

11. The term presiding officer could mean either vice president or president pro tem. When Calhoun became vice president in 1825 he exercised this power so firmly that it was taken away from him by the Senate after four months. See George H. Haynes, *The Senate of the United States* (Boston: Houghton Mifflin Co., 1938), p. 274.

caucus, usually without dissent; and the whole Senate votes on the adoption of the party lists.

Senate Rule XXIV is somewhat more detailed than House Rule X concerning the method of making assignments to committees, though it reveals little more about the actual process:

> In the appointment of standing committees, the Senate, unless otherwise ordered, shall proceed by ballot to appoint severally the chairmen of each committee, and then, by one ballot, the other members of the same. A majority of the whole number of votes given shall be necessary to the choice of a chairman to a standing committee, but a plurality of votes shall elect the other members thereof.

The procedure followed during the period under consideration was to suspend the rules by unanimous consent and to adopt resolutions designating the members of committees. Unlike procedure in the House, these resolutions are subject to amendment by striking out and adding names, though there was but one instance of this during the period. In the 83rd Congress when the then independent Senator Wayne Morse's committee positions were at stake, assignments to all committees were agreed to except those for Armed Services and Labor and Public Welfare. (Morse's former committees) and District of Columbia and Post Office (those to which he was assigned by the Republican conference).[12] When appointments to Armed Services were taken up, Leverett Saltonstall was approved separately as chairman, but the other members were selected by ballot. Senators were to cast their votes for the list of eight Republicans and seven Democrats nominated by their respective parties, or they could cross out the name of one Republican or Democrat and insert Morse's name in its place. Morse was defeated in this quest for his old committee positions

12. The committee-on-committees proposed that Morse be allowed to retain his seat on Armed Services but be removed from the more partisan Labor Committee. The conference, however, voted to remove him from both his former positions on the grounds that he had been disloyal to the Republican party in the 1952 presidential election.

by a vote of 81 to 7.[13] Following this decision, Morse asked that his assignment be postponed until a resolution had been acted upon that would add himself and one majority member to each of his former committees. The other committee positions were then filled in the usual manner.[14]

The task of handling initial assignments and transfers from one committee to another is formally consigned to committees-on-committees. For Senate Democrats, this committee is called the steering committee, a group of between twelve and seventeen members chosen by the floor leader. Once appointed, they serve until they leave Congress.[15] As it has been constituted from the 80th through the 90th Congresses, the committee has reflected the regional strength of the Democratic party in the Senate fairly accurately, as may be seen from table 5:1. Most members had either liberal or moderate voting records, according to the way

TABLE 5:1

Regional Representation of Democrats on the Steering Committee and in the Senate, 80th through the 90th Congresses

	EAST	MIDWEST	SOUTH	WEST
Percentage of steering committee members by region	21.3	12.5	42.5	23.7
Percentage of Democratic senators by region	17.3	15.3	42.2	25.2
Disproportion in committee representation	+4.0	−2.8	+0.3	−1.5

13. Because Senators Richard B. Russell and Robert A. Taft felt that using a secret ballot would be a dangerous precedent, especially when the partisan division was as close as it was in 1953, each senator's ballot was printed in the *Congressional Record*.

14. Morse's resolution was eventually reported unfavorably by the Committee on Rules and Administration and voted down by the Senate. For the entire discussion, see *Congressional Record*, 83rd Cong., 1st sess., 1953, pp. 327-52, 5421-44.

15. Joseph S. Clark notes that John W. Kern, majority leader under Woodrow Wilson, chose an entirely new committee-on-committees of nine, seven of whom were loyal to the president. See his *Congress: The Sapless Branch* (New York: Harper and Row, 1964), p. 120.

in which these terms are used in chapter 6, though Lyndon B. Johnson's appointments increased the number of conservative members, in interesting contrast with his liberalization of some of the key committees. Taken for the entire period, 41.9 percent had liberal voting records during the Congresses in which they served, 34.9 percent had moderate records, and 23.2 percent had conservative records.

The Senate Republican committee-on-committees has varied in size between eight and twenty-three members. It has generally included senior Republicans, but it has tended to have a greater sprinkling of less-senior members than its Democratic counterpart —in fact, one-third of its total membership has been made up of senators who have served for two years or less. The committee, for the eleven Congresses under consideration, has reflected the Republican regional strength nearly as closely as the Democats, as may be seen from table 5:2. Taken for the entire period, 60.7 percent of the members had conservative voting records, 32.1 percent moderate, and 7.2 percent liberal.

TABLE 5:2
Regional Representation of Republicans on the Committee-on-Committees and in the Senate, 80th through 90th Congress

	EAST	MIDWEST	SOUTH	WEST
Percentage of committee-on-committee members by region	33.6	43.8	2.8	20.6
Percentage of Republican senators by region	34.8	37.4	4.9	22.9
Disproportion in committee representation	−1.2	+6.4	−2.1	−2.3

Seniority in the Senate is an important factor in committee assignments. Senators are ranked according to the length of their uninterrupted service, dating in most cases from the opening day of the Congress to which they were elected.[16] Those entering on

16. If they were appointed to fill an unexpired term, they started accumulating seniority on the date on which a governor certified the appointment.

the same day are listed according to previous political experience, preference being given to former senators, then to former members of the House, and finally to former governors. If two members have had similar political experience, the one who served in the office longest takes precedence. Members who have had no experience in these offices are ranked according to the date when their state came into the Union by the Democrats and on the basis of lot by the Republicans.

The individual preferences of senior party members largely determined the choice committee assignments prior to the 83rd Congress for the Democrats and the 86th Congress for the Republicans. When vacancies occurred on committees, each senator was asked, in order of his Senate seniority, if he desired to make the move, with the least desirable openings left for the least-senior members. This procedure was as automatic as possible, though there was some leeway even here. In the 82nd Congress, for example, Senator Morse, whose seniority ranking was twenty-two, campaigned for an assignment on the Foreign Relations Committee, arguing that it lacked membership from the West Coast. Republican conservatives urged Homer Capehart, whose ranking was also twenty-two but who was listed ahead of Morse, to take the position. Liberals, thereupon suggested George Aiken, fifteenth in rank. In the end, the liberal, Charles Tobey, thirteenth in rank, took the opening.[17]

Beginning in 1953, Democratic Leader Lyndon B. Johnson departed from such rigid application of the seniority rule in handling transfers and initial appointments. The so-called Johnson Rule provides that no member of the party, regardless of his Senate seniority, is to receive a second top committee seat until every Democratic senator has been given at least one such assignment.

If they were chosen at a special election to fill an unexpired term, seniority commenced on the day on which the new senator took the oath of office if the Senate was in session, or on the day after the election if the Senate was not in session.

17. Bertram M. Gross, *The Legislative Struggle* (New York: McGraw-Hill, 1953), p. 277.

The idea was not a new one. Republican Senator Prescott Bush had made this same suggestion in 1951,[18] but Johnson was the first leader able to convince senior party members of the advisability of such a procedure.

With the abandonment of strict application of seniority principles, the work of the floor leader, the committee-on-committees, and the secretary of the party became far more than routine. Lyndon Johnson dominated his committee-on-committees while his successor, Mike Mansfield, the possessor of a very different style, did not. Mansfield did seek to liberalize what had become an increasingly conservative committee under Johnson, with such additions as Joseph S. Clark, Paul H. Douglas, William Proxmire, Stuart Symington, and Harrison A. Williams.

All freshmen committee assignments for the entire period are summarized in table 5:3. For the Democrats, with the exception of the tiny class that entered in the 90th Congress, the 83rd Congress freshman class did more poorly in its initial assignments than any other, but this was a Republican Congress and the majority party always receives a greater share of good positions. On the other hand, the 86th Congress class did better than any other. Sixteen new Democrats had been elected and, in order to give good assignments to as many as possible, Johnson, with the agreement of Everett M. Dirksen, worked out "the great juggle of 1959." Plans were kept secret so that all senators would not be requesting improved assignments. The size of the more important committees was increased, that of the housekeeping committees reduced, so that there would be more plums to pass around. Even Senator Clark, one of the most consistent critics of Democratic committee assignments, agrees that the work done in this year was good.

At the commencement of the 87th and the 88th Congresses, however, complaints were made concerning the operation of the Johnson Rule. Senators criticized the increased power of the party leaders, as in this statement by Senator John Carroll: "When

18. U.S. Senate, Committee on Expenditures in the Executive Departments, *Organization and Operation of Congress,* Hearings, 82d Cong., 1st sess., 1951, p. 42.

TABLE 5:3

*Senate Freshmen Committee Assignments, By Political Party, 82nd Through 90th Congresses**

Congress	Number of Freshmen Democratic Senators	Average Value of Their Committee Assignments	Number of Freshman Republican Senators	Average Value of Their Committee Assignments
82 (1951–52)	5	12.0	8	13.1
83 (1953–54)	6	10.4	10	10.6
84 (1955–56)	8	8.5	7	12.7
85 (1957–58)	9	10.1	5	11.7
86 (1959–60)	16	7.8	4	9.7
87 (1961–62)	9	9.6	3	10.7
88 (1963–64)	9	9.3	4	9.2
89 (1965–66)	7	9.6	3	8.7
90 (1967–68)	2	10.5	5	10.0

* Freshmen include all senators appointed or elected to a Congress in the two-year period that began six months before the opening of that Congress. Each member's committee assignments were given the value of their preference ranking as determined in table 6:5. For example, an assignment to Foreign Relations scored one point, one to Banking and Currency scored ten points, and if these were a member's two assignments, he had a total score of eleven. (Assignments to Aeronautical and Space Sciences were not included since this is a relatively new committee.) The scores for the entire class were totaled for each Congress and averaged on the basis of the total number of committee assignments of the senators involved. The lower the score, the more favorable the assignments.

favors can be used in this body or in any other body by a small core of people to reward their friends and to punish others, I think the question should be looked into."[19] They also claimed that liberals had not been treated as well as they deserved. Senator Clark complained that seniority "can be used with great effect to maintain the status quo, to keep in positions of power those who do not wish to change in a changing world. But when seniority is suggested in behalf of some of us who are not in the status quo group, it is very easy to pass it over."[20] At another point in the discussion of 1961 committee assignments, Carroll said that "when

19. *Congressional Record*, 87th Cong., 1st sess., 1961, p. 629.
20. Ibid., p. 627.

some of us have seniority and seek to assert it, we are given the alibi of geography, but when we assert geography, we are confronted with seniority." Clark added to this, "and sometimes when we assert philosophy, we are given the gate."[21]

Liberal senators also claim that favorable assignments have been given to members of newer classes as a means of blocking a liberalization of cloture. Senator Mansfield summed up the charge somewhat facetiously during the 1963 discussion: "We have indeed come full circle from the days when freshmen were given the leftovers after the seniors had feasted on the choice assignments. Now, we learn, we are force-feeding them like prize livestock."[22] In support of this claim, Senator Clark noted that of the twenty-two nonfreshmen senators seeking new positions in 1963, seven of the eight who voted against liberalizing cloture received their first choice and only one of the fourteen (Senator Mansfield) who voted for the rules change received his first choice.[23] Senator Mansfield's rebuttal gives support for the force feeding theory. He noted that of the nine freshmen senators, all but two received at least one first choice in spite of the fact that seven voted for liberalization of cloture.[24] Frank E. Moss gave evidence that a senator's stand on cloture had a bearing on his committee assignments. He testified that secretary for the majority, Bobby (Robert G.) Baker, had assured him that he could receive a desired appointment "if I could tell him or Senator Russell that the Senate is a continuing body"[25]—that is, if he would agree that the Senate should not adopt its rules (including cloture) anew at the beginning of each Congress.

An ingenious analysis has recently been made by Wayne Swan-

21. Ibid., p. 629.
22. *Congressional Record*, 88th Cong., 1st sess., 1963, p. 2920.
23. Ibid., p. 2530.
24. Ibid., p. 2769.
25. *Congressional Quarterly Weekly Report*, May 27, 1964, p. 986. During the Senate investigation of Baker, it was also brought out that he deprived Senators Stephen M. Young and Quentin N. Burdick of coveted positions on the Judiciary Committee by reporting falsely to the steering committee in 1961 that they no longer wished these appointments.

son that supports Clark's charges that the Johnson Rule has modified the seniority system in such a way as to help support the
Establishment.[26] He took all Democratic senators who had served
for at least four Congresses in the period between the 80th and
the 88th and determined the number who had succeeded during
the first eight years of their tenure in winning a position on one
of the major committees. He then divided the Senators into conservatives, moderates, and liberals (see table 5:4).

TABLE 5:4
*Percentage of Democratic Senators' Assignments to Major Committees
After Four Congresses, By Ideological Groupings**

Conservatives	59.1
Moderates	50.0
Liberals	38.2

* The major committees are the top six as listed in table 6:5. The ideological
groups were determined in much the same way as in table 6:4.

Swanson made a further breakdown by dividing the liberals
into those who had received a major committee assignment and
those who had not, by the end of their first eight years. He then
determined the percentage of support the members of the four
groups had given the Establishment on six votes taken between
1961 and 1963 on liberalization of cloture and expansion of the
Appropriations and Finance committees. Table 5:5 shows that the

TABLE 5:5
*Percentage of Democratic Senators' Support
For the Establishment, By Ideological Groupings*

Conservatives	93.3
Moderates	86.1
Liberals (with major committees)	42.7
Liberals (without major committees)	11.5

26. Wayne R. Swanson, "Committee Assignments and the Nonconformist
Legislator: Democrats in the United States Senate," *Midwest Journal of
Political Science* (Feb. 1969), 84.

liberals who had been willing to go along on such issues had fared much better than their more independent colleagues—Joseph S. Clark, Paul H. Douglas, Ernest Gruening, Pat McNamara, Frank E. Moss, Edmund S. Muskie, William Proxmire, Jennings Randolph, and Harrison A. Williams.

Republicans, less given to favor-swapping and less inclined to centralize power in one party leader than the Democrats, did not adopt a procedure similar to the Johnson Rule until 1959.[27] The Republican rule provided that no Republican senator already serving on one of the top four committees (Appropriations, Armed Services, Finance, and Foreign Relations) should serve on another of these until all Republican senators had been canvassed, but with the "grandfather clause" proviso that senators already on two of these committees could maintain their positions and even move from one top position to another.[28] The change was made easier at this time by the retirement of sixteen Republicans who held a total of twenty-two major committee positions, and by a somewhat greater willingness on the part of senior Republicans to bow to the desires of junior senators. Floor Leader Dirksen set an example by shifting from the Appropriations Committee to Labor and Public Welfare, which caused Senator Richard B. Russell to exclaim, "I cannot understand the Senator from Illinois. He never seems to want to have any seniority."[29]

The effect of the new, more flexible procedures can be seen from table 5:6, which gives the percentages of Democratic and Republican senators who had important committee assignments in the 90th Congress and compares them with assignments in the 82nd Congress before the Johnson Rule went into effect in either party. All but five Democratic and four Republican senators in the 90th Congress had membership on at least one of the top eight committees as ranked in table 6:5 below.

27. The minority party (and Republicans have been in the minority for all but two of these nine Congresses) has less chance to provide its members with choice assignments, for it receives a smaller proportion of positions.
28. *Congressional Quarterly Weekly Report*, Jan. 15, 1965, p. 83.
29. Congressional Record, 88th Cong., 1st sess., 1963, p. 2540.

TABLE 5:6
*Percentage Distribution of Top Senate Committee Assignments**

	90th Congress	82nd Congress	90th Congress	82nd Congress
None	8%	16%	8%	26%
One	39	45	42	38
Two	53	39	50	36
	100%	100%	100%	100%

* The Democrats without a major committee in the 90th Congress were Robert F. Kennedy (elected in 1964), Edmund S. Muskie (1958), Jennings Randolph (1958), William B. Spong Jr. (1966), and Harrison A. Williams Jr. (1958). The Republicans were Howard H. Baker Jr. (1966), Edward W. Brooke (1966), George Murphy (1964), and Charles H. Percy (1966). Senator Muskie reminisced during his vice presidential campaign that former Majority Leader Lyndon Johnson "didn't let you come on too fast. . . . He felt he had to punish me [for supporting a liberalization of cloture] by giving me three committees I didn't want" (*New York Times*, September 10, 1968).

These departures from the seniority rule have made it possible to use different criteria in making committee assignments. Undoubtedly, as has already been noted, one of the major considerations in receiving a favorable position is whether the member is a "Senate man"—that is, whether he has by hard work mastered the specialized committee work he has been given, shown a willingness to compromise on his objectives based on an understanding of the problems of other senators, demonstrated loyalty to the Senate as an institution, and been cooperative with party leaders.[30]

Geographical, ideological, and religious factors may also play a role in the complex negotiations over assignments, though it is impossible to weigh the importance of each. No two senators from the same party from the same state may serve on any committee. This practice not only assures some geographical distribution of committee seats, but it eliminates what might become a source of intrastate jurisdictional disputes between senators. Vacancies are often filled with a senator from the same section of the

30. Donald R. Matthews, *U.S. Senators and Their World* (Chapel Hill: University of North Carolina Press, 1960), chap. 5.

country as the person who has retired. A member's political ideology has undoubtedly been important in some instances. Much
attention has been given to appointments to the powerful Finance
Committee, for example.

Committee Seniority in House and Senate

While congressional seniority plays an important role in the making of committee assignments, committee seniority is all-important in promotions once assignments have been made. If two or
more members go on a committee at the same time, note is taken
of previous political experience. If previous political experience
is equal, procedure is determined by lot, by alphabetical arrangement of names, or by the date when the incumbent's state came
into the Union. Once established, the seniority order is not dis-
turbed. John M. Vorys of Ohio, for example, lost the draw to
Robert Chipperfield of Illinois in 1939 when both were assigned
as Republican freshmen to the House Foreign Affairs Committee.
Both came from equally safe districts, and twenty years later,
when Vorys retired, he still ranked second to Chipperfield, though
he had been the Republican mainstay of the committee for most
of that period.

When the committee party ratio changes because of a change
in the party ratio of the house, members of the minority party
with the least seniority may lose their committee positions. Otherwise the right to remain on a committee and to move up the ladder
is generally unquestioned. Those who have been "bumped" are
nearly always given the chance to return when an opening develops.

Congress is thoroughly attuned to its loose two-party system
and it has no set pattern for handling third-party members, party
bolters (those who support another party's presidential condi-
date), or those who switch their party designation. Generally, it
penalizes third-party members only if the division between the
two major parties is so close that assignment would hurt party

regulars. Since 1947 the problem has not come up with the frequency that it did in the earlier history of Congress,[31] only four examples having occurred in the House. Vito Marcantonio, a member of the American Labor party from New York, voted for Sam Rayburn for Speaker in 1947. Democrats, however, refused to assign him unless the controlling Republicans gave them an extra position, for otherwise they would have had to drop one of their own members. After a year without assignment, he was finally placed by the Republicans on the Committee on House Administration. Leo Isaacson, another member of the American Labor party who served in Congress only in 1948 was placed on Government Operations. Frazier Reams, former Democrat who served two terms as an independent from Ohio, was assigned by the Democrats to the Post Office Committee. Vincent Dellay of New Jersey, who changed parties in the middle of the 85th Congress was merely switched from the Republican to the Democratic side of the Merchant Marine Committee.

A study of committee assignments of Senate party bolters since 1925 shows only two examples of removal from a committee (Lynn J. Frazier in 1925 and Wayne Morse in 1953) and three examples of members remaining on their committees but losing seniority (Edwin F. Ladd, Smith W. Brookhart, and Robert M. LaFollette in 1925) as punishment for supporting another party's presidential candidate. In all other cases, no retaliatory action was taken. The House has seen examples of such punitive action in 1925 and 1933 when Republicans who failed to support their presidential candidate were either demoted or removed from their important committee assignments. There was considerable discussion of punishing Democratic House defectors in the postwar period (Adam Clayton Powell for his support of Eisenhower in 1956, William Colmer for refusing to support Kennedy in

31. For experience prior to the 80th Congress see Clarence A. Berdahl, "Some Notes on Party Membership in Congress," *American Political Science Review* (April, June, August 1949): 309, 492, 721; and Ralph K. Huitt, "The Morse Committee Assignment Controversy," *American Political Science Review* (June 1957): 313.

1960), but no action was taken until 1965. The heavily Democratic 89th Congress, however, took precedent-making action. The Democratic caucus voted to punish Representatives John Bell Williams of Mississippi and Albert W. Watson of South Carolina for having publicly supported Goldwater in the 1964 elections. Watson, who had been a freshman in the 88th Congress, was kept in the bottom position on the Committee on Post Office and Civil Service. He resigned from Congress, ran successfully as a Republican in a special election, and was assigned by his new party to the Interstate Commerce Committee. Williams was dropped to the bottom from the fifth position on District of Columbia and the second position on Interstate Commerce, and thus missed the chance to become chairman when Oren Harris retired in 1966. He asked to be returned to the ranking position on the Commerce Committee at the commencement of the 90th Congress, and when the Democratic caucus turned him down he refused any assignments. He was elected governor of Mississippi later in the year and resigned from the House.

The most celebrated assignment controversy during the period concerned Senator Wayne Morse, a party switcher. He broke with the Republican party in October 1952, when he announced his support for Adlai Stevenson. He remained an independent during the 83rd Congress, but he voted with the Democrats to organize the 84th Congress and formally joined the Democratic party on February 17, 1955. In the 83rd Congress he sought to maintain his committee membership on Armed Services and Labor and Public Welfare, though he did not expect to maintain his seniority ranking on these committees. The parties were so closely divided that Republicans, who organized the 83rd Congress, placed him on District of Columbia and Post Office and Civil Service, in spite of three attempts by Morse to regain his former assignments. They expected Morse to vote with the Democrats on committee matters and preferred what amounted to an even division on these two less important committees. In a more recent case of party change, Senator Strom Thurmond of South Carolina moved from the Democratic to the Republican party in 1964. Republicans kept him on the Armed Services Committee and gave him a position on Banking and Currency. On both committees he was placed in third position, immediately behind the two Republican holdovers.

If a ranking member leaves a committee because of transfer to another committee or retirement from Congress, all his fellow party members on the committee who were beneath him move up in rank. The career of Representative Adolph J. Sabath gives a unique illustration of what can be accomplished by transfer, if it is combined with longevity. He entered Congress in 1907, transferred to the Rules Committee in 1929 (after twenty-two years of service), became its chairman in 1939 after another ten years, and remained the ranking Democrat on the committee for thirteen more years.[32]

The stress on committee seniority is often justified on the grounds that promotion should be based on legislative and subject-matter experience. A peculiar departure from this principle is the fact that a member who is defeated or who fails to run, and is later returned to Congress, loses his committee seniority. This practice has its justification, at least to the congressman who replaces the retiring member, for he does not wish to lose his own rights if his predecessor returns. This occurs fairly infrequently. (In the 90th Congress, only two senators and twenty-three representatives had had interrupted previous service in their respective houses.) Two midwestern Republican victims of Democratic landslides will serve as examples. Ralph Harvey and Earl Wilson, both from Indiana, had served consecutively five and nine Congresses respectively before they were unseated in the 1958 Democratic landslide. Both returned to Congress and to their same committees in the 87th Congress. Harvey had been appointed to the Agriculture Committee in the 82nd Congress and had worked his way to sixth place on the Republican side, but when he returned he ranked tenth. Wilson had been appointed to the Appropriations Committee in the 82nd Congress and had worked his way up to eleventh place, only to be dropped back to the very bottom as a result of his de-

32. Roland A. Young, *The American Congress* (New York: Harper, 1958), p. 71.

feat in the 86th Congress.[33] An unusual exception took place in the case of Henry Cabot Lodge Jr., who resigned from the Senate in 1944 to enter the service. When he returned in 1947, a move was made to restore his former seniority rights both in the Senate and on the Foreign Relations Committee. He declined to accept his previous rank on the committee, but accepted enough Senate seniority to enable him to return to that committee as its lowest ranking Republican member.

In short, to become a committee chairman, a legislator must remain continuously on a given committee longer than any other fellow party member, and be of the majority party. It is not uncommon to find men on a given committee of higher House and Senate rank than the committee chairman. This is partly a matter of luck and partly a feeling on the part of some that it is better to be second or third on an important committee than chairman of a minor one. In the 90th Congress, for example, fifteen Democratic senators who were not chairmen had seen greater service in the upper house than Senator Jennings Randolph, the Public Works Committee chairman, and one hundred Democratic representatives who were not chairmen had seen greater service in the lower house than Congressman Thaddeos J. Dulski, chairman of the Post Office Committee. But other members will stay with an early assignment, preferring to be bigger fish in smaller ponds.

While the selection of committee chairmen by the seniority system is "as popular a target as sin itself,"[34] relatively little critical attention has been paid to the method of making initial appointments. Suggestions that have been made tend to concentrate either

33. An interesting example of the peculiarities of the system took place in the House Committee on Science and Astronautics in 1961. Emilio Daddario, whose name had been mistakenly omitted from the committee list approved by the House, was returned to the committee at his former rank. J. Edward Roush, who was not seated for several months until his contested election was decided, was also returned to the committee at his former rank. John McCormack, however, who had resigned to make room for Daddario, was later restored to the committee but at the bottom of the list (though he continued to sit at the right of the chairman).
34. Emanuel Celler, "The Seniority Rule in Congress," *Western Political Quarterly* 14 (1961): 160–67.

on reform of the appointing agency or on criteria for making appointments that should be made binding on that agency.

Since both houses are too large to vest the appointing power in the full membership, the complex task must be delegated to some single person or small group. Both the House and the Senate have in the past clearly reacted against vesting the power in its presiding officer. This power, though it has been given to four party committees-on-committees, has gravitated to the floor leaders of the two parties. Because of the size of the task in the House, the party leaders exercise their power mainly in connection with assignments to the major committees. In the smaller Senate, greater control by the party leaders is possible, if they desire it and if their party members allow them to exercise it. Certainly Lyndon Johnson dominated committee assignments when he was floor leader, and the Republicans moved in this direction in the 86th Congress. Critics who favor greater party responsibility would have the floor leaders share their power to a greater extent with party policy committees that give proportionate representation to the less senior, more liberal members of their parties.[35]

Other suggestions would bind the committees-on-committees, however they are constituted, to follow certain criteria in making appointments. Some propose that all sections of the country should have representation on all committees in proportion to their strength in Congress. Others propose that a variety of economic interests be represented on each committee. Still others ask for a greater reflection of current political attitudes—either by giving a seniority bonus to members from two-party districts, or by distributing committee seats among recently elected members in proportion to their strength in Congress. Those who stress party re-

35. Stephen K. Bailey, *The Condition of Our National Political Parties* (Santa Barbara, Calif.: Fund for the Republic, 1959), p. 15. In 1910 Representative George Norris proposed that the appointment power be taken away from the Speaker and given to a newly constituted Rules Committee that would represent the entire country and every interest in the country (George W. Norris, *Fighting Liberal* [New York: Macmillan Co., 1945], p. 123).

sponsibility are likely to call for an overrepresentation of the majority party on all committees and for a complete by-passing of seniority in making appointments and promotions on the so-called control committees concerned with appropriations, revenues, and House rules.[36]

No system will satisfy everyone so long as there are a limited number of committee positions and fairly clear agreement as to which ones are the most prestigious. The present methods have been followed without major change since 1846 in the Senate and 1911 in the House, and so long as the senior members, who have the greatest power to change the system, show the least disposition to do so, drastic reform seems unlikely. Senior party members have not been entirely inflexible, however, as may be seen by the modifications brought about by the adoption of the Johnson Rule in the Senate.

36. For suggestions see Bailey, *Political Parties,* pp. 16, 23; and Ted F. Silvey of the National Planning Association as he testified on the Legislative Reorganization Act, Joint Committee on the Organization of Congress, Hearings, *The Organization of Congress,* pursuant to H. Con. Res. 18, 79th Cong., 1st sess., 1945, pp. 881–82.

6.

Committee Variety

A VISIT to a hearing or a talk with a member of each of the now thirty-seven "little legislatures" gives insights into the immense variety of these very human institutions. The nature of a committee's assigned jurisdiction is basic. It determines the groups, both inside and outside the government, with which a committee is primarily concerned, and sets its work load. These activity factors, in turn, affect a committee's membership. Both the decisions of the party agencies that make assignments and the preference of the members of the House and Senate work to produce recognizable committee types. Many committees have a strong regional or ideological flavor. In all this, congressmen, by showing preferences for certain committees, have created fairly recognizable "pecking orders." All these factors—the scope of issues handled, the work load, regional representation, ideological balance, and membership preference—are discussed in this chapter.

Table 6:1 classifies committees according to the scope of the issues they handle, and, as a result, the groups with which they are most directly concerned. Committees in the national issue category deal with the broadest questions. They are no less subject to external pressures than other committees, but the pressures are likely to come from a greater variety of sources. Clientele-oriented committees are more involved in the reconciliation of economic and regional demands and are concerned with a smaller number of interest groups. Housekeeping committees concern themselves primarily with matters internal to the government. It must be clearly noted that this is a generalized grouping and many specific

TABLE 6:1
Committees Classified According to the Scope of the Issues Handled*

SENATE COMMITTEES	HOUSE COMMITTEES

National Issue Committees

	Science & Astronautics (Dis.)
Aeronautical & Space Sciences (Dis.)+	Appropriations (Dis.)
Appropriations (Dis.)	Armed Services (Dis.)
Armed Services (Dis.)	Ways and Means (Redis.)
Finance (Redis.)	Foreign Affairs
Foreign Relations	Judiciary (Redis.)
Judiciary (Redis.)	Rules
	Un-American Activities

Clientele-oriented Committees

	Agriculture (Dis.)
Agriculture & Forestry (Dis.)	Banking & Currency (Reg., Redis.)
Banking & Currency (Reg., Redis.)	Interstate & Foreign Commerce (Reg.)
Commerce (Reg.)	Interior & Insular Affairs (Dis.)
Interior & Insular Affairs (Dis.)	Education & Labor (Reg., Redis.)
Labor & Public Welfare (Reg., Redis.)	Merchant Marine & Fisheries (Dis.)
Public Works (Dis.)	Public Works (Dis.)
	Veterans' Affairs (Dis.)

Housekeeping Committees

| District of Columbia | District of Columbia |
| Government Operations | Government Operations |

Post Office & Civil Service (Dis.) Post Office & Civil Service (Dis.)
Rules & Administration House Administration
 Standards of Official Conduct

* Donald R. Matthews uses a somewhat different grouping of committees, that of "top," "interest," "pork," and "duty." The "top" committees were Appropriations, Armed Services, Finance, Foreign Relations. The "interest" committees were Agriculture, Banking and Currency, Commerce, Judiciary, Labor and Public Welfare. The "pork" committees were Interior and Insular Affairs, Post Office and Civil Service, Public Works. The "duty" committees were District of Columbia, Government Operations, Rules and Administration. See Donald R. Matthews, *U.S. Senators and Their World* (Chapel Hill: University of North Carolina Press, 1960), p. 154.

† Chapter 8 describes a categorization of domestic issues according to whether they are distributive (involving government subsidy, with decisions reached relatively easily since no one group stands to lose much), regulatory (involving government regulation, with hard-fought decisions since some groups do stand to lose), and redistributive (involving government manipulation with class overtones and resulting especially hard-fought decisions). According to this breakdown, distributive policies tend to be handled by clientele committees (Agriculture, Interior, Merchant Marine, Public Works, Veterans'), though three national issue committees (Appropriations, Armed Services, Science) and one housekeeping committee (Post Office) are also involved. Regulatory policies tend to be handled by clientele committees (Banking, Commerce, Labor). Redistributive policies also tend to be handled by clientele committees (Banking, Labor), though two national issue committees are also involved (Finance for social insurance, Judiciary for civil rights).

The abbreviations in parentheses after the committee titles designate which of the categories the committees involved with such policies tend to fall into.

exceptions can be found, yet this categorization was held satisfactory by staff members of each committee.

A somewhat different way of looking at committees is to group them according to the variety of government organizations with which they have direct contact. Most committees are concerned with a given function, agriculture, for example, which has most of its government contacts with the Department of Agriculture. Some committees have broader contacts, and in some instances greater power. The Government Operations committees, for example, are concerned with all executive agencies. The administration committees of the House and Senate are concerned with certain aspects of the work of all other committees. Of greatest importance, the House Rules Committee controls the access of most House committees to the floor; the two revenue and the two Appropriations committees are concerned with every committee and every government agency. These five are often referred to as the control committees of Congress.

Attempting to measure work load is yet another way of classifying committees to show how their assigned jurisdictions affect them. A variety of measurements could be used—the number of bills assigned, the number and length of hearings, the number of measures reported, the size of the staff, the amount of money spent by each in performing its functions. By almost any of these tests the two Judiciary committees would come out on top, yet this is largely because of the large number of private bills they introduce. A useful single test is the number of roll-call votes held on committee measures, for a floor roll call is a good sign of the importance of legislation in most cases. It is by no means an infallible sign, however. It can denote a seriously divided committee or an unskillful chairman. Table 6:2 ranks committees according to the number of roll calls held on their measures from the 8oth through the 9oth Congresses (1947–68). Most of the national issue committees fall in the upper half of the index, with Appropriations in the lead. The only two exceptions are the two House national issue committees that originate little legislation, Un-American Activities being primarily an investigating committee and Rules a scheduling committee. Clientele committees fall in the middle range (with Banking and Currency and Labor leading in both houses), and housekeeping committees fall at the bottom.

Congressmen, under the guidance of the various party committees-on-committees, sort themselves out among these standing committees according to certain definable patterns that relate to the regions from which they come, their ideological bent, and their attitude towards their committee role. Table 6:3 relates a region's strength in Congress to its strength on each committee. By all odds, the Interior committees stand out in this sort of analysis. The overrepresentation of westerners is more than twice as great as any other example discovered on any committee. The West has also tended to dominate the Public Works committees, especially in the Senate. The East has been overrepresented on the Labor and the Commerce committees. The South and the Midwest have tended to dominate the Agriculture committees; the East and the Midwest, the Foreign Affairs committees; the East and West, the House Merchant Marine Committee.

A glance at the five most powerful committees (House Appropriations, Rules, Ways and Means; Senate Appropriations, Finance) shows that the South has been overrepresented on all but House Appropriations, the Midwest on all but Senate Appropriations, and the West on both Appropriations committees. The East has been underrepresented on all five committees. In the 90th Congress (1967–68), six southern states (Arkansas, Florida, Georgia, Louisiana, Tennessee, and Texas) had a member on at least four of these five so-called control committees. This was true of only one state in each of the other three regions—New York in the East, Illinois in the Midwest, and California in the West.

A congressman's ideology has an effect on his committee preferences, as well as on his ability to get on those of his choice. Committees, themselves, tend to take on ideological positions. There is, for instance, a great ideological gap between the Senate Committee on Finance and the Senate Committee on Labor and Public Welfare. It is less obvious, however, where many other committees fall on the conservatism-liberalism axis, an axis that stretches

TABLE 6:2
*Committees Ranked According to the Number of Roll Calls Held on Their Measures, 80th through 90th Congresses**

HOUSE COMMITTEE

	Type of Committee	Number of Roll Calls Held	Percentage
1. Appropriations	(N)	438	18.58
2. Banking & Currency	(C)	213	9.03
3. Ways & Means	(N)	206	8.74
4. Judiciary	(N)	196	8.31
5. Education & Labor	(C)	165	7.00
6. Foreign Affairs	(N)	162	6.87
7. Agriculture	(C)	138	5.85
8. Interstate & Foreign Commerce	(C)	133	5.64
9. Armed Services	(N)	129	5.47
10. Public Works	(C)	108	4.58

SENATE COMMITTEE

	Type of Committee	Number of Roll Calls Held	Percentage
1. Appropriations	(N)	632	18.47
2. Foreign Relations	(N)	468	13.68
3. Finance	(N)	428	12.51
4. Judiciary	(N)	362	10.58
5. Labor & Public Welfare	(C)	318	9.29
6. Banking & Currency	(C)	312	9.12
7. Agriculture & Forestry	(C)	208	6.08
8. Armed Services	(N)	140	4.09
9. Commerce	(C)	119	3.48

11.	Interior & Insular Affairs	(c)	104	4.41
12.	District of Columbia	(H)	84	3.56
13.	Post Office & Civil Service	(H)	81	3.44
14.	Veterans' Affairs	(c)	51	2.16
15.	Un-American Activities	(N)	43	1.82
16.	Government Operations	(H)	36	1.53
17.	Merchant Marine & Fisheries	(c)	31	1.31
18.	Rules	(N)	24	1.02
19.	House Administration	(H)	16	0.68
			2,358	100.00

10.	Public Works	(c)	115	3.36
11.	Interior & Insular Affairs	(c)	99	2.89
12.	Post Office & Civil Service	(H)	80	2.34
13.	District of Columbia	(H)	49	1.43
14.	Government Operations	(H)	47	1.37
15.	Rules & Administration	(H)	45	1.31
			3,422	100.00

* Includes all roll calls that were listed by *Congressional Quarterly* on measures that originated in a specific committee. The recently created space and standards committees were not included. The letter in parentheses after each committee's name denotes its type: national issue (N), clientele (c), or housekeeping (H).

TABLE 6:3
*Index of Regional Overrepresentation on House and Senate Committees, 80th through 90th Congresses**

Committee	Type Committee	Total Under- Or Over- Representation	East	Midwest	South	West
HOUSE COMMITTEE						
Interior & Insular Affairs	(C)	3.79	.61	.63	.57	3.60
Agriculture	(C)	1.18	.42	1.09	1.50	1.01
Foreign Affairs	(N)	1.18	1.20	1.28	.65	.65
District of Columbia	(H)	1.18	.83	.90	1.47	.60
Merchant Marine & Fisheries	(C)	1.14	1.34	.72	.80	1.32
Un-American Activities	(N)	1.06	.55	1.27	1.04	1.30
Judiciary	(N)	1.00	1.30	.79	1.09	.60
Education & Labor	(C)	.94	1.31	1.00	.58	1.21
Government Operations	(H)	.78	1.10	1.21	.80	.73
Rules	(N)	.78	.72	1.11	1.24	.85
Banking & Currency	(C)	.70	1.31	1.04	.81	.84
Interstate & Foreign Commerce	(C)	.57	1.20	.96	.99	.68
Armed Services	(N)	.55	1.02	.79	1.12	1.20
House Administration	(H)	.54	1.00	1.10	1.06	.62
Ways & Means	(N)	.51	.81	1.10	1.13	.91
Veterans' Affairs	(C)	.41	1.04	.82	1.17	.98
Appropriations	(N)	.37	.90	1.13	.90	1.04
Public Works	(C)	.21	.92	1.00	1.04	1.09
Post Office & Civil Service	(H)	.15	.99	.99	1.07	1.06

SENATE COMMITTEE

Interior & Insular Affairs	(C)	4.89	.05	.38	.18	3.50
Agriculture & Forestry	(C)	2.54	.42	1.67	1.57	.28
Labor & Public Welfare	(C)	1.54	1.78	.73	.58	.93
District of Columbia	(H)	1.35	1.60	.66	.68	1.09
Armed Services	(N)	1.25	1.25	.53	1.36	.83
Judiciary	(N)	1.23	.83	1.41	1.19	.54
Banking & Currency	(C)	.99	1.40	1.09	.98	.52
Rules & Administration	(H)	.99	1.33	1.18	.58	.94
Appropriations	(N)	.93	.76	.77	1.26	1.20
Finance	(N)	.92	.87	1.07	1.32	.70
Post Office & Civil Service	(H)	.79	1.10	.97	1.28	.62
Public Works	(C)	.79	.90	.85	.86	1.40
Foreign Relations	(N)	.78	1.12	1.20	1.06	.60
Commerce	(C)	.61	1.35	.87	.87	1.00
Government Operations	(H)	.44	.96	1.02	.91	.71

* The index of overrepresentation is determined by dividing the percentage of members from a given committee from one of the four regions by the percentage of members of the full house from that region. An index figure smaller than 1.0 means that the region has been underrepresented; one greater than 1.0 means that it has been overrepresented. The regions are those used by *Congressional Quarterly*. The committees are listed in the order of the cumulative amount of over-or under-representation found. The recently created space and standards committees were omitted from this table. The letter in parentheses after each committee's name denotes its type: national issue (N), clientele (C), and housekeeping (H).

between a concept of strictly limited government to one that advocates active government participation in the economic and social life of the country. In an attempt to rank committees according to the conservatism of their members, the proportion of conservative votes cast by each member of Congress from 1947 through 1968 was determined. The conservatism score for each member was credited to each of his committees, and an average conservatism score was determined for each committee. Table 6:4 shows the results for the House and the Senate. In reading it, one should keep in mind the fact that the index reflects the general ideological position of a committee's membership, not its ideological position on the issues that come within its specific jurisdiction.

The Senate and House patterns are somewhat different. In the Senate, all but one of the national-issue committees fall in the upper or more conservative half of the index, with both control committees (Appropriations and Finance) at the top. Foreign Relations, the outstanding exception, comes at the bottom, largely because its subject matter has more appeal to those of a liberal persuasion and to those more interested in a national political reputation than a strictly legislative one. The clientele committees are spread throughout the index, with Agriculture near the top and Labor and Public Welfare 26.3 points below, at the very bottom. The housekeeping committees, made up mostly of junior members, fall in the more liberal half of the index, with the exception of Government Operations which has been powerful enough, especially through its permanent subcommittee on investigations, to attract and hold conservatives.

In the House, of the control committees, only Rules falls in the upper half of the index, with both Appropriations and Ways and Means showing themselves to have more liberal memberships than their opposite numbers in the Senate. Foreign Affairs, like its Senate counterpart, is one of the more liberal committees. Clientele committees in the House, as in the Senate, are spread over the index, with Agriculture at the top and Banking and Currency at the bottom. The housekeeping committees in the House tend to be more conservative than those in the Senate, with District of Columbia being outstanding for its conservatism ranking. It is generally known that membership is sought by southerners in an endeavor to keep an eye on the civil rights situation in the capital city.

Members of Congress have established a "pecking order" of committees, even though there are many personal variations: Interior is a top committee to a westerner, Banking and Currency to a man with business experience, Labor to a liberal, for example. There is a clear tendency of members, as they gain seniority, to move from certain committees to certain other committees. Since change of assignment means starting at the bottom of the new committee seniority list, the sacrifice will be made only if the new position is considered more important or if the leadership has requested that a member make a change.

In 1963 Senator Joseph S. Clark, a member of the Democratic committee-on-committees, gave some insights into the Senate Democratic "pecking order" of committees when he was discussing the so-called Senate "Establishment."[1] He referred to Appropriations, Armed Services, and Foreign Relations as "prize committees;" suggested that a senator had to be "hog tied" to get him to agree to go on Agriculture and "shanghaied" to go on Labor; he spoke of "the poor District of Columbia Committee" and referred to Banking and Currency as "another Orphan Annie."

One way of attempting to determine committee preferences in a less impressionistic manner is to note the positions of the most senior members of Congress. At the start of the 90th Congress, there were sixteen senators (twelve Democrats and four Republicans), and fifty-three representatives (forty-seven Democrats and six Republicans) who had served for twenty years or more. Senate committees with the largest number of these old timers were Appropriations (9), Foreign Relations (6), Agriculture (5), and Aeronautical and Space Sciences (5). The House committees with the largest number of these senior members were Armed Services

---

1. *Congressional Record*, 88th Cong., 1st sess., 1963, pp. 2559–2562.

TABLE 6:4

*Committees Ranked According to Their Conservatism, 80th through 90th Congresses**

HOUSE COMMITTEE	Type Committee	Conservatism Score	SENATE COMMITTEE	Type Committee	Conservatism Score
1. Agriculture	(C)	61.3	1. Finance	(N)	60.4
2. Un-American Activities	(N)	59.2	2. Agriculture & Forestry	(C)	57.4
3. District of Columbia	(H)	56.9	3. Appropriations	(N)	55.7
4. Armed Services	(N)	54.7	4. Armed Services	(N)	55.2
5. Rules	(N)	52.6	5. Government Operations	(H)	50.9
6. Veterans' Affairs	(C)	52.3	6. Judiciary	(N)	48.8
7. House Administration	(H)	51.8	7. Commerce	(C)	48.6
8. Interstate & Foreign Commerce	(C)	50.8	8. Public Works	(C)	46.3
9. Interior & Insular Affairs	(C)	50.2	9. Rules & Administration	(H)	46.3
10. Post Office & Civil Service	(H)	49.9	10. Interior & Insular Affairs	(C)	46.1
11. Public Works	(C)	49.4	11. Banking & Currency	(C)	45.7
12. Judiciary	(N)	48.8	12. Post Office & Civil Service	(H)	45.7
13. Appropriations	(N)	48.5			

14. Ways and Means	(N)	48.1	13. District of Columbia	(H)	43.0
15. Merchant Marine & Fisheries	(C)	45.8	14. Foreign Relations	(N)	42.7
16. Government Operations	(H)	43.5	15. Labor & Public Welfare	(C)	31.1
17. Education & Labor	(C)	41.0			
18. Foreign Affairs	(N)	40.3			
19. Banking & Currency	(C)	40.2			

* The letter in parentheses after each committee's name denotes its type: national issue (N), clientele (C), and housekeeping (H). The new space and standards committees were not included in this table.

For the 80th through the 85th Congresses, conservative votes were those so designated in the "Congressional Scoreboard" published by the *New Republic*; for the 86th through the 90th Congresses, they were "conservative coalition support scores" published by *Congressional Quarterly*. In determining a committee average, only members who served for the greater part of each two-year Congress were counted.

The author is aware of the difficulties connected with this approach. He is dependent upon the subjective judgment of the editors of the *New Republic*, and yet a comparison of these scores derived from vote analyses made by Americans for Constitutional Action, a conservative organization, shows almost identical results. The *New Republic* source was chosen because it covered the entire portion of the period before *Congressional Quarterly* started with its less subjective, more thorough tabulation in the 86th Congress.

TABLE 6:5
*Preference Ranking of Congressional Committees, 81st through 90th Congresses**

	Type Committee	A (To)	B (From)	C (Net Shifts (A-B))	D (Number of Committee Members)	E (Net Transfers Per Unit of Membership (C÷D))
HOUSE COMMITTEE						
1. Rules	(N)	32	8	24	132	.182
2. Ways and Means	(N)	44	5	39	250	.157
3. Appropriations	(N)	72	13	59	496	.119
4. Foreign Affairs	(N)	43	9	34	316	.108
5. Armed Services	(N)	38	9	29	368	.079
6. Un-American Activities	(N)	12	5	7	90	.078
7. Interstate & Foreign Commerce	(C)	37	23	14	314	.045
8. Judiciary	(N)	28	16	12	323	.037
9. Agriculture	(C)	30	22	8	331	.024
10. District of Columbia	(H)	27	26	1	249	.004
11. Public Works	(C)	33	35	-2	321	-.006
12. Education & Labor	(C)	17	23	-6	293	-.020
13. House Administration	(H)	38	43	-5	250	-.020
14. Government Operations	(H)	42	52	-10	302	-.033
15. Interior & Insular Affairs	(C)	28	43	-15	302	-.050
16. Banking & Currency	(C)	26	41	-15	301	-.050
17. Merchant Marine & Fisheries	(C)	28	48	-20	299	-.067
18. Post Office & Civil Service	(H)	26	48	-22	250	-.088
19. Veterans' Affairs	(C)	16	53	-37	253	-.146

SENATE COMMITTEE		A	B	C	D	E
1. Foreign Relations	(N)	30	2	28	160	.175
2. Finance	(N)	25	3	22	156	.141
3. Appropriations	(N)	37	6	31	245	.127
4. Judiciary	(N)	23	5	18	148	.122
5. Armed Services	(N)	20	5	15	157	.096
6. Commerce	(C)	25	10	15	158	.095
7. Agriculture & Forestry	(C)	15	15	0	152	.000
8. Interior & Insular Affairs	(C)	8	9	−1	155	−.006
9. Labor & Public Welfare	(C)	9	15	−6	142	−.042
10. Banking & Currency	(C)	9	19	−10	144	−.069
11. Public Works	(C)	10	27	−17	145	−.117
12. Rules & Administration	(H)	15	29	−14	98	−.143
13. Government Operations	(H)	9	29	−20	127	−.157
14. Post Office & Civil Service	(H)	8	29	−21	114	−.184
15. District of Columbia	(H)	6	38	−32	89	−.360

* Information in this table was gathered from appropriate volumes of the *Congressional Directory*. Column A gives the number of members who transferred to each committee during the 81st through the 90th Congresses. (Initial 80th Congress appointments, when the new committee system went into effect, and freshmen appointments are excluded.) Column B lists the number of members who transferred off each committee during the same period. Column C gives the number who transferred on to the committee less the number who transferred off. Column D lists the total number on each committee for the period under study. Column E, which gives the net transfers per unit of membership, was arrived at by dividing column C by column D.

(9), Appropriations (8), Agriculture (6), District of Columbia (5), Foreign Affairs (5), Government Operations (5), and Ways and Means (5).

A more systematic way to measure the desirability of committees is to find the relation between the number of members who transfer to, and the number who transfer from each committee over a period of time. If these numbers are weighted according to the number of members on each committee, a fairly accurate indication of the committee caste system can be made. Table 6:5 presents this ranking for the House and Senate.[2] In the House, national issue committees are given the highest ranking. Clientele committees come next, with the Committee on Interstate and Foreign Commerce being more popular even than the lowest national issue committee, Judiciary. Clientele committees with a favorable balance of transfers are Interstate Commerce and Agriculture. The most popular of the housekeeping committees, District of

2. On the basis of their experience, staff members of the House of Representatives would give a somewhat different listing of preferences:

Most Sought After Committees	Committeess With Sectional Appeal
1. Ways and Means	11. Agriculture
2. Appropriations	12. Public Works
3. Rules	13. Merchant Marine and Fisheries
4. Interstate and Foreign Commerce	14. Armed Services
5. Science and Astronautics	15. Interior and Insular Affairs
6. Judiciary	Bobtail Committees
7. Banking and Currency	16. Government Operations
8. Foreign Affairs	17. House Administration
9. Education and Labor	18. District of Columbia
10. Post Office and Civil Service	19. Veterans' Affairs
	20. Un-American Activities

This listing is in a letter from D. B. Hardeman, former member of the whip staff of the House, to the author, August 12, 1968.

Louis Gawthrop reaches different conclusions than both of these lists. He arranges committees according to the percentage of members with single committee assignments on each. See his "Changing Membership Patterns in House Committees," *American Political Science Review* (June 1966): 366–73.

For a detailed treatment of the Senate committee caste system, see Donald R. Matthews, *U.S. Senators and Their World* (Chapel Hill: University of North Carolina Press, 1960), pp. 148–52.

Columbia, falls into tenth place, largely because of a desire of southern Democrats to maintain control of the capital city.

With one or two notable exceptions, Senate committees fall into about the same index positions as House committees. National issue committees are given the highest priority, Foreign Relations being the most sought after (Foreign Affairs is fourth in the House). The clientele committees lie in the middle, Commerce and Agriculture being the favorites, as in the House. And the four housekeeping committees fall into place at the very bottom.

Certain committees, therefore, in spite of the attempt of the framers of the Legislative Reorganization Act of 1946 to make all committees as equal as possible in functions and importance, are more equal than others. Their members tend to be the more effective legislators. The lower ranking committees tend to be apprentice stations, with high membership turnover and a lack of continuity.

7.

Committee People

SENIORITY, more than any other single factor, determines who holds the power within committees. A study of the nature and effects of the seniority system, therefore, is necessary to an understanding of the people who run the "little legislatures"—committee members and their staff.

The Seniority System

It is well to remember that very few human organizations ignore seniority entirely. Champ Clark, in his autobiography, noted that it is practiced in all the affairs of life:

> No sane man would for one moment think of making a graduate from West Point a full general, or one from Annapolis an admiral, or one from any university or college chief of a great newspaper, magazine or business house. A priest or a preacher who has just taken orders is not immediately made a bishop, archbishop or cardinal. In every walk of life "men must tarry at Jericho till their beards are grown."[1]

The reason seniority pervades Congress more than most other organizations can be explained by the fact that ultimate control over members of Congress resides in their constituencies, not in

1. Champ Clark, *My Quarter Century of American Politics*, 2 vols. (New York: Harpers, 1920), 1:209.

the legislature itself. Political parties have not been able to build very effective sanctions over these members, partly because American constituents have not allowed them to do so, partly because the parties are too internally divided to agree on the use of sanctions. Under these conditions there are such clear advantages to an automatic system of choosing chairmen that few members of Congress have advocated any other method.[2]

The debate over the seniority system, which is generally carried on outside the Congress, centers on the choice of committee chairmen. The unfavorable arguments stress the effect of the system on party responsibility and presidential leadership, the lack of any dependable relationship between seniority and qualified leadership, and the fact that the committee leaders in Congress are by no means representative of many of the dominant interests either in the party or in the nation. They tend, generally, to be made by proponents of greater party power. The favorable arguments, generally made by advocates of the status quo, stress the harmony that results from the system, the emphasis that it places on legislative experience, and the lack of any more suitable alternative.

The most telling argument of the critics of the seniority system is that it promotes people to power regardless of their support for the program of their president and their party. A proponent of this theory has said: "A chairmanship, after all, is the position of a quarterback on a football team. It should not be given to someone who refuses to be part of the team or who might even carry the ball across the wrong goal line."[3] In fact, many hold that the people most likely to become chairmen—the members from one-party constituencies—are the ones most likely to be out of tune with their party's program.

The system, the critics argue, is no guarantee that chairmen

2. Charles L. Clapp, *The Congressman: His Work as He Sees It* (Washington, D.C.: The Brookings Institution, 1963), p. 227.
3. Committee on Political Parties of the American Political Science Association, *Toward a More Responsible Two-Party System* (New York: Rinehart and Co., 1950), p. 62.

will be well qualified. A hardy constitution and the ability to be reelected in the home district do not necessarily fit a man to preside over committee meetings or to defend committee reports on the floor. Two often cited examples of serious failures of the system are Fred A. Hartley Jr., chairman of the House Education and Labor Committee in 1947 and 1948, and Thomas S. Gordon, chairman of the House Committee on Foreign Affairs during most of the 85th Congress (1957–58), for neither had learned his committee's business during his apprenticeship period. There have been examples, also, of chairmen who were too senile to be effective. When Senator Arthur Capper became chairman of the Agriculture Committee he could neither make himself understood, nor understand others. If the system puts so much emphasis on experience, why, they ask, is a man who leaves to take an administrative post, but who returns later to Congress, given little or no credit for his previous experience? The late Alben W. Barkley is an example of this. They conclude that "the seniority principle is followed mainly because the seniors are pleased with themselves and see no sufficient reasons for consigning their powers to others."[4]

Finally, the critics suggest that the system produces a large number of chairmen who are representative of only one element of the party, and that, generally, a minority element. They represent stagnant districts made safe by restrictions on voting, by a one-party monopoly, by the ascendance of a major interest group, or by an effective rural or urban political machine.[5] Thus, the leaders of Congress produced by the seniority system are almost guaranteed to oppose the president, regardless of party; and a new nonconstitutional dimension is added to our constitutional system of separation of powers.

The most telling argument of the proponents of seniority is that the system promotes legislative harmony. It prevents hurt feelings on the part of those passed over in the struggle for appointment, and incidentally, it keeps pressure groups out of this struggle at the

4. Alfred De Grazia, *The Elements of Political Science* (New York: Alfred A. Knopf, 1952), p. 331.
5. George B. Galloway, *Legislative Process in Congress,* (New York: Thomas Y. Crowell Co., 1953), p. 271.

stage where a chairman is chosen. As a result, it helps to create a more clublike atmosphere, both in the legislative body as a whole, and on the various committees. Committees can act as more of a unit, and in a more nonpartisan manner. As Roland Young has pointed out, "The adjustment of rival claims must precede the adjustment of major conflicts without being permitted to divert attention for long from the larger task at hand. Some harmony within the legislature—including agreement on the location of internal authority—must exist before the legislature can itself promote harmony between conflicting groups."[6]

Senator Barkley spoke in similar terms when he opposed the Morse-Lehman attempt to prevent Senator James O. Eastland from becoming Judiciary chairman in 1956: "The element of favoritism would come into play, and there would be log-rolling and electioneering for the votes of the committee members by those who wanted to be committee chairmen. . . . Jealousies, ambitions, and all the frailties of human nature would crop out in the electioneering methods of men who wanted to be chairmen of committees."[7]

Another argument of the proponents is that the system produces experienced chairmen. Congressman Robert Luce has suggested that "though not the only factor in deciding merit, experience is the most important factor."[8] This experience must be with the subject matter within the committee's jurisdiction, with the people who serve on the committee, and with legislative procedure on the floor. (A chairman is also likely to be better acquainted with the officials at the working levels of the executive branch with whom he has to deal than the more transient department heads, who come and go with changes of presidents.) The proponents agree that the system doesn't always bring forth the right person, but they note that a Capper, a Gordon, and a Hartley do not last

6. Roland A. Young, *The American Congress* (New York: Harpers, 1958), p. 46
7. *Congressional Record*, 84th Cong., 2nd sess., 1956, p. 3822.
8. Robert Luce, *Congress: An Evaluation*, (Cambridge: Harvard University Press, 1926), p. 9.

long. The skill that most of the products of the system have developed is necessary to bring order out of chaos. According to Russell Baker: "The small group from the rotten boroughs, running sometimes unopposed, sometimes with token opposition, stays on for twenty, thirty, forty years, to become committee chairman, master the mysteries of the House and make it work, or make it stall. Without them, the House might slide into chaos like the Assembly of the late Fourth French Republic."[9]

The proponents also argue that the system is better than the alternatives. Those who testified before the Joint Committee on the Organization of Congress in 1945, and again in 1965, explored nearly every conceivable one of these alternatives. Of the proposals that would operate automatically, one calls for rotation in office, another for seniority bonuses for members elected from competitive districts. Rotation in office could take the form of passing the chairmanship around among all majority members with six years or more service, after a chairman had been in office for an equal length of time, or after he had reached the age of sixty-five.[10] It could also take the form of placing a limit on the length of time a legislator can spend on any committee or in Congress. Another proposal would allow a higher seniority rating to members whose opponents received more than 20 percent of the vote in any general election.[11]

The other broad category of alternatives involves giving some constituency the power to choose chairmen on the basis of certain rationally thought out criteria. Members of the various committees could be given the power to choose their own chairmen,[12]

9. Russell Baker, *An American in Washington* (New York: Alfred A. Knopf, 1961), p. 167.
10. See testimony of Representative Albert Gore in U.S. Congress, joint Committee on the Organization of Congress, Hearings, *The Organization of Congress*, pursuant to H. Con. Res. 18, 79th Cong., 1st sess., 1945, p. 389; see also *Toward a More Responsible Two-Party System*, p. 37.
11. Stephen K. Bailey, *The Condition of Our National Political Parties* (Santa Barbara, Calif.: Fund for the Republic), p. 16.
12. See testimony of George Smith and of Representative Albert Gore, Joint Committee on the Organization of Congress, Hearings, 1945, pp. 406, 888.

or at least to override the seniority system when a majority (or two-thirds) of the committee so decides.[13] Another possibility would be to have the chairman chosen by the entire house, by secret ballot. Senator Wayne Morse argued for this when he objected to the choice of Senator James O. Eastland as Judiciary Committee chairman in 1956. He reasoned that senators have a right to sit in Congress, unchallenged, as agents of their states, but that senators, themselves, should be able to choose their own agents, even if they are members of the minority party.[14] These alternatives may give a chance to choose chairmen on the basis of ability or devotion to the public interest or some other criterion. Others propose choosing chairmen, on the basis of their party loyalty, by one of a number of party organs: the caucus, the committee-on-committees, the Rules Committee, the policy or steering committee, the floor leader, or the presiding officer. Many who testified in 1965 called for the removal of chairmen who failed to support their party's presidential candidate or who consistently disagreed with their party's platform.[15]

In reaction, the proponents of the status quo feel that the automatic proposals tend to make too little use of invaluable, accumulated experience; that majority choice of chairmen is impractical for a full house and highly divisive for a committee; and that party choice is either impossible of accomplishment because of the lack of party responsibility, or simply unwise. Senator Harry F. Byrd played up to widely held American attitudes in his reply to Senator Joseph S. Clark's proposal that both he and Senator Eastland be denied their chairmanships for lack of support of the national Democratic ticket in 1960: "You are apparently proposing that questions of great public importance should be considered in the United States Senate on a partisan basis alone. I propose to

13. See testimony of Senator Estes Kefauver, ibid., p. 72. One staff member suggested that the committee members choose a member of the staff as chairman, without vote (George Smith, ibid., p. 406).
14. *Congressional Record*, 84th Cong., 2nd sess., 1956, p. 3816.
15. Joint Committee on the Organization of Congress, Hearings, *The Organization of Congress*, pursuant to S. Con. Res. 2, 89th Cong., 1st sess., 1965, p. 1504.

act on these matters and others on the basis of my most considered judgment and conviction after study of all the facts available and all the circumstances, existing and foreseen."[16]

Strong backers of seniority take the essentially conservative position that there is no reason to change from a system that is working satisfactorily to a system about which the results are largely unknown. Some also wonder if the system has not turned out to be a "rather handy scapegoat for Congressional inertia."[17]

Finally, the proponents argue that there are more ways to get around the occasional ill effects of the seniority system than its critics recognize. Party leaders and their committees-on-committees have selected new members to the more important committees with an eye to their potential as eventual chairmen. They have found face-saving means to remove members from committees when they felt it necessary. In 1949, for example, the complexion of the House Un-American Activities Committee was changed markedly when John E. Rankin, already chairman of Veterans' Affairs was removed on the grounds that chairmen should have only one committee assignment, and F. Edward Hebert, on the grounds that only lawyers should serve on the committee.[18] When, in 1958, Speaker Sam Rayburn and Majority Leader John W. McCormack became worried that Overton Brooks might succeed to the chairmanship of the important Armed Services Committee they removed him from the line of succession by persuading him to become head of the newly created Science and Astronautics Committee.[19] Both Thomas S. Gordon of House Foreign Affairs and Theodore Francis Green of Senate Foreign Relations were persuaded to step down from their chairmanships, and Adam Clayton Powell was removed from the chairmanship of the Education and Labor Committee. There is still some leeway to choose among

16. *New York Times*, December 4, 1960.
17. Stewart L. Udall, "A Defense of the Seniority System," *New York Times Magazine*, Jan. 13, 1957, p. 64.
18. Robert K. Carr, *The House Committee on Un-American Activities* (Ithaca: Cornell University Press, 1952), pp. 470–74.
19. Actually, Brooks died in 1961, three years before Carl Vinson retired from Congress at the age of 82.

committees (and committee chairmen) when important bills are assigned, though the Legislative Reorganization Act partially closed this door by defining committee jurisdiction in detail. And occasionally, certain matters can be assigned to select committees, for the seniority custom does not operate here. In short, party leaders are not as hopelessly bound by seniority as is generally pictured.

Although it is impossible to prove the correctness of many of these appraisals of the seniority system, some can be analyzed statistically. Charges have been made, for example, that chairmen are approaching senility, that certain sections enjoy a disproportionate share of the chairmanships, that chairmen come from districts that are socially and politically stagnant, and that they vote against their party and the president a great percentage of the time.

The period covered in this analysis, 1947 to 1968, includes two Republican and nine Democratic Congresses. Counting each chairmanship anew for each Congress, there were a total of 140 Democratic and 30 Republican chairmen in the Senate; 176 Democratic and 38 Republican chairmen in the House of Representatives.[20] Altogether, 141 individuals occupied the 36 chairmanships during the twenty-two year period. Nine senators (and no members of the House) moved from one chairmanship to another.

It is certainly true that chairmen are older than their colleagues, although perhaps not as markedly as is commonly believed. Table 7:1 shows the age distribution of all chairmen at the commencement of each of the eleven Congresses studied. The greatest percentage of both Senate and House chairmen have been in their sixties but some have reached the position in their forties. The youngest chairmen were Representative Harold H. Velde (42) and Senator Joseph R. McCarthy (43), both in the Republican 83rd Congress. The oldest chairmen, both Democrats, were Representative Robert L. Doughton (87) in the 82nd Congress and

20. If a chairman died less than halfway through a particular Congress, his successor is counted as if he had been chairman throughout in the statistical presentations made here.

TABLE 7:1

Age Distribution of House and Senate Chairmen,
80th through 90th Congresses

	HOUSE		SENATE	
Age Range	Number	Percent	Number	Percent
Under 50	10	5	9	5
50–59	62	29	55	32
60–69	79	36	57	34
70–79	51	24	36	21
80–89	12	6	13	8
	214	100	170	100

Senator Theodore Francis Green (89) at the commencement of the 85th Congress.

It is also true that the South provides a large percentage of the chairmen when the Democrats are in control, as does the Midwest when the Republicans are in control. Maps 7:1 and 7:2 show the states from which chairmen have come during the period under study. Perhaps this material can be better grasped in connection with table 7:2. Taking both parties together, the South has filled nearly one-half of all chairmanships in both houses. The East and Midwest lie within five percentage points of each other within each house, though they produced markedly more chairmen for the House than the Senate. The West, on the other hand, produced far fewer House than Senate chairmen. Undoubtedly the frequent redistricting made necessary by rapid population growth has had something to do with the lack of seniority and, therefore, chairmanships for that area. Looking at the parties separately, it is clear that well over half of all Democratic chairmen have come from the South, and well over half of all Republican chairmen have come from the Midwest.

There are a number of ways of attempting, very roughly, to identify the more stagnant states to see if they tend to produce the greatest percentage of chairmen. Presumably, in our urban-industrial society, rural states and states with low total personal income would fall into this category. Furthermore, in this two-party country, one-party states and states with low voter turnout would also tend to produce more chairmen.

TABLE 7:2
Percentage Distribution of Committee Chairmen
By Geographical Region, 80th Through 90th Congresses*

| | HOUSE | | | SENATE | | |
	Democrats & Republicans	D	R	Democrats & Republicans	D	R
East	24.6	22.2	33.4	11.5	3.8	36.0
Midwest	20.7	9.1	62.9	16.4	3.8	56.0
South	46.0	58.6	0.0	45.2	59.5	0.0
West	8.7	10.1	3.7	26.9	32.9	8.0
	100.0	100.0	100.0	100.0	100.0	100.0

* The regional groupings, which are marked on maps 7:1 and 7:2, are those used by *Congressional Quarterly*.

Table 7:3 groups the states in quintiles according to their degree of urbanism and shows the percentage of committee chairmen coming from each division. The Senate has drawn its chairmen from the more rural states. The twenty least urban states (the first and second quintiles) have had 43 percent of the Democratic and 50 percent of the Republican chairmen. In sharp contrast, the House chairmen have tended to come from more urban states. When the analysis is made by congressional districts instead of by states, however, House results look different. Taking the 88th Congress only, 75 percent of House chairmen came from the 203 districts classified by *Congressional Quarterly* as rural, 25 percent from the 103 urban districts, and 5 percent from the 50 suburban districts.[21]

Another of the social and economic characteristic of the states that have produced chairmen is found in table 7:4. The states are divided into quintiles according to total per capital income for 1966, with the thought that the poorest states are more likely to be stagnant. Because of the difficulty of gathering data for the entire period, the table covers Democratic chairmen and Republican ranking committee members for the 90th Congress only. The

21. No chairmen came from the 79 districts classified as "mixed." See *Congressional Quarterly*, 1963, pp. 1173–84. Because of the great amount of redistricting that has taken place in recent years, it is impossible as yet to make this breakdown for a later Congress.

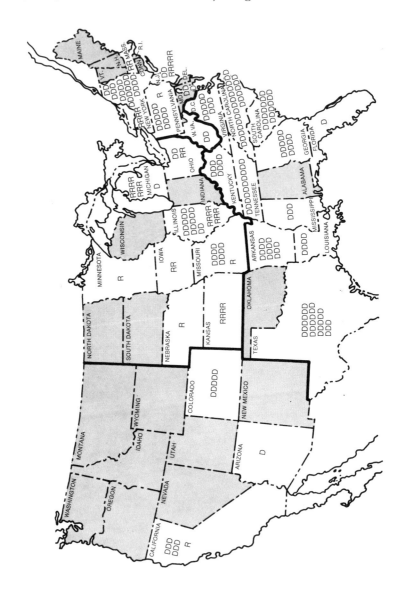

MAP 7:1 *States From Which House Chairmen Have Come,
80th–90th Congresses**

*Shaded states produced no chairman. A "D" or an "R" is placed within a state for each Democratic or Republican chairman. A chairman for more than one Congress is counted anew for each. A successor for a man who died less than halfway through is counted as chairman throughout. Neither Alaska nor Hawaii produced chairmen.

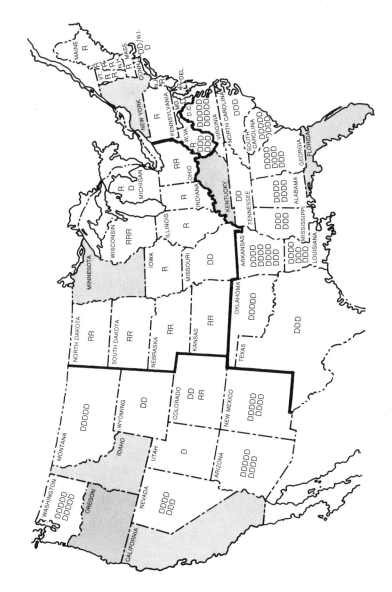

MAP 7:2 *States From Which Senate Chairmen Have Come,*
80th–90th Congresses

TABLE 7:3

Percentage Distribution of Committee Chairmen by States, Grouped According to Degree of Urbanism, 80th through 90th Congresses*

	HOUSE			SENATE		
	Both Parties	D	R	Both Parties	D	R
Least urban quintile	13	16	0	28	29	23
2nd quintile	19	18	28	16	14	27
3rd quintile	14	17	3	24	25	20
4th quintile	17	14	31	18	18	17
Most urban quintile	37	35	38	14	14	13
	100	100	100	100	100	100

* The states have been ranked and divided into quintiles according to the percentage of the population classified as urban. *Congressional Quarterly*, 1963, pp. 1173–84. The first quintile (0.0% to 14.2% urban) includes Alaska, Idaho, Vermont, Wyoming, Mississippi, North Dakota, South Carolina, South Dakota, Arkansas, West Virginia. The second quintile (14.5% to 22.8%) includes Maine, New Hampshire, Kentucky, Montana, North Carolina, New Mexico, Delaware, Iowa, New Jersey, Kansas. The third quintile (24.0% to 30.0%) includes Oregon, Georgia, Virginia, Tennessee, Florida, Alabama, Minnesota, Oklahoma, Wisconsin, Indiana. The fourth quintile (30.3% to 34.4%) includes Maryland, Nebraska, Pennsylvania, Washington, Louisiana, Missouri, Michigan, Rhode Island, Connecticut, Ohio. The fifth quintile (35.4% to 57.5%) includes Utah, Massachusetts, Colorado, California, Nevada, Illinois, Texas, Hawaii, Arizona, New York.

TABLE 7:4

Percentage Distribution of Chairmen and Ranking Minority Members from States Grouped According to 1966 Per Capita Personal Income, 90th Congress*

		HOUSE			SENATE		
		Both Parties	D	R	Both Parties	D	R
Lowest quintile	($1,751–2,310)	17.5	35.0	0.0	34.4	62.4	6.2
2nd quintile	($2,311–2,576)	17.5	25.0	10.0	25.0	18.8	31.3
3rd quintile	($2,576–2,872)	5.0	5.0	5.0	15.6	0.0	31.3
4th quintile	($2,931–3,220)	32.5	15.0	50.0	3.1	0.0	6.2
Highest quintile	($3,271–3,678)	27.5	20.0	25.0	21.9	18.8	25.0
		100.0	100.0	100.0	100.0	100.0	100.0

* Figures from U.S. Department of Commerce, *Statistical Abstract, 1967* (Washington, D.C.: Government Printing Office, 1967), p. 327.

two houses differ markedly. Of the Senate chairmen and ranking minority members, 59.4 percent came from the twenty states with the lowest per capita income while 20 percent came from the states with the highest income. In the House the pattern is almost the reverse, with 60 percent coming from the states with the highest income and 35 percent from the states with the lowest. There is also a clear difference between the parties. Well over a majority of the Democrats in both houses came from the twenty states at the low end of the scale while a majority of the House Republicans and 31.2 percent of the Senate Republicans came from the twenty states at the upper end of the scale.

Turning now to more clearly political classifications, table 7:5 divides the states and congressional districts from which chairmen have come according to their degree of electoral competition. An election won by greater than 60 percent of the two-party vote can be called safe. Constituents have elected 88 percent of the House chairmen and 62 percent of the Senate chairmen by safe margins. Republicans, who served as chairmen in only two Congresses in the period under consideration, fell well below Democrats, especially in the Senate. An election contest won by less than 55 percent of the vote is close. Only 2 percent of the House chairmen fell into this category. A considerably larger number of Senate chairmen, 23.5 percent, had close races, as could be expected from the fact that states are usually larger and more heterogeneous than congressional districts.

TABLE 7:5
*Percentage Distribution of Chairmen from States and Congressional Districts Grouped According to Electoral Competition, 80th through 90th Congresses**

	HOUSE			SENATE		
	Both Parties	D	R	Both Parties	D	R
Over 60% (safe)	88.0	91.0	74.0	62.4	68.6	33.4
55 to 60% (fighting)	10.0	7.0	23.0	14.1	14.3	13.3
Under 55% (close)	2.0	2.0	3.0	23.5	17.1	53.3
	100.0	100.0	100.0	100.0	100.0	100.0

* In the computation, each election was counted separately.

A final test to see if chairmen come from the more stagnant states, as is so often claimed, is to divide the states into quintiles according to the percentage of adult population voting in the 1964 election, and to relate this classification to the distribution of chairmen. The results are presented in table 7:6. Because of the difficulty of obtaining data for all previous elections and the considerable variations in turnout over the years, this analysis was made for the 90th Congress only. When both parties are considered together, a fairly even division among the quintiles appears, except for House chairmen from the states with the greatest turnout. Marked differences again show up between the two parties, however. A large percentage of House and Senate Democratic chairmen come from the ten states with the lowest voter participation—nearly all of them southern.

Based on voting records, table 7:7 compares the party loyalty of committee chairmen with that of the rest of their parties. A party "unity score" is used that indicates the percentage of times a member votes in agreement with a majority of his party, when a majority of the other party votes in opposition. The table shows the party unity average for chairmen (or ranking minority members) for the 80th through the 90th Congresses, by house and by

TABLE 7:6
*Percentage Distribution of Chairmen and Ranking Republican Committee Members from States Grouped According to 1964 Voting Percentage of the Population, 90th Congress**

	HOUSE			SENATE		
	Both Parties	D	R	Both Parties	D	R
Lowest quintile	25.0	50.0	0.0	25.0	50.0	0.0
2nd quintile	17.5	25.0	10.0	21.9	31.2	12.5
3rd quintile	40.0	15.0	65.0	21.9	0.0	43.8
4th quintile	5.0	0.0	10.0	12.5	12.5	12.5
Highest quintile	12.5	10.0	15.0	18.7	6.3	31.2
	100.0	100.0	100.0	100.0	100.0	100.0

* Figures as to voting percentage of population taken from *World Almanac, 1966* (New York: World Telegram and Sun, 1966), p. 384.

TABLE 7:7

*Average Party Unity Score for Chairmen (or Ranking Minority Members) Compared with Average for All Party Members and for Floor Leaders, 80th through 90th Congresses**

	HOUSE		SENATE	
	Democrats	Republicans	Democrats	Republicans
Average chairmen's (or ranking members') party unity score	65.9%	75.6%	63.9%	71.4%
Average members' party unity score	73.2%	75.5%	70.9%	72.0%
Average floor leaders' party unity score	89.6%	77.4%	79.8%	83.3%

* Data for this table are taken from appropriate volumes of *Congressional Quarterly*, for the 80th through the 90th Congresses. For example, see p. 24 in the 1957 volume.

party. For purposes of comparison, it also shows the party unity average for all party members and for the party's floor leader. With the exception of Republican chairmen and ranking minority members in the House, which show .1 percent greater party unity than all members of the Republican party in that body, the average of chairmen lags behind that of their fellow party members —by 7.3 percent for House Democrats, by 7.0 percent for Senate Democrats, and by .6 percent for Senate Republicans. And chairmen lag well behind the average for floor leaders—by 23.7 percent for House Democrats, by 15.9 percent for Senate Democrats, by 11.9 percent for Senate Republicans, and by 1.8 percent for House Republicans. Well over half the chairmen are close to the top in party unity. However, the average is pulled down by the party mavericks who hold two or three chairmanships in most Congresses.[22]

22. A check for chairmen whose party unity score is 20 percent or more below the chairmen's average in one or more Congresses turns up the following names: Senate Democrats Harry F. Byrd (Va.), James O. Eastland (Miss), Edwin C. Johnson (Colo.), Pat McCarran (Nev.), John L. McClellan (Ark.), A. Willis Robertson (Va.), Richard B. Russell (Ga.);

Voting records also lend themselves to analysis of the degree of support that party chairmen, or ranking minority members, have accorded the chief executive. Table 7:8 compares the support given the president by his committee leaders, by all members of his party, and by his party leaders.[23] The average for chairmen or ranking minority members is 4.6 percent below that of the party members' score for the Senate, 5.4 percent below in the House. The House committee leaders' score averages 24.0 percent below that of the floor leaders, while the gap in the Senate is 18.6 percent.

In conclusion, a comparison should be made between the seniority system as it operates in the House and as it operates in the Senate, as well as a comparison of its operation under Democrats and Republicans. Turning first to its operation in the two houses, the analyses show some interesting differences. Senate chairmen have represented more competitive electoral districts. The House, on the other hand, though it has had a large number of chairmen from rural districts, also has had a large number of urban-based chairmen. This helps to explain the fact that they have tended to come from more urban high-income areas, and that they, on the average, have shown a little more party unity and presidential support than Senate chairmen.

There are also partisan differences. Democratic chairmen have come from electoral districts that are more southern and slightly more rural, that have lower incomes, that tend more strongly to one-partyism, and that have a lower voter turnout. It is not

Senate Republicans George D. Aiken (Vt.), William R. Langer (N. Dak.), Charles W. Tobey (N.H.); House Democrats Graham H. Barden (N.C.), Charles A. Buckley (N.Y.), Omar Burleson (Tex.), William M. Colmer (Miss.), Robert L. Doughton (N.C.), John L. McMillan (S.C.), Tom Murray (Tenn.), John E. Rankin (Miss.), L. Mendel Rivers (S.C.), Howard W. Smith (Va.), Thomas B. Stanley (Va.), Edwin E. Willis (La.), John S. Wood (Ga.); House Republican Richard T. Welch (Calif.).

23. During the 81st, 82nd, 87th, 88th, 89th, and 90th Congresses both the presidency and Congress were controlled by Democrats; during the 83rd Congress both were controlled by Republicans; during the 80th there was a Democratic president and a Republican Congress; and during the 84th, 85th, and 86th there was a Republican president and a Democratic Congress.

TABLE 7:8
*Presidential Support Scores for Members of the President's Party,
80th through 90th Congresses**

	HOUSE	SENATE
Average chairmen's (or ranking members') presidential support score	61.6%	58.1%
Average members' presidential support score	67.0%	62.7%
Average floor leaders' presidential support score	85.6%	76.7%

* *Congressional Quarterly* has done a thorough analysis of presidential support since the 83rd Congress, and its data are used above. See, for example, *Congressional Quarterly*, 1957, p. 102. In order to get a crude check on presidential support in previous Congresses, the author made, for each Congress, a tally of ten votes (five on foreign and five on domestic issues) on matters about which the president's stand was clear. The procedure used was similar to *Congressional Quarterly*'s but it was not exhaustive.

too surprising, therefore, that a greater percentage of Democratic chairmen have been out of line with their party.

The picture is far from the ideal held by many of the proponents of majority rule, yet this empirical analysis does not make as clear a case against seniority as many of the critics claim. Chairmen are older on the average than their colleagues, and yet with luck a number of younger men are singled out for chairmanships. The districts that produce chairmen are not as much backwaters as is often suggested, and the degree of party unity and presidential support among chairmen is not as low as many believe. A discussion of the interactions between chairmen and others on their committees will help to give a more human picture of the effects of the seniority system.

Committee In-Groups

There are all sorts of ways to get things done in Congress. The best way is to live long enough to get to be a committee chairman, and resilient enough to be a good one. Chairmen complain to me that they are frustrated too, but this is really beside the point. If things can be done, they can do them; we are very sure of that.[24]

Many factors work to give a chairman power: the experience that generally comes from seniority, the demands for leadership that come from both within and outside a committee, control over the parliamentary process by virtue of being a focal point, and the availability of rewards and punishments. Yet a chairman is dependent, at a minimum, on the toleration of his fellow committee members. Clues as to both a chairman's power and its limits can be gathered from studying the various divisions within committees—the chairman (and perhaps the ranking minority member) versus the rest, the majority versus the minority party delegation, the senior members versus the junior members, the activists versus the inactivists. Generalizations are of value only if it is remembered that these relations vary from Congress to Congress, from committee to committee, and even from one legislative proposal to another.

The skills that a chairman is likely to have acquired while gaining seniority help him to build his power. He will have worked with the members of his committee longer than any other members of the majority party, known their strengths and weaknesses, and discovered how to make the best use of their talents. He will also have developed an invaluable knowledge of the subject matter handled by his committee, along with its legislative, administrative, and judicial history.

Demands for leadership increase a chairman's power. Congressmen admit that their committees are so large and so full of individualists that they soon learn that they can accomplish little without strong chairmen. Sociologists have found that group life can be far more pleasant in situations where leadership is clearly recognized, and legislators agree that this holds for such special

24. Clem Miller, *Member of the House* (New York: Charles Scribner's Sons, 1962), p. 39.

types of groups as congressional committees.[25] Groups outside the committee have also found it advantageous to deal with chairmen and inconvenient to deal with all committee members.

The mere fact that chairmen are important points of focus gives them great control over communications between the committee and the Congress, the parties, the interest groups, the executive agencies, and the press. Being a focus of attention also gives a chairman power over the parliamentary process. What goes in and what stays out of a measure is of great importance, and a chairman can build his power by combining in the right proportion the tantalizing with the unpalatable. Control over committee procedure adds to this power. And, of course, the unusual degree of control that Congress gives a chairman when his measures reach the floor and conference stages, adds even more to his strength.

A wide variety of rewards and punishments is available to help chairmen keep their members in a cooperative frame of mind.[26] While the late Clarence Cannon probably thought more in terms of punishments, the average chairman is likely to emphasize rewards. Even those stereotyped villains, the southern chairmen, are unrivaled in encircling their colleagues with love, perhaps because they know that they are in a minority position. Rewards can be in many forms—a word of praise, the chance to have one's name attached to an important administration measure, the offer of a subcommittee chairmanship, having a pet provision included in a committee proposal, being asked to speak for the committee on the floor, membership in the conference, the offer of staff assistance, an assignment to travel for the committee. Punishments can be the denial of any of these. They range from making a member feel "like a first grader at a seventh grade party"[27] to juggling a man out of a desired subcommittee chairmanship. Chair-

25. Robert T. Golembiewski, *Behavior and Organization* (Chicago: Rand McNally and Company, 1962), p. 105; Clapp, *The Congressman*, p. 227.
26. For a perceptive treatment of the reward and punishments available to chairmen of the Appropriations committees, see Richard F. Fenno Jr., *The Power of the Purse* (Boston: Little, Brown & Co., 1966), pp. 136–60.
27. Udall, *Seniority System*, p. 15.

man Cannon did this in 1955, for example, when he moved J. Vaughan Gary from the foreign operations subcommittee by making him chairman of another subcommittee.[28]

All powerful as he appears, a chairman is dependent on the support of his committee, his party and his house. Richard F. Fenno Jr. quotes a committee member who was speaking of his chairman: "If he can handle people and play his cards right, he can have a lot of power. But if he can't carry the Committee with him, he'll lose it."[29] And the description by Ways and Means Chairman Wilbur Mills of his approach reveals implicit limitations: "Well, I try to get a consensus of the Committee and then a consensus of the House."[30]

In the House, an increasing number of committees have adopted specialized rules of operation. Change is likely to grow out of a committee's opposition to its chairman, though there are exceptions, such as Chairman Clair Engle's encouragement of the adoption of rules by the Interior Committee during the 84th Congress (1955–56). Committee victories are usually won by dissident members of the majority working in combination with minority party members, in coalitions not unlike the one that stripped the Speakership of its powers in 1910. The reforms, therefore, usually increase the powers of a bipartisan majority of the whole committee and not those of the dominant party. If the committee majority delegation is large and united, however, it can work to increase its own powers, as in the case of the Education and Labor reform during the 89th Congress. A number of recent reforms have taken steps to limit the powers of the chairman by making certain types of decisions automatic—subcommittee jurisdictions

28. Otto E. Passman was then raised to the chairmanship, a position from which he was able to cut foreign aid appropriations. To give an idea of how important Cannon's change was, in 1962 Congressman Gary voted 83 percent of the time to support President Kennedy's foreign policy programs, Passman 33 percent. See *Congressional Quarterly*, 1962, p. 711.
29. Fenno, *Power of the Purse*, p. 137.
30. *Nation's Business*, Feb. 1968, p. 50. See the perceptive article by John F. Manley, "Wilbur D. Mills: A Study in Congressional influence," *American Political Review* (June 1969): 442.

are spelled out so as to leave little choice in the reference of measures, subcommittee chairmen must be chosen on the basis of seniority, and the senior men who handled measures in subcommittee must be chosen as conferees.

In nearly every recent Congress examples can be found of committee rebellions. In the 83rd Congress, Chairman Clare E. Hoffman lost effective control of the Committee on Government Operations, with the resulting development of autonomous subcommittees. In the following Congress, House Education and Labor Chairman Graham A. Barden was forced to submit to a democratic set of committee rules in a rebellion engineered by Stuart Udall and other committee liberals. In the 89th Congress, as a result of Chairman Adam Clayton Powell's much publicized absenteeism and capricious activities, Education and Labor revised its rules further to tighten majority party control over staff and to enable the committee to limit the chairman's delaying powers. Also in the 89th Congress, members of the Post Office and Civil Service Committee adopted rules that took power from Chairman Tom Murray and placed it largely in the hands of subcommittee chairmen who were given great independence in hiring staff and conducting investigations. In the 90th Congress, a new chairman, Thaddeus J. Dulski, took over the committee and the rules were modified to give a committee majority somewhat greater control over subcommittee actions. In 1967 members of the Committee on Banking and Currency, partly in reaction to Chairman Wright Patman's populistic distrust of banks, tightened the committee majority's control over staff and investigations. At the same time, with the change of chairmanship of the Agriculture Committee, rules were adopted giving minority members a greater voice in committee affairs.

Such victories over a chairman are not easily won, as a member of Congress noted in the round-table conference on Congress organized by the Brookings Institution:

> The toughest kind of a majority to put together is one to reform a committee in the face of opposition from the chair-

man. As you get closer to the top of the hierarchy, the pressures on people who normally would be counted on to aid reformers are enormous and even people who would be classified as among the "good guys" rather than the "bad guys" tend to chicken out. It is the second and third termers who really have to lead the rebellion. The new fellows are still in a dream world and after you get beyond two or three terms you are a part of the team and begin to see some merit in the system.[31]

The more resilient chairman is so sensitive to rumblings of committee discontent that such showdowns never materialize. He will keep an eye on the various divisions within his committees, conciliate the dissident elements, and alternately loosen and tighten his reins of control.

The ranking minority member on a committee shares some of the chairman's powers, if only because he may well become chairman if the control of Congress changes. One ranking member explained the relationship in this manner during the 83rd Congress:

> The gentleman and I have been see-sawing back and forth on this committee for some time. He was chairman in the 80th Congress. I had the privilege of serving as chairman in the 81st and 82nd Congresses. Now he is back in the saddle. I can say that he has never failed to give me his utmost cooperation, and I have tried to give him the same cooperation during his service as chairman of this Committee. We seldom disagree, but we have found out that we can disagree without being disagreeable. Consequently, we have unusual harmony on this committee.[32]

Many chairmen, especially of committees that do not divide too clearly along party lines, consult regularly with their ranking minority members on staff hiring, allocation of funds, committee agenda, and the form of legislative proposals. Committees that

31. Clapp, *The Congressman*, p. 223.
32. *Congressional Record*, 83rd Cong., 1st sess., 1953, p. 4933; quoted in Richard F. Fenno, Jr., "The House Appropriations Committee," *American Political Science Review* (June 1962): 319.

handle divisive measures concerned with labor, taxes, housing, and governmental operations are less inclined to peaceful cooperation and have even, at times, operated under conditions of open warfare or cold hostility between the chairman and his opposite number. Sometimes these quarrels are given public airing, as when Carroll D. Kearns refused to move his Education and Labor minority staff into "one stinkey little room" at the request of Chairman Adam Clayton Powell, or when Banking and Currency Chairman Wright Patman complained that Clarence E. Kilburn was "putting things in the *Record* time after time, claiming I was a laughing stock."[33]

The party division within committees is clearly recognizable. The delegations sit on opposite sides of the committee table, they often caucus separately, and they may well use different committee staff people. These divisions may be very important on committees that handle measures on which the national parties are divided, although committee groupings are most generally formed along subject-matter, regional, or ideological divisions which cross party lines.

Bipartisan groups of senior committee members are then of greater importance than the party groupings. Those who have served on committees for a number of years have some of the same seniority-accrued advantages of the chairman that greatly increase their importance in committee proceedings. In a situation where "power is in silence, in committee, in personal relations,"[34] the junior member is at a disadvantage. There is evidence that the rule that freshmen are to be seen and not heard has eroded gradually since World War II,[35] but it is still safe to say that junior committee members are not as influential as other members until they have proven their knowledge of subject matter and procedures, and have shown an ability to work well with other members.

33. *New York Times*, March 13, 1961; *Congressional Record*, 88th Cong., 2nd sess., 1964, p. 14717.
34. Miller, *Member of the House*, p. 104.
35. Jerry Voorhis, *Confessions of a Congressman* (Garden City: Doubleday & Co., 1947), p. 28.

Skillful activists can exert real influence on committee decisions without being in formal positions of authority. Holbert N. Carroll refers to the group within a committee that takes initiative in connection with a certain measure as the "efficient part."[36] Probably at one time or another most congressmen have belonged to the efficient part of their committees. Most visible are those who become so much the masters of certain specialties that when these specialties are involved they are thrust into positions of temporary leadership. Examples here would be Senator A. S. Mike Monroney when Congress was considering airline matters, or the late Representative John Fogarty when it was concerned with medical research. A somewhat rarer type is the person who comes to dominate a committee because of superior ability, including the ability to take leadership without giving a less able chairman the feeling that he is usurping power. One of the most frequently cited examples of such a person is John M. Vorys who was the real leader in the House Committee on Foreign Affairs under the chairmanships of both Carles A. Eaton (80th Congress) and Robert B. Chipperfield (83rd Congress). The late Senator Robert S. Kerr clearly dominated the Public Works Committee when Dennis Chavez was chairman, as he dominated the Finance Committee towards the end of Harry F. Byrd's chairmanship. Even in a seniority-conscious Congress, legislators can play effective roles without great seniority, without formal positions of power, and even without being members of the majority party. This fact acts as a real limitation on authoritarian chairmen.

Hired Help: Committee Staff[37]

One of the major changes brought about by the Legislative Reorganization Act of 1946 was the creation of professional com-

36. Holbert N. Carroll, *The House of Representatives and Foreign Affairs* (University of Pittsburgh Press, 1958), p. 27.
37. Much of the material in this section is drawn from Kenneth Kofmehl, *Professional Staffs of Congress* (Lafayette, Ind.: Purdue University, 1962).

mittee staffs.[38] The Joint Committee on the Organization of Congress found a "shocking lack" of skilled staff and proposed, in order to lessen congressional dependence on executive departments and on interest groups, the appointment of qualified committee personnel "without regard to political affiliation" and with qualifications determined by a director of congressional personnel.[39] The provision calling for a personnel director was deleted on the floor of the Senate, but the other committee proposals were adopted.[40] While the law gave the Appropriations committees the power to determine the size staff they needed, all other committees were allowed to hire four professional and six clerical staff people. A majority of a committee's members are authorized to hire, to fire, and to allocate these staff members between the party delegations. Two provisions of the law, it was hoped, would slow the rate of exchange of staff between the legislative and executive branches. One required written permission of the House or Senate administration committee in order to be able to augment committee staff by borrowing personnel from executive agencies. The other prohibited professional staff members from working for the executive branch for a year after leaving congressional employment. The latter provision was repealed early in 1949, shortly after the Democrats regained control of Congress and a number of staff members showed a strong desire to return to the executive branch.[41]

38. The first staff appropriation was made in 1856 for hiring of clerks of the House Ways and Means and Senate Finance committees. By 1900 funds were being provided for clerks for most other committees but the four money committees were the only ones to develop professional staffs with continuity of service before 1947.
39. Joint Committee on the Organization of Congress, *Organization of Congress,* Senate Report 1011, pursuant to H. Con. Res. 18, 79th Cong., 2nd sess., 1946, pp. 9–11.
40. See Section 202, Public Law 601, 79th Congress.
41. Daniel A. Reed argued for the repeal, claiming that the restriction placed serious limits on the development of a government career service. A. S. Mike Monroney argued that the provision had been inserted in order to encourage a congressional career service and to limit the exchange between the two branches. See *Congressional Record,* 81st Cong., 1st sess., 1949, p. 535.

George H. E. Smith, the secretary of the Republican Senatorial Policy Committee, issued an important *Memo on Committee Staffing* in 1946, claiming that "few requirements of the new law will be as important or as full of risks."[42] He suggested that it was inadvisable to hire "mere fact finders," public relations experts, or narrow specialists, and that staff members need not be either male or lawyers. They should have inquiring minds, a background in the area related to the committee's activity, and an ability to communicate. Gladys M. Kammerer found a fairly high degree of professionalism in the appointments made in the 80th Congress and no decline in quality on most committees in the 81st Congress, when the Democrats again took control. This shift brought relatively little staff turnover—the greatest change, she found, took place on the tax and labor committees of the two houses.[43]

The Legislative Reorganization Act vested the hiring and firing function in the committee majority, though the general pattern has been to delegate the power to the chairman, who often consults with the ranking minority member. One congressman gave the reason for this at the Brookings round table on Congress:

> I am a firm believer in letting the chairman select the staff and holding him responsible for its quality and performance. If the staff isn't good you can raise hell with him. Having a committee try to supervise a staff is impossible. The committee should, however, have a clearly understood power to veto staff nominations of the chairman and to direct discharge of an unsatisfactory employee.[44]

It is not uncommon for chairmen to use committee staff very much like their own office staff, to work on constituency and campaign matters. Struggles between members and chairmen con-

---

42. Quotations are taken from the copy of the *Memo* in the files of the Senate Republican Policy Committee.
43. Gladys M. Kammerer, *The Staffing of the Committees of Congress* (Lexington: University of Kentucky Bureau of Government Research, 1949); idem, *Congressional Committee Staffing Since 1946* (Lexington: University of Kentucky Bureau of Government Research, 1951).
44. Clapp, *The Congressman*, p. 257.

cerning use of staff have made news from time to time. Two examples will be cited to show that committee members are not powerless. In the 81st Congress, in reaction to chairman John Lesinski's highhandedness, the majority of the House Committee on Education and Labor established a subcommittee on staffing matters. In the 83rd Congress, the minority members of Senator Joseph R. McCarthy's permanent investigations subcommittee resigned in protest over a resolution granting the chairman total control over staff hiring and firing. They stayed away until the rule was rescinded and they gained a new position of minority counsel.[45]

A survey of the size of committee staffs in the 90th Congress (1967–68) shows a total of 1,083 employees of the thirty-seven standing committees and their subcommittees.[46] Five hundred and sixty-three were employed by the Senate and 520 by the House. The runaway committee, by all odds, was Senate Judiciary, with a total of 150. Senator Eastland ran it with a loose rein, save in the field of civil rights, and it was a tradition for a subcommittee chairman to build his own staff empire. The closest House rival was Government Operations with a staff of 54. These committees have had to seek permission from their respective houses to hire more than their allotted 10 staff members. At the other extreme are a number of committees that fail to hire the authorized number of staff personnel. For the 90th Congress these were the House Rules Committee with 5, the House Administration Committee with 7, and the Senate Agriculture Committee with 7. The chairmen of all three of these committees, incidentally, were conservative southerners of some seniority.

Throughout most of the period covered by this study, the senior committee staff man had been Everard H. Smith who had joined

45. Kofmehl, *Professional Staffs of Congress*, pp. 70, 238. For a full-scale description of a dispute over staff, see the account of the counsel to the House Interstate Commerce Committee's subcommittee on legislative oversight (Bernard Schwartz, *The Professor and the Commission* [New York: Alfred A. Knopf, 1959]).
46. Charles E. Brownson, *1968 Congressional Staff Directory* (Washington, D.C.: The Congressional Staff Directory, 1968).

the Senate Appropriations Committee in 1913, become chief clerk in 1939, and served in that capacity for nearly eighteen years. As of the 90th Congress, however, Boyd Crawford of the House Foreign Affairs Committee and Charles J. Zinn of the House Judiciary Committee, both of whom had joined their respective committees in 1939, were the senior committee staff people. To get a more detailed view, a survey was made of the 217 biographies of committee employees listed in the 1968 edition of the *Congressional Staff Directory*. Nearly half of the group had law degrees and a significant number had had teaching or journalistic experience. Sixty-two had had previous congressional jobs before joining the committee that employed them during the 90th Congress. Eighty-two had had previous experience in the executive branch. Of this group, the largest number, twenty-four, had worked for the Department of Justice. A change of control of the executive branch is likely to start a move from one end of Pennsylvania Avenue to the other. As an example, *Roll Call* noted that thirty-nine staff members, the largest percentage of whom had worked for congressional committees, had moved to the executive branch in the first three months of the Kennedy administration.[47]

Wherever the committee performs its functions, staff members play an important role—in all stages of the legislative process, in detailed supervision of the executive branch, and in day-to-day contacts between the committee and the interested public. Surprisingly little of a specific nature has been said about what staff people do, however, probably because it involves continuous, specialized, self-effacing, nondramatic work.

One hint as to importance of the staff members is the widespread use of the privately published *Congressional Staff Directory* by members of the executive branch and interest groups. Another is the sense of personal power that so many staff members conveyed to the author during his interviews. Though some legislators make a habit of praising their staff members in floor discussion, they generally work in anonymity. Philip W. Kelliher, coun-

47. *Roll Call*, April 8, 1961.

sel for the House Armed Services Committee, used poetry to describe his role:

> Silent he sits
> Amid the applause,
> Words,
> His words still echoing in his ears.
> Warmed only by an inward smile
> The pro, the cynosure of no one,
> Basks in the infra red light
> Of anonymity.[48]

Two case studies of specific legislative victories in which staff figured importantly give further insights. Stephen K. Bailey, in his *Congress Makes a Law*, which describes the passage of the Full Employment Act of 1946, shows how staff gathered basic economic data, prepared the case as it was to be made by the measure's legislative sponsors, and arranged committee hearings, all with the goal of arousing public interest, unifying support, and splitting the opposition.[49] Richard Harris, in *The Real Voice*, which describes the passage of the Kefauver drug bill of 1961, shows how crucial a role staff played at every stage, from suggesting an investigation of the drug industry to proposing strategy to be followed in the final Senate-House conference.[50]

The amount of staff influence will vary with congressional and staff concepts of the proper role for committee staff, as well as with the amount of time committee members can give to overseeing staff work.

Annually, when committee appropriations are voted, a few congressional voices, generally on the Senate side, are raised against "government by staff." Though the number of critics is narrowing, Senators Allen J. Ellender and Carl T. Curtis can always be counted on. Senator Curtis has said, in a typical comment, "We

48. *New York Times*, July 23, 1962.
49. Stephen K. Bailey, *Congress Makes a Law* (New York: Columbia University Press, 1950).
50. Richard Harris, *The Real Voice* (New York: Macmillan Co., 1964).

are having legislation by staff rather than by elected officials. Far be it from me to challenge the qualifications of any of the staff members. So far as I know, all of them are brilliant and well educated, but they are not elected by anyone. They do not represent the people. They are not answerable to the people. The public does not know who they are."[51] To this Senator John A Carroll, much more of an organization man, replied that staff was necessary so that Congress could hold its own in an increasingly complex world and in competition with an expanding executive branch.

Charles Clapp found little feeling among House members that committee staffs exerted too much influence. They tended to resent too much staff partisanship. One member said, "I would much prefer to have a quite dispassionate professional than a partisan professional. I think I can provide the partisanship myself."[52] And Congressman Clem Miller said, noting the value of the differing approaches of legislator and staff, "a good chairman working with a good staff man can be a joy to behold, one complementary to the other."[53]

Staff attitudes towards their proper role fall into three patterns with a certain degree of neatness. Two reflect their committee situation, one in a nonpartisan fashion and the other in a partisan manner. The third is somewhat more independent of committee. The first group of staff members stated in interviews that they felt their role was to service the needs of the various committee members, feeding them questions, background papers, and reports expressing the members' points of view, and never taking a stand themselves. This type tends to serve on the less partisan committees where the chairman and ranking minority member work in close cooperation. A second group, made up largely of those who

---

51. *Congressional Record*, 86th Cong., 1st sess., 1959, p. 2193.
52. Clapp, *The Congressman*, p. 261.
53. Miller, *Member of the House*, p. 12. This type of relationship is similar to the one praised by Dean Acheson that sprang up between Senator Arthur H. Vandenberg and Under Secretary of State Robert Lovett (Dean Acheson, *A Citizen Looks at Congress* [New York: Harper and Bros., 1957], p. 73).

worked for strongly partisan chairmen on committees most concerned with domestic economic policy, played actively partisan
roles. One staff man said he delighted in writing reports that made
Republican members of the committee squirm. Like the first type,
he was closely attuned to his committee situation. If he remained
on the staff at all with a change of party, he would become an
earmarked adviser to the minority. However, a majority of the
senior staff members interviewed spoke of a role somewhat more
independent of their committee. They would serve all members
to the best of their ability, but they would argue for their own
point of view. They explained their survival through changes in
party control as a result of their valuable services to members,
fast footwork, and never pushing their point of view too far.

The limits on committee members' time also have an effect on
the degree of influence exerted by staff. According to perceptive
staff people on both sides of the Capitol, committee members who
have relatively few conflicting demands on their time, who are
vitally concerned because of the importance of the subject matter
handled, and who have long experience on a committee tend to
limit the freedom of their staffs. To state the situation conversely,
staff generally has greater influence on Senate committees, on
committees that handle routine matters, and on committees with
high membership turnover.

Attempting to earmark staff for minority members is a difficult
problem. In 1960 the author interviewed a number of people who
were designated as representing the minority, either in the *Congressional Staff Directory* or on a list made available by the Republican staff member of the Ways and Means Committee, and he
found these designations to be very misleading. About half of
those interviewed were openly partisan. Another half claimed to
be professional, not partisan, and further checking showed that
most of these were so regarded by their fellow staff members. One
minority staff position was filled by a southern Democrat since
this seemed to be the only way to keep her on the payroll. Further
than this, a number of people who were nowhere designated as
minority staff really served that function.

Max Kampleman, a former Democratic Senate staff member, claimed that it is "ridiculous to expect committee chairmen to surround themselves with staff people who hold views contrary to their own."[54] Looking at it from the standpoint of the minority party, a congressman has said, "when the chips are really down, the staff is tipped towards the majority and the minority doesn't get much help."[55] Congressman Fred Schwengel, a leader in the drive for minority staffing, bases his argument on party ratios, saying "we have to work with a situation in the House of Representatives and in the Senate where Democrats outnumber Republicans three-to-two and three-to-one, yet staff responsible to the Democrats out-numbers staff responsible to the Republicans ten-to-one and eleven-to-one."[56]

When the minority party in Congress can make use of executive agencies, as Democrats could in the 80th Congress and Republicans could in the 84th, 85th, and 86th Congresses, there is less need for minority committee staffing. Demands increase when the minority party lacks this source of assistance. It is not surprising that the greatest demands for minority staff came when the Democrats regained control of the executive branch in 1961. Another factor that has increased demands for earmarked committee staff has been disregard for the minority position in committee investigations with strong partisan overtones. Most chairmen bury the partisan hatchet when seeking to win acceptance for their legislative proposals, but they seem to take the hatchet out during investigations. Nearly half of the twenty-nine committee staff members with "minority" in their title in the 88th Congress (1963–64) were concerned with committee investigations.

There is no easy solution to the problem. Staff work is often so complex that continuity of service is highly desirable. Minority staffing on a spoils basis without regard to competence is generally recognized as unwise, and a wholesale shift in staff with each party

54. "The Legislative Bureaucracy: Its Response to Political Change," *Journal of Politics* 16 (1953): 549.
55. Clapp, *The Congressman*, p. 259.
56. *Congressional Record Appendix*, 88th Cong., 1st sess., 1963, p. A5164.

change is considered inconceivable. Minority staffing on an ideo-logical basis presents its difficulties, also. One staff member com-mented that "the same staff can't serve both Democratic Senator Joseph Clark and Republican Barry Goldwater." Then he re-flected, "for that matter he can't serve both Senator Goldwater and his Republican colleague, Jacob Javits." A congressman at the Brookings round table said, in summing up the problem, "A committee staff can be bipartisan and still be biased. You must re-member that the splits within the two parties are sometimes more strained than between the two parties. You can end up with a bipartisan staff that is loaded one way or the other, conservative or liberal."[57] Generally, the staffs are tipped in the direction of the conservative position, a fact that satisfies most of the seniority leaders and most of the staff members, and that disturbs the "young turks."

The Joint Committee on the Organization of Congress called for a nonpartisan, professional staff. George H. E. Smith of the Senate Republican Policy Committee hit a more realistic note in his *Memo on Staff Organization:*

> In certain committees dealing with statistics and similar factual data, it will be possible in time to build a professional staff capable of serving both political parties alike. The na-ture of the subject matter itself minimizes partisan leanings. Staff personnel on the Appropriations Committee and the Joint Committee on Internal Revenue have practically achieved this result.
>
> Nonpartisan staff operations will not be so easily achieved in other committees where political differences generate sharp controversies. This is likely to be the case with the greater number of committees.

In spite of forces working for conservative, permanent staffing, the clientele committees in fields that come closest to dividing the parties have been the ones most likely to provide staffs with

57. Clapp, *The Congressman,* p. 260.

differing points of view. The most notable example is the Senate Labor and Public Welfare Committee where the split is clearer than anywhere else—with House Education and Labor not far behind. The Banking and Currency and the Commerce committees also tend to have aggressive, ideologically scrappy staffs.

A related staff problem concerns the access to staff of junior committee members, regardless of party. This has not been touched on so much in public discussion, though it is of concern to members of Congress as can be seen from the number of times it came up during the 1965 hearings of the Joint Committee on the Organization of Congress. Senator James B. Pearson of Kansas suggested that "each member of a committee be allotted a committee staff position regardless of his ranking as a member of the committee."[58] Representative Kenneth Hechler, a member of the Joint Committee, was interested in the suggestion on the grounds that "it would not only take care of both majority and minority staffing but in addition it would take care of some of the alleged abuses in the seniority system."[59]

These are the people—some elected and some hired hands, some hoary with seniority and others relatively young, some conservative and some liberal—who carry out the activities of congressional committees.

58. Joint Committee on the Organization of Congress, Hearings, 1965, p. 238.
59. Ibid., p. 363.

III
Committees &
Congressional Procedure

8.

Committee Business: Prepartum

"CONGRESS IN ITS committee rooms is Congress at work," said Woodrow Wilson. There are hundreds of these committee rooms in the Capitol and its satellite office buildings, overflowing with staff members, filing cabinets, and potted philodendron. Of central importance, of course, are the hearing rooms of the thirty-seven standing committees. These are painted and decorated predictably, yet physical facilities vary greatly. In the House Committee on Rules, for example, members are likely to conduct their hearings quite informally as they sit around a large table that nearly fills the room and leaves little space for spectators. A hearing by the House Committee on Ways and Means, however, is conducted far more formally. The members sit behind a long raised dais that is slightly curved at the ends. They face a large auditorium and speak into microphones. The tone of committee hearings varies greatly, also, as can be seen by attending a hearing in the hushed academic atmosphere of the Senate Committee on Foreign Relations and then moving to the county courthouse atmosphere of the Senate Post Office Committee.

These rooms see the greater part of the maturing of legislative proposals, a process that is sometimes characterized as "kneading" or "stewing." The late Speaker Sam Rayburn used to compare it to the aging of good bourbon. Here public hearings are held, measures are marked up in executive session, floor strategy is worked out, meetings of conference committees take place, and the execution of the law by administrative agencies is surveyed.

Rules Governing Committees[1]

Before discussion of the various committee activities, however, one should look at the rules and customs that serve to control them. The committee is the child of the house and the house has sanctions with which to control it. Neither branch of Congress, however, has seen fit to regulate committee activities to any great extent, though the Legislative Reorganization Act of 1946 sought to regularize committee procedure and to wrest some control from chairmen, giving it to committee members. Relatively few changes have been made since then, with the exception of House rules adopted in 1955 to protect the rights of witnesses, a reaction to the McCarthy period, and 1963 House rules regulating committee travel.

The Legislative Reorganization Act required all but the Appropriations committees to set regular meeting dates. According to the *Congressional Directory* for the 90th Congress (1967–68), five House and three Senate committees had not complied with this regulation (House committees on Appropriations, Interstate Commerce, Public Works, Veterans' Affairs, and Ways and Means; Senate Committees on Appropriations, Interior, and Judiciary.[2] To encourage floor attendance, all Senate and House committees, except the House committees on Government Operations, Rules, and Un-American Activities, are denied the right to sit when their respective houses are in session unless they receive specific permission. This was an old House rule that the Legislative Reorganization Act applied to the Senate as well. The possibility that a point of order may be raised in either house, noting that committee action was taken when the parent body was in session, serves to

1. Walter Kravitz of the Legislative Reference Service was helpful in checking the details of this section. See also Robert P. Griffin, "Rules and Procedure of the Standing Committees" in *We Propose: A Modern Congress*, Ed., Mary McInnis (New York: McGraw-Hill, 1966), p. 37.
2. Of the remaining twenty-eight committees, eleven had chosen weekly meetings, ten bimonthly, and seven monthly. Thirteen meet on Tuesday, eight on Wednesday, four on Thursday, two on Friday, and one on Monday.

enforce the provision. Both houses are generous in granting permission to sit; almost invariably the Appropriations committees are allowed to sit at will during an entire session of Congress by adoption of a resolution to that effect. Nevertheless, permission must be granted by unanimous consent, thus allowing a single individual to block committee action for extended periods of time during filibusters, for example. As a result, proposals have been made to change the rule in order to allow committees to sit unless permission is specifically denied.[3]

The problem of committee attendance is a difficult one—more so for Senate than House committees, for senators have more competing demands on their time. The rules hold that a majority of a committee constitutes a quorum. Committee action may be challenged on the floor on the grounds that a quorum was not present when a vote was taken, though the House has seen fit to hedge such a potentially dilatory motion with safeguards—it must be made by a member who was present at the meeting and before floor debate starts. For the purpose of taking sworn testimony, a committee may determine a smaller quorum—not less than two for the House or less than one-third of its members for the Senate.[4]

Each house exercises purse-string control over its committees. Individual committees receive $10,000 for routine expenditures plus the salaries for four professional and six clerical staff members. (The Appropriations committees are excluded from these restrictions.) Requests for funds above this amount must be passed on by the administration committees and the full houses. Generally, there is little opposition to a committee's requests, although unfavorable publicity may cause a restriction of committee freedom. The House, which is more sensitive to public clamor, for

3. A 1964 Senate rules change allowed committees to sit while that body is conducting the routine business of the morning hour.
4. House Rule XI, 26h; Senate Rule XXV, 3. These changes came in reaction to *Christoffel v. the United States*, 338 U.S. 84 (1949). In this case the Supreme Court invalidated the punishment of a witness for giving false testimony before the House Education and Labor Committee, on the grounds that a quorum (a majority of the members) was not present and that therefore it was not a "competent tribunal."

example, placed strict limits on committee travel abroad in reaction to publicity given to the trips of Education and Labor chairman, Adam Clayton Powell. Another means of congressional control of general committee activity is the requirement that when a committee reports a measure changing an existing statute, it must show clearly the revisions it is making.

Some of the regulations concerning committee procedures—the requirement that regular meeting dates be set and the provision that no action be taken unless a quorum is present, for example—serve to increase the power of the majority of committee members in relation to the chairman. House rules provide that a committee majority may call meetings over the opposition of the chairman.[5] Since the 1946 act, the rules instruct chairmen to honor majority decisions and to take steps to bring committee proposals to a floor vote. Complete committee records are called for, separate from the records of the chairman and available to the members of the respective houses.

Congressional regulations also cover the relationship between committees and the public regarding investigatory procedures and secrecy. As a timesaving device, the Legislative Reorganization Act requests that those who testify before committees submit written statements in advance and limit their formal presentations to brief summaries—a provision that is rarely followed to the letter. All Senate and three House committees (Appropriations, Government Operations, and Un-American Activities) have the power to issue subpoenas, while the other House committees must receive specific authorization.[6] In 1955 the House adopted a series of procedural safeguards for witnesses appearing before its committees.[7]

5. Three members of a committee may request a special meeting. The chairman has three days in which to determine whether he shall schedule a meeting within the succeeding seven days. If he fails to do so, a majority of the members can call such a meeting over his opposition. See House Rule XI, 25.
6. Telford Taylor suggests that one way in which Congress could regain some control over its investigating committees would be to repeal the provision of the Legislative Reorganization Act granting Senate committees the subpoena power automatically (*Grand Inquest* [New York: Ballantine Books, 1955], p. 286).
7. House Rule XI, section 26, h–g.

A chairman is to make a clear statement of the purpose of an investigation before its start. A witness is guaranteed the right to counsel. If, in the opinion of a committee, testimony would tend to defame a person, the committee is to go into executive session, testimony from which is to be made public only with the consent of the majority of the committee. The person in question has the right to receive a transcript (at his own expense) of the public and committee-released testimony, to appear in his own defense, and, if the committee approves, to subpoena witnesses. At the same time the right of the committee to punish "obstructive" witnesses was strengthened.

The Legislative Reorganization Act sought to encourage more committees to take action in public, calling for open hearings except for executive sessions for the marking up of bills and voting, or when the committee by majority vote calls for a closed meeting. The House Appropriations Committee has ignored this directive but all others have at least some open meetings.[8] The televising of committee hearings has been a matter of some controversy. The Senate has allowed it under Rule xxxiv, while the House, under Speakers Sam Rayburn and John McCormack, has not. Rayburn stated that he did not find television conducive to "decorum or orderly procedure."[9] He held that the rules of the House are the rules of committees and that television is not allowed by House rules. Speaker Joseph Martin, in the 83rd Congress, however, did allow the televising of House hearings, claiming that this was in the spirit of the Legislative Reorganization Act which called for more open meetings of committees.

Committees may go further than these congressional regulations and frame their own rules of procedure. As of the 90th Congress, twenty-four of the thirty-seven standing committees (as well as

8. The following committees reported that over 50 percent of their meetings were closed during the 89th Congress: in the House—Appropriations, Armed Services, Foreign Affairs, House Administration, Judiciary, and Ways and Means; in the Senate—Armed Services, Foreign Relations, and Rules and Administration (*Congressional Quarterly Weekly Report*, April 21, 1967, p. 643).
9. C. Dwight Dorough, *Mr. Sam* (New York: Random House, 1962), p. 516.

a number of investigating subcommittees) had adopted some written rules. No such rules had been adopted by seven Senate committees (Agriculture, Appropriations, Finance, Interior, Labor, Public Works, and Rules and Administration) and six House committees (Appropriations, House Administration, Interstate Commerce, Judiciary, Veterans' Affairs, and Ways and Means). The committees without special rules include four of the five so-called control committees (the two revenue and the two Appropriations committees), and the fifth, the House Committee on Rules, adopted a limited set of rules for the first time in 1967. Even granting the fact that the work of these committees is different from that of the others, the chairmen of these important committees clearly guard their prerogatives with unusual care. Beyond that, committees without special rules tend to be those whose work is of a relatively routine, nonpartisan nature that does not invite committee revolts, and those whose work is not primarily investigative; for such committees have nearly all drawn up procedural safeguards. Senate committees have found special rules less necessary than have House committees. When they have adopted them, their rules have generally been brief and perfunctory.

A survey of these committee regulations shows concern with each of the three fields covered by congressional regulations: regularized procedures, chairmen-membership relationships, and committee-public relationships.

As to regularized procedures, proxy voting and docket days have been matters of some concern. While proxy votes are not allowed in either house, they are allowed in a committee when authorized by its rules. For example, George Galloway found that in the 85th Congress (1957–58) in the House one committee (Judiciary) allowed both general and special proxies, thirteen allowed special proxies, and six allowed none.[10] Docket days, when

10. The six that prohibited proxy voting were Appropriations, Banking and Currency, House Administration, Interstate and Foreign Commerce, Rules, and Veterans' Affairs (George B. Galloway, *History of the House of Representatives* [New York: Thomas Y. Crowell Co., 1961], p. 87). The House Administration Committee has recently allowed proxies.

a member of Congress can appear before a committee and speak for bills he is sponsoring, were favored by the Joint Committee on the Organization of Congress, though a provision calling for their use was deleted from the Legislative Reorganization Act. The House Committee on Interstate and Foreign Commerce experimented with the procedure in the 80th and 83rd Congresses, and the House Foreign Affairs Committee, in the 81st. Staff members reported that the procedure was abandoned because it forced consideration of measures that lacked substantial support.

Committee rules can also influence the relations among members of a committee by increasing the powers of a majority at the expense of the chairman. A survey of committee rules shows relatively few that spell out democratic procedures. There are more examples in the House than in the Senate, and they usually denote a successful little rebellion in the committee's past. (Some of these have been discussed in chapter 7.)

On paper, the most democratic rules are those of the House Committee on Interior and Insular Affairs.[11] According to its provisions, the majority, if it desires, can exercise detailed control of committee affairs. It can change the rules, call special meetings, refer matters to subcommittees, discharge them, establish a quorum, make decisions, and have them carried out. The regularization of procedures further limits the discretion of the chairman by setting a regular meeting date, establishing subcommittees with clear subject- matter jurisdiction, setting their size and party ratios, and requiring that the chairmen be chosen on the basis of seniority (though they are to be replaced if they have a record of excessive absences). Proxies are allowed but they must be written and the purpose for which they are to be used must be clearly stated. Full committee records are to be kept. In the process of establishing limits on the chairman, care is taken to see that the minority is not allowed undue dilatory action. Roll calls are limited to the taking of record votes and the determination of the

11. See Steward L. Udall, "A Defense of the Seniority System," *New York Times Magazine*, Jan. 13, 1957, for a description of these rules under the benevolent chairmanship of the late Clair Engle.

presence of a quorum, and minority reports are to be "prepared with such expedition that the submission of the report of the committee will not be delayed."

Some committee rules also go further than general congressional regulations in outlining the rights of those testifying before them. These are found in the greatest detail in committees and subcommittees most frequently exercising the investigatory function. In the House these are Government Operations, the investigations subcommittee of Interstate and Foreign Commerce, claims subcommittees of Judiciary, and Un-American Activities. In the Senate, these are the permanent investigations subcommittee of Government Operations and privileges and elections subcommittee of Rules and Administration. Nearly all provide for the right to counsel, and for notice of date and nature of questioning. Some give individuals who have been mentioned unfavorably rights to attempt to clear themselves.

There is ample evidence that, although these regulations of the activities of congressional committees are important, they alone are not enough. As Robert F. Kennedy has said, "in the final analysis, if the chairman, members of the committee and the committee counsel are going to be unfair [to witnesses] there is nothing in the way of rules, regulations or laws that can really stop them."[12] And rules can no more harness a committee to the will of the house or force it to operate democratically than they can guarantee fair treatment of witnesses. It is also important to note that the most democratic procedures do not always guarantee the "right" committee decision. Senator Joseph Clark blames the long years of opposition by the House Interior Committee to the Senate-passed wilderness bill to "an absence of effective committee procedures."[13] Actually, the cause stems from the personnel of the committee, not its procedures, which could hardly be more democratic.

12. Robert F. Kennedy, *The Enemy Within* (New York: Harper and Bros., 1960), p. 311.
13. Joseph S. Clark, *Congress:The Sapless Branch* (New York: Harper and Row, 1964), p. 186.

Committees and the Legislative Process

Committees operate under these regulations—some of which stem from the full legislature, some of which are self-imposed—as they go about their legislative work. For an individual measure, the usual first stage of committee activity is to seek a report from the executive agency concerned, though the practice varies according to the people involved and whether or not the two branches are controlled by the same party. After this comes the public hearing, which is often described with some cynicism. A railway executive once wrote that hearings "are largely matters of scenery to satisfy the public," but he lived to regret the statement when his letter was produced at a hearing of the Senate Committee on Interstate and Foreign Commerce that was investigating the railroads.[14]

Hearings perform a variety of functions. David Truman describes them in this manner:

> First, the hearing is a means of transmitting information, both technical and political, from various actual and potential interest groups to the committee. This is the most familiar function, and probably the least important. From the standpoint of the interest group or the committee member, . . . the hearing is usually a haphazard and unsatisfactory device for giving and receiving information. This is one function of such proceedings, but it alone would not account for their continued vitality. A second use is as a propaganda channel through which a public may be extended and its segments partially consolidated or reinforced. A third function is to provide a quasi-ritualistic means of adjusting group conflicts and relieving disturbances through a safety valve.[15]

14. U.S. Senate, Committee on Interstate and Foreign Commerce, *Investigation of Railroads*, hearings on S. Res. 71, 1935, p. 10457.
15. David B. Truman, *The Governmental Process* (New York: Alfred A. Knopf, 1951), p. 372.

Clem Miller places more importance on the classical function of hearings than does Truman:

> Congressional hearings serve many purposes. The principal one is to build the recorded base of knowledge upon which legislation can be constructed. Even where there is the honest desire of the committee, its crabbed way must seem strange to the untutored bystander. Many of the issues before Congress have been around for years. The chairman may be excused if he leaves holes in his investigation. Why develop a long line of inquiry when it was fully covered by Report umpty-ump of the 84th Congress?[16]

Ralph Huitt has noted that hearings also serve purposes of individual committee members:

> He may wish to make himself a national leader, build a reputation as a subject-matter expert, advertise himself to the constituency, do a favor for a supporter, discharge some of his own aggression—the list could be a long one. What is important is to see that in every aspect of congressional life it is necessary to satisfy both the system needs and the largely personal needs of the member who must keep himself solvent in a free-enterprise politics.[17]

The chairman and his chief staff people are in the best position to determine such important matters as when hearings should be scheduled, who should testify and in what order, and how the questioning of witnesses should be carried out. The setting of a date for hearings involves consideration of not only the total work load of a committee but also the schedule of the committee in the opposite house that will also be conducting hearings. Since most legislation is in fields in which committees have acted before, the members and staff have a good idea of the groups that will want

16. Clem Miller, *Member of the House* (New York: Charles Scribner's Sons, 1962), p. 8.
17. David B. Truman, ed., *The Congress and America's Future* (Englewood Cliffs, N.J.: Prentice-Hall, 1965, p. 92.

to make presentations and of the positions that each will take. While there is no general right to testify and some may be denied the opportunity, those in charge of hearings are likely to see that each viewpoint, if not each group, is represented, if only to forestall charges of bias. In answer to criticisms that hearings often show too little planning and too little interest in "the inconvenient facts," some interesting innovations have been tried in recent Congresses. Hearings have been held in the field, and advisory panels of experts have been organized. These devices have been most frequently used in committees handling technical subjects, such as the Joint Committee on Atomic Energy and the Joint Economic Committee. Often hearings fall into a certain pattern, administrative officials appearing first, followed by proponents of the measure under consideration, then opponents.

In investigations, a staff member may be given the main task of asking questions; however, in ordinary hearings members do their own questioning. Usually the chairman starts, then the ranking minority member, then the ranking majority member, and so on down the line as established by seniority. Both time and important questions have often been exhausted when the junior members have been reached. One newcomer to the House Armed Services Committee managed to gain the recognition of his chairman, Carl Vinson, by tinkling the glass bells on the wall lights, until one day he found they had been wrapped in soundproofing tape.[18]

There is no hard and fast line between an investigation and an ordinary hearing. An investigation may be conducted by a special committee rather than by a standing committee, though this is not necessarily the case; it is usually concerned with the consideration of a special problem rather than a special legislative proposal; and the procedures of an investigating committee are likely to be more courtlike. Throughout Congress's history, many examples of both productive and destructive investigations can be found, but the latter type seems to have become increasingly prevalent. This can be explained in part by Congress's increasing concern with polit-

18. Russell Baker, "Again Vinson Mounts the Ramparts," *New York Times Magazine*, May 4, 1958, p. 78.

ical ideology and its disinclination to protect certain types of underdogs. Committees that show some restraint when they investigate a J. P. Morgan-type witness lose it, at times, when investigating an Earl Browder-type witness. Since much has been written about congressional investigations, this book makes reference to them only in passing.[19]

The Joint Committee on the Organization of Congress favored joint committee hearings as a means of bridging the gap between the House and the Senate and of relieving the burden on those who testify, but the provision was deleted from the Legislative Reorganization Act in the House. There is, of course, nothing to block joint action, but a survey of all committees produced a very small number of examples of this kind of cooperation between parallel committees in opposite houses, or even between committees in the same house with overlapping jurisdiction. The reasons most often given are that the two houses have markedly different procedures and different timetables, and that they are jealous of one another to a point that makes it difficult to work out acceptable protocol for joint hearings. A joint hearing means that the junior members have even less chance to question witnesses. And there are undoubtedly occasions, according to both legislators and representatives of interest groups, when a second set of hearings serves an important appellate function, for new and important facts are brought out. Further, different chairmen may represent widely differing interests and these interests don't want to put all their eggs in one basket.[20] Few can conceive of—or would advocate—a joint hearing on civil rights with Senator James O. Eastland of Mississippi and Representative Emanuel Celler of New York as cochairmen.

Malcolm E. Jewell and Samuel C. Patterson suggest a number

19. See Taylor, *Grand Inquest*; Alan Barth, *Government By Investigation* (New York: Viking Press, 1955); "Congressional Investigations," *University of Chicago Law Review* 18 (Spring 1951).
20. This was a phrase used by a small business lobbyist when the author asked him if he would prefer more joint committee action.

of roles that a committee member may play at hearings.[21] If the role is interpreted in national terms he may be either administration loyalist or opposition spokesman. If it is conceived in more parochial terms, he may be pressure group advocate, representative of a local constituency interest, or errand boy for a constituent. He may also play a role derived from his position on the committee, particularly that of expert or prosecutor. Obviously, these roles change with differing subject matter, and also with differing committee situations. For example, at an open committee hearing, the committee member is more likely to react to the expectations of outside groups; in executive session, he is more likely to react to the expectations of his fellow committee members.

On the basis of his important study of Senate Banking and Currency Committee hearings on price control legislation, Ralph Huitt found that committee members were more likely to play the roles of political participant than objective judge:

> The members of this Committee did not sit as legislative judges to discover an abstract general interest, nor did they seem concerned with presenting a balanced debate for public consideration. On the contrary, most of them did take sides. The Committee hearings clearly were used as a public platform for opposing groups with which the Senators identified. A great deal of information was received from interested groups, which the Senators accepted or rejected in accordance with their preconceived notions of the facts.[22]

The stage that follows the public hearing, the closed committee meeting at which a measure is marked up, is of vital importance, for committee autonomy is so great that a measure is likely

---

21. Malcolm E. Jewell and Samuel C. Patterson, *The Legislative Process in the United States* (New York: Random House, 1966), pp. 456–59. Jewell and Patterson have based their analysis on Ralph K. Huitt, "The Congressional Committee," *American Political Science Review* (June 1954): 340.
22. Ibid., p. 365.

to pass on the floor in the form in which it was reported out of committee. Former Speaker Rayburn is said to have advised President Eisenhower that "it's much easier to influence committee action before damage is done than it is to undo such action after a committee has acted."[23]

While the mark-up sessions of each committee vary according to its chairman's style and the respect with which he is held, there tends to be informal give-and-take among the members that crosses party and seniority lines with considerable freedom. Perceptive staff members say that at this stage the "gallery player" declines in importance and the member who has "done his homework" takes the lead.

These meetings are nearly always closed to the public, though in 1968 the House Education and Labor Committee experimented with a number of open mark-up sessions, primarily as a means of encouraging better committee attendance. Most members want some point in the legislative process when interest groups and constituencies are not looking over their shoulders. (If they prefer not to be heard by their fellow committee members of the opposite party, they may well caucus in order to take a party stand before meeting with the full committee.) Secrecy serves the useful function of allowing relatively free discussion among a number of specialized legislators of the possible political and technical difficulties presented by a legislative proposal. A by-product of this secrecy that appeals to many legislators, as Bertram Gross has pointed out, is the fact that committee members build up an "oligopoly of information" that is of interest to members of the executive branch and various interest groups.[24]

If a committee handles issues that divide the national parties (public housing, for instance) and the majority party can count on clear sailing on the floor, there may be little attempt made to conciliate members of the minority party. Generally, however, the goal is to work out a compromise that will be accepted

23. Dorough, *Mr. Sam*, p. 497.
24. Bertram M. Gross, *The Legislative Struggle* (New York: McGraw-Hill, 1953), p. 310.

by as many members of both parties as possible. A senior subcommittee chairman of the House Committee on Appropriations explained this to Richard Fenno: "I tell them we should have a united front. If there are any objections or changes, we ought to hear it now, and not wash our dirty linen out on the floor. If we don't have a bill that we can all agree on and support, we ought not to report it out. To do that is like throwing a piece of meat to a bunch of hungry animals."[25]

At the Brookings Institution round table, a less senior member gave his view of committee decision-making:

> A feeling of comraderie develops in the committees. You tend to go along with your fellow committee members on bills in which they are particularly interested. I find myself going along sometimes even with members of the other side, although for some that principle works in reverse: they irritate you so much that you are against anything they are for.[26]

Richard Fenno, in his study of appropriations politics, quotes a member of the House Committee on Appropriations as saying, "If there's anything members don't like it's someone who keeps quiet in Committee and then pops up on the floor with an amendment."[27] That committee has developed a custom of "reserving," that is, of a member's notifying his colleagues that he may disagree openly at some later point. Other committees have not developed the custom of reserving quite so formally, but there is widespread agreement with the unwritten rule that a member should not express any stand on the floor that he has not previously stated in committee. One of the legislative charges most frequently brought against Senator Joseph McCarthy was that he failed to abide by this unwritten rule.

25. Richard F. Fenno Jr., "The House Appropriations Committee," *American Political Science Review* (June 1962): 317.
26. Charles L. Clapp, *The Congressman: His Work as He Sees It* (Washington, D.C.: The Brookings Institution, 1963), p. 15.
27. Richard F. Fenno Jr., *The Power of the Purse* (Boston: Little, Brown & Co., 1966), p. 205.

Proxy voting by committees presents difficult problems. During the hearings of the Joint Committee on the Organization of Congress in 1965, it was pointed out that trustees and directors are forbidden to cast proxies because they have been selected "to exercise their judgment based on what they see and hear."[28] The Joint Committee report, which asked that proxies be forbidden, stated, "You cannot argue with a proxy; a proxy cannot consider an offered amendment; a proxy cannot compromise."[29] Proxies, in short, are not very subtle legislative instruments and they do give great added power to a chairman and his ranking minority member. Yet there is a real problem of committee attendance. Generally, even the most stringent committee rules merely circumscribe their use by demanding that they be filed with the clerk before a meeting and that they be as specific as possible as to the position of the absent member.

The mark-up session concluded, a committee report is written. Writing is generally done by committee staff, often with the help of the administrative agency concerned. Many staff people know their committee members and their subject matter so well that they can write both majority and minority reports and have almost no changes made by the committee. On the more partisan committees, of course, separate minority staff members write the dissents.

A dissenting report is the exception. Richard Fenno writes, "A minority report, written in opposition to the majority report of a committee, is the outward visible symbol of inward invisible committee disunity. It publicizes, prosecutes, and sharpens internal committee conflict."[30] A survey of over 2,000 committee reports written during the 86th Congress (1959–60) showed that only 112, or 5 percent, had dissents. Of these 112, all but 10 of the minority reports were divided along party lines. The House com-

28. Joint Committee on the Organization of Congress, Hearings, *The Organization of Congress*, pursuant to S. Con. Res. 2, 89th Cong., 1st sess., 1965, p. 351.
29. Joint Committee on the Organization of Congress, Senate Report 1414, 1966, p. 9.
30. Fenno, *Power of the Purse*, p. 203.

mittees that produced the greatest number of minority reports were Interstate and Foreign Commerce with 8, Ways and Means and Government Operations with 7 each, and Banking and Currency with 6.[31] The Senate committees with the greatest proportion of dissents were Judiciary and Labor and Public Welfare with 11 each, and Interstate and Foreign Commerce and Finance with 8 each.[32]

31. Other House committees with minority reports lined up as follows: Agriculture, Judiciary, Public Works with 5 each; Foreign Affairs with 4; Education and Labor with 3; Science and Astronautics with 2; Appropriations, Armed Services, Interior and Insular Affairs, Post Office and Civil Service, Merchant Marine and Fisheries with 1 each. No minority reports were filed by District of Columbia, Rules, Un-American Activities, Veterans' Affairs, or House Administration.

32. Other Senate Committees with minority reports lined up as follows: Public Works with 4; Banking and Currency and Foreign Relations with 3; Government Operations, Interior and Insular Affairs with 2; Agriculture and Forestry, Post Office and Civil Service, Rules and Administration with 1. No minority reports were filed by Aeronautical and Space Sciences, Appropriations, Armed Services, or District of Columbia.

9.

Committee to Floor:
The House

The task of narrowing down the thousands of measures introduced in Congress each year is monumental. To give it to the full membership is inconceivable, though some state legislatures are still in a position to make these decisions by majority vote. The major alternatives, then, are to entrust the task to the standing committees or to the leadership of the majority party. It is also possible to devise rules so that bipartisan majorities within Congress can overrule the decisions made by either the committee or the party leaders.

Congress has left the major task of screening with the committees. These "dim dungeons of silence," as Woodrow Wilson characterized them, have eliminated all but roughly 20 percent of the measures introduced in Congress in recent years, as may be seen from table 9:1.

Congress has never been entirely satisfied with placing so much power in the hands of committees, however, and it has also vested considerable power in the hands of majority party leaders. They can influence committees, though they have no absolute power over them. Working in tandem with the seniority leaders who dominate the committees, the party leaders can greatly increase the chances of a bill passing. If they have strong backing from the members of their house they can occasionally force out of committee measures that are strongly opposed by the seniority leaders.

Especially at the time of the Cannon revolt in 1910, congressmen found themselves at odds with both the committee leaders

TABLE 9:1
*The Fate of Bills in Congress, 80th Through 90th Congresses**

	80th	81st	82nd	83rd	84th	85th	86th	87th	88th	89th	90th
ACTION IN THE HOUSE											
Bills introduced House bills	7,163	9,994	8,568	10,288	12,467	13,876	13,304	13,420	15,299	18,552	20,587
reported House bills	1,410	1,837	1,456	1,535	1,739	1,392	1,216	1,455	1,119	1,271	1,021
passed House bills	1,192	1,687	1,340	1,392	1,562	1,253	1,083	1,301	934	1,109	792
ACTION IN THE SENATE											
Bills introduced Senate bills	2,945	4,275	3,494	3,893	4,315	4,329	3,926	3,810	3,937	3,931	4,199
reported Senate bills	765	1,100	883	1,173	1,255	1,179	866	926	586	747	812
passed Senate bills	636	913	775	1,027	1,159	1,062	768	834	540	688	720
ACTION IN CONGRESS											
Bills enacted	1,364	2,024	1,617	1,783	1,921	1,719	1,292	1,569	1,026	1,283	1,002

* This information is taken from the appropriate resumes of congressional activity published in the "Daily Digest" of the *Congressional Record*. Only bills are tabulated, no resolutions. The markedly larger number of bills introduced in the House can be explained in part by the fact that, until recently, in that body there could be no multiple sponsorship of legislation. In order for representatives to be on record as favoring a bill in its initial stages, therefore, many identical measures were introduced.

and the party leaders. They created unique procedures whereby bipartisan majorities could bring out on the floor measures that had been blocked by both committee and party leaders.

The scheduling of legislative business has been likened to railroading. Though he was writing of the House, what De Alva S. Alexander says applies nearly as well to the Senate:

> The running of trains on a single track railroad may be likened to the passage of measures through the House. The freight gives way to a local passenger train, which sidetracks for an express, which in turn sidetracks for the limited, while all usually keep out of the way of a relief train. Meantime, when a train having the right of way passes, the delayed ones begin to move until again obliged to sidetrack. . . .[1]

Bertram Gross has carried this analogy still further:

> One should assume that this railroad has no fixed schedule of priorities. One should think of many trains being run by canny engineers who will try to hold back on some occasions and to plow ahead on others. One should then visualize a tremendous number of trains lined up in the railroad yard, with their crews eager to devise means of getting a favorable signal and with gangs of switchmen roaming the yards making efforts to insure that certain trains are permanently sidetracked. Finally, one should realize that every week new trains are lined up in the yards and that every week brings closer the end of Congress when the yards and tracks are all completely cleared and the entire process of lining up starts all over again.[2]

This and the succeeding chapter concentrate on party leadership and on the rules and customs of the House and the Senate that shape the leadership's power to screen and schedule. The

1. De Alva Stanwood Alexander, *History and Procedures of the House of Representatives* (Boston: Houghton Mifflin Co., 1916), p. 222.
2. Bertram M. Gross, *The Legislative Struggle* (New York: McGraw-Hill, 1953), pp. 338–39.

infinitely more complex pattern of the House will be discussed in this chapter. Here scheduling is performed primarily by the majority leader and the Speaker. The leaders have tended to consult regularly with a group of intimates and have not made effective use of formalized steering or policy committees. They have also had to reckon with an independent source of power, the House Rules Committee, which is a bipartisan standing committee organized under the seniority system, and which has the ability to suppress major legislation. Further, the leaders have to operate under complex rules, precedents, and customs that sometimes act to limit them, giving some guarantees to minorities and to bipartisan majorities.

Party Leadership

For a time the House gave the Speaker almost complete control over allocation of legislative priorities, but it revolted against the authoritarian power of Joseph Cannon in 1910 and, rather than trying to harness it, pulled apart a centralized power structure that had been years in the making. It has never been willing to trust any one person or group with such formal power since that time. As a result, militant coalitions of House members are in a somewhat better position than prior to 1910 to push the party leaders further than they might like to go. Also, strategically placed individuals are in a considerably better position to veto the program proposed by the party leaders. In spite of this, the contemporary Speaker and majority leader play the central role in legislative scheduling, for in them resides most of the power to take positive action.

Prior to the Cannon revolt, the Speaker was unlimited in his freedom to determine whom to recognize, and had the power to appoint the members of all standing committees, to choose their chairmen, and to serve as the chairman of the Rules Committee. The House rebellion brought a curtailment of his powers to the point that no Speaker can successfully ignore the rank and file, as Cannon did. As the late Sam Rayburn described his role, "My experience with the Speakership has been that you can't lead people by driving them. Persuasion and reason are the only ways to lead them. In that way, the Speaker has influence and power in the House."[3] At another time he commented, "You can't really say how you lead. You feel your way, receptive to those rolling waves of sentiment. And if a man can't see and hear and feel, why then, of course, he's lost."[4]

If the modern Speaker cannot dictate, his powers are still great. Randall Ripley categorizes the resources on which he bases his power as "use of rules, influence on tangible rewards or preferment for individual members, influence on psychological rewards or preferment, and dominance of the communications process."[5] As presiding officer, he interprets the rules. His right to determine whom to recognize when two or more congressmen address the chair, though circumscribed, is still great.[6] He appoints members of all select committees and House members of conference committees and he has great influence in determining who shall be appointed to standing committees. He decides who is to preside over the Committee of the Whole House. Perhaps most important, without his help very little can be accomplished and with it a great deal can be, for he commands most of the available routes through the complex labyrinth of the House. As one congressman described the members' relationship to the Speaker, "You feel lonesome when you are not in his good graces." Congressman Richard

3. *Time*, October 13, 1961, p. 26.
4. Neil MacNeil, *Forge of Democracy* (New York: David McKay, 1963), p. 75.
5. Randall B. Ripley, *Party Leaders in the House of Representatives* (Washington, D.C.: The Brookings Institution, 1967), p. 193.
6. In the matter of recognition, the Speaker is now bound by a complex set of rules regarding the handling of various types of measures. For example, he must recognize the chairmen of Appropriations and Ways and Means when they move consideration of money bills and he must allow committee members in charge of other types of legislation to control the time allotted for general debate. One of the few times when he can exercise complete discretion is on two days a month when motions are made to suspend the rules and pass legislation under special procedure.

Bolling has said, in describing the position of his party's leader, "A modern Democratic Speaker is something like a feudal king— he is first in the land; he receives elaborate homage and respect; but he is dependent on the powerful lords, usually committee chairmen, who are basically hostile to the objectives of the national Democratic party and the Speaker."[7]

It is not easy to determine where the Speaker's role stops and the majority leader's begins. The Speaker's position is recognized by the Constitution and by the rules of the House, while that of the majority leader is not. Yet the majority leader operates more in the limelight and, as a result, it is easier to understand the role he plays. Speakers, being leaders of the whole House, have tended to limit their participation in floor debate and in voting, while majority leaders have played exceedingly active roles here.

The majority leader has achieved a position of greater importance since the 1910 revolt. Prior to 1910, he was chosen by the Speaker; now, he is chosen by secret ballot of the caucus.[8] Sam Rayburn has claimed that one "can run the House from the floor or from the chair."[9] but unless the majority leader can clearly dominate the Speaker by strength of personality, as did Oscar Underwood under Champ Clark and Rayburn under William B. Bankhead, he is likely to be forced into the role of second man in the party hierarchy, working in close collaboration with the Speaker.[10]

Nevertheless, the majority leader has both stature and room for independent action. He is the field general of his party on the floor of the House. He guides his party's legislative program, following closely the fortunes of the various measures in committee, making

7. Richard Bolling, *House Out of Order* (New York: E. P. Dutton, 1965), p. 70.
8. Democrats prefer the term caucus and Republicans conference. Both refer to the meetings of all the members of a political party in a single house for the purpose of selecting party leaders or discussing party policies. The term caucus will be used here unless specific reference is being made to the Republican organization, for it is a more generic term.
9. MacNeil, *Forge of Democracy*, p. 70.
10. Ripley, *Party Leaders*, pp. 92, 95.

major decisions as to scheduling (in cooperation with the Speaker, committee chairmen, and the minority leader), and leading in floor debate.

In spite of many individual variations, all majority leaders enjoy certain powers inherent in their office. An organization of any size has to accept a certain amount of leadership in order to accomplish its tasks. The mere fact of being the leader gives the majority leader superior access to information about both legislation and procedure. The skillful leader will be able to reinforce his power by winning the support of the members. This can be done by showing sensitivity to the demands of the constituencies of the different members, by helping the members make legislative records that will aid them in reelection, and, in general, by granting or withholding favors that make a legislator's role easier and more effective.

A perusal of the statements made at least weekly (usually more frequently) by the majority leaders of the House helps in an understanding of their peculiar position. They are likely to speak with a certain sense of power, using such personal phrases as "I plan to . . ." and "I would hope very strongly that. . . ." At the same time, the impression is constantly given that the power is tenuous, that it depends on a number of factors beyond the majority leader's control.

The greatest limit on the majority leader is the existence of the other members, each with independent sources of strength, with personal and constituency-based idiosyncrasies. A congressman's constituency makes the decision to hire and fire. The legislative party leader cannot change this decision. He cannot remove the legislator who is well entrenched at home; he cannot save the legislator who is not. "Every member is elected in his own right," said former Majority Leader John McCormack, "and all we can do is try in a refreshing way to press and press and press."[11]

One gets the impression, startling at first, that most majority

11. *Congressional Record*, 86th Cong., 2nd sess., 1960,, p. 11391.

and minority leaders have gotten along better with each other than each has with many of the members of his own party. As leaders, the two men have many common interests that they do not share with their fellow party members.

The fact that committees are independent units of power also acts as a limit on the majority leader. They can act too slowly for his taste. McCormack commented with a note of frustration in May 1961, "I have sent letters around to chairmen of committees on two occasions asking them to get bills out of committees that could be acted on before this session closes."[12] Committees can so alter legislative proposals as to change the whole tenor of floor action. They can refuse to act at all.

The House has had only three majority leadership teams throughout the period under study here. Speaker McCormack and Majority Leader Carl Albert served together, starting in 1962. Speaker Rayburn and Majority Leader McCormack served together from 1940 through 1961, with the exception of two Republican-controlled Congresses. For men of markedly dissimilar backgrounds and temperaments, they worked in tandem effectively. Republican Speaker Joseph W. Martin Jr. and Majority Leader Charles A. Halleck served together in the 80th and the 83rd Congresses. They worked fairly cooperatively, according to most contemporary observers, though the relations must have been strained at times, judging from a number of controversies that arose when Halleck announced the schedule and from the bitterness that was shown when Halleck displaced Martin as minority leader in the 86th Congress, and again, when Gerald R. Ford replaced Halleck in the 89th Congress.

Randall B. Ripley, in his study of House party leaders, found two important differences between the Democratic and Republican parties, regardless of whether they were in the majority or minority position. Republicans are more inclined to govern themselves by committee, while Democrats have established a more

12. Ibid., p. 11390.

centralized rule. Republicans demand more ideological agreement among their members than do Democrats. He concludes:

> These two differences are related to one another. Rank-and-file Republican members are more concerned with internal democracy because they realize that party leaders exercise considerable power over their careers and futures in the House. Thus, they constantly seek a greater voice in internal party decisions as a means of self-protection. When a leader stands in their way, as Charles Halleck did in 1965, they replace him with a more malleable man. Democrats on the other hand are willing to give their leaders more security (and the power that stems from security) because these leaders exercise less immediate power over their careers. Democratic leadership is centralized, but more willing to tolerate dissent. Part of the price for centralization is the tacit understanding that the leaders will not punish individuals except in extreme cases, but will instead be tolerant with all members calling themselves Democrats.[13]

Though the Joint Committee on the Organization of Congress advocated the formation of party policy committees to work with the party leaders in determining and effectuating policy, little has come of the proposal in the House. As "coachman of a poorly harnessed team," Speaker Rayburn did not care to be tied too closely to institutionalized party organizations that could act as a further limitation on his powers.[14] He preferred to work with an informal group of personally selected and congenial members referred to as the "Board of Education." Speaker McCormack, on the other hand, had no such informal advisory body and he drew very heavily on the advice of his floor leader and whip.[15]

13. Ripley, *Party Leaders*, p. 192.
14. Clem Miller, *Member of the House* (New York: Charles Scribner's Sons, 1962), p. 90.
15. Robert L. Peabody, *"Party Leadership Change in the United States* House of Representatives," *American Political Science Review* (Sept. 1967): 690.

Steering or policy committees have existed for many years in the House, but they have never played a significant role. Democrats had created a steering committee in 1933 as a consolation prize for the two Democratic leaders who lost the Speakership to Henry T. Rainey. Democrats have treated it very casually, and it fell into general disuse under Speaker Rayburn who was not interested in sharing his power (and restricting his maneuverability) with an elective body. In more recent years it was generally referred to as the policy committee, though it was never formally designated as such. Committees were apparently appointed for every Congress until the 86th, but, to paraphrase the report of the first Joint Committee on the Organization of Congress, they seldom met and never steered. After a lapse of three years and with the pushing of the liberal Democratic Study Group,[16] a new steering committee was established in March 1962 by Speaker McCormack. Congressman Ray J. Madden was chosen chairman after much maneuvering, but little was heard from the committee in the 87th Congress and it was not recreated in the 88th. The Democratic Study Group asked for and won its revival at the start of the 89th Congress, but under Madden's chairmanship, it took no action in that or in the succeeding Congress.

House Republicans have made more use of their policy committee than the Democrats. Republicans had a steering committee that had been created in 1919. At the beginning of the 81st Congress, after their 1948 election defeat, they formally designated this as their policy committee.[17] The floor leader served as chairman until the 86th Congress when Halleck designated John W. Byrnes for that position, undoubtedly the result of an agreement which helped enable Halleck to succeed Martin in that year. He was succeeded by John J. Rhodes in 1965, when Gerald R. Ford took over as minority leader.

16. The Democratic Study Group is an informal organization, formed in 1956, that has provided policy research, a whip organization, and even financial campaign assistance for liberal Democrats.

17. George B. Galloway, *History of the House of Representatives* (New York: Thomas Y. Crowell Co., 1961), p. 151 gives the resolution of creation.

House Committee on Rules[18]

The party leadership of the House shares its screening and scheduling tasks with the Rules Committee. This unique institution started its life as a legislative committee. It gradually developed into a vehicle for the leadership of the majority party. Since 1937, however, when the southern Democratic-Republican coalition took shape in Congress, it has played an independent role, frequently modifying measures in ways not desired by the party leaders and occasionally blocking them entirely.

DEVELOPMENT OF THE RULES COMMITTEE

Many students of Congress see a certain inevitability to the gradual accretion of powers of the House Rules Committee, and the literature is full of statements similar to this one written by Congressman Robert Luce: "The story of the Committee on Rules of the National House is the story of development of power made necessary by the growth of business."[19]

The committee's first function was to report changes in the rules of the House. This is an important but limited power which it still exercises today. It is the only channel through which rule

18. In preparation for this section, the author interviewed all members of the Rules Committee in the 86th Congress, John McCormack, and Joseph Martin. Three doctoral dissertations were of great assistance in providing background information: Lewis J. Lapham, "Party Leadership in the House Committee on Rules" (Harvard University, 1953); James A. Robinson, "Decision-Making in the Committee on Rules" (Northwestern University, 1957); Christopher Van Hollen, "The House Committee on Rules (1933–1951): Agent of Party or Agent of Opposition" (John Hopkins University, 1951). See also James A. Robinson, *The House Rules Committee* (Indianapolis: Bobbs-Merrill Co., 1963); and "The Enlarged Rules Committee" in Robert L. Peabody and Nelson W. Polsby, *New Perspectives on the House of Representatives* (Chicago: Rand McNally and Co., 1963).

19. Robert Luce, *Legislative Procedure* (Boston: Houghton Mifflin Co., 1922), p. 478. See also Legislative Reference Service, "A Short History of the Development of the House Committee on Rules," *Congressional Record*, 86th Cong., 2nd sess., 1960, pp. A 7098–99.

changes may be made, except at the beginning of each new Congress when the rules come up for adoption.

In 1858, the Speaker of the House was made an ex officio member of the Rules Committee, and gradually, by Speakers' interpretations and by rules changes, it began to acquire the extensive powers that it exercises today.

The committee's most important advance took place in 1883 when it received the power to hasten or to block floor action on legislation. Prior to this year, the rules governing the order of business could be suspended in order to hasten the consideration of important business only by unanimous consent or by a two-thirds vote. In 1883 the Ways and Means Committee had reported a high tariff measure but was unable to win House acceptance. The high tariff Republican leadership did not want to risk a House vote on the lower version which had passed the Senate and it lacked the necessary support to suspend the rules by a two-thirds majority. To solve the dilemma, future Speaker Thomas B. Reed of the Rules Committee devised a resolution that provided that it would be in order to take the Senate bill from the Speaker's Table, to declare disagreement, and to ask for a conference.[20] In this manner, the leadership was able to suspend the rules by a majority vote. In 1886 the Speaker specifically upheld this new power of the Rules Committee—to report in the nature of a rule a regulation of debate intended for a single day. The power was exercised infrequently at first, but by 1890 it came into general use as an efficient means of doing business. Gradually the custom of allowing individual committees to propose special rules (to be adopted by unanimous consent or by a two-thirds vote) has declined, and the Rules Committee has been placed in a dominant position as a governor of both procedure and policy.

It is interesting to note that this power of the committee was first devised as a means of sending a measure to conference in order to carry out party policy. The rules of the House concerning the sending of bills to conference provided, until 1965, that

20. Democratic Study Group, *Memorandum on Sending a House Bill to Conference*, Sept. 30, 1960, pp. 7–8.

a House Bill that involved new expenditures and that had been amended by the Senate was to be referred again to the standing committee that handled it originally.[21] (In most cases a special rule would then be needed to bring the measure before the House for action.) This provision could be by-passed by unanimous consent, suspension of the rules, or by a special rule, so that immediate action might be taken. Thus when the sending of a measure to conference did not command at least the two-thirds support necessary for suspension of the rules, the House Rules Committee was in a position to grant or deny access to the conference stage of legislative proceedings. It generally used its power to grant access, but since 1937 it has occasionally denied it. A statehood bill in 1954 and a school construction measure in 1960 are outstanding examples. At the start of the 89th Congress, this power was taken away from the Rules Committee. A new rule was adopted that allowed the Speaker to recognize a member for the purpose of offering a motion that would permit the sending of a bill to conference by a simple majority vote.[22]

By 1892 the committee won the power to have its reports called up for immediate consideration, with severe limitation on dilatory tactics.

In 1893 the committee was granted the power to sit while the House is in session without having to receive special permission.[23] In that year it was also authorized, by Speaker's interpretation, to report special rules on legislation not referred to it by committees of original jurisdiction. In answering a point of order that held the Rules Committee had no jurisdiction over such bills, a later Speaker found adequate precedent for the exercise of power by

21. House Rule XXIV, clause 2, Disposal of Business on the Speaker's Table. Senate-amended House bills that do not involve new expenditures are made privileged in that motions are in order to send them to conference.
22. See the proviso added to House Rule XX, clause 1. At the same time the House adopted a 21-Day Rule (an amendment to Rule XI, clause 23) and amended Rule XXI, clause 1, by eliminating a provision permitting a single member to delay action by demanding that a measure be read in full.
23. Since 1957 this privilege has been shared with the committees on Government Operations and Un-American Activities.

the Rules Committee. He further stated that, "even if there were no precedents the Chair would be inclined to overrule the point of order, because the Committee on Rules is the executive organ of the majority of the House."[24]

Changes in committee membership have taken place from time to time. The Speaker served as chairman from 1858 until 1910. As a result of the Cannon revolt, the Speaker was removed from the committee and denied the right to name its members. Although a rules change in 1947 repealed this 1910 prohibition against having the Speaker as a member, no incument has chosen to take a position on the committee.

In the nineteenth century, Rules was generally a five member committee, with three members of the majority and two of the minority party. In 1910 it was raised to ten and it has been pegged at eleven, twelve, fourteen, and fifteen at various times since.[25] Between 1945 and 1960, the size remained at twelve, with an 8 to 4 ratio by agreement between party leaders Rayburn and Martin. In the 87th Congress (1961), it was increased to fifteen members, in an attempt to bring the committee more into line with party policy.

THE ROLE OF THE RULES COMMITTEE

There is little agreement as to the proper role for the House Committee on Rules. It became important, originally, as a committee of the Speaker and the majority party. The revolt against Speaker Cannon in 1910 by a bipartisan majority of the House left a confused situation. Some who testified before the Joint Committee on the Organization of Congress in 1946 questioned whether the

---

24. *Congressional Record*, 67th Cong., 2nd sess., 1922, p. 9577.
25. In 1911 it was set at eleven (with a 7 to 4 ratio). In 1917 it was raised to twelve. (In the 65th Congress there were 6 Democrats, 4 Republicans, and 2 Progressives; and in the 66th Congress there were 7 Republicans, 4 Democrats, and one Progressive. In all other Congresses in this period the ratio was 8 to 4.) The Committee was increased to a membership of fourteen in 1935. (The party ratio was 10 to 4, except during the 78th Congress when it was fixed at 9 to 5.)

committee should have a policy role at all, or whether it should merely act as a "traffic cop," speeding up some matters, slowing down others, but never thwarting the desires of a majority of the members.[26] If it should be a policy committee, should it be a spokesman for the majority party, for the bipartisan House majority, or for some concept of the national interest not always expressed by either the majority party or a bipartisan majority?

No member of the committee interviewed during the 86th Congress was willing to accept the traffic cop role as the sole function of the committee, and it is doubtful that members ever have.[27] As one committeeman stated, "If the committee's role is merely to be that of directing traffic, I might as well join the Post Office Committee where I can help to color the stream of legislation." In one sense, the traffic cop–policy committee debate is academic. Inevitably, with the large number of bills introduced in Congress and with the limited amount of time available for their handling, any committee that singles out some bills for quick passage and holds up others until there is no hope for legislative action becomes a policy forming committee.

Generally, those who favor the traffic cop approach feel that the committee should not be allowed to exercise what amounts to an absolute veto. They may admit that the committee can effectively review the quality of legislative drafting, that it is in a good position to plan the timing of the legislative program with an eye to grass-roots reaction, that it may be more capable of taking a broad view than some of the specialized legislative committees—yet they feel that there should be relatively easy ways for a determined majority of the House to take action on proposals held up by the Rules Committee.

26. "It seems to me that the Rules Committee job is more that of a traffic director than one to pass on the merits of the bills that have been heard very completely by the individual committees" (Joint Committee on the Organization of Congress, Hearings, *The Organization of Congress*, pursuant to H. Con. Res. 18, 79th Cong., 1st sess., 1945, p. 104).

27. On the basis of interviewing members during the 87th Congress, Robert L. Peabody reached a similar conclusion (Peabody and Polsby, *House of Representatives*, p. 185).

Others feel that shifting, bipartisan House majorities are unorganized and irresponsible. They believe that the functions of the Rules Committee should be performed by a body that is completely integrated with the majority party, an organization that can be held responsible for its actions at the polls. This body should have the power to veto the wishes of a numerical majority whenever they are in conflict with responsibly determined majority party policy.

Another group feels that the committee should not necessarily be responsive to the majority or the majority party, but should act as platonic guardians who best express the conscience of the House.[28"] Claire Hoffman has spoken of the committee as protecting "a member of Congress from being required to vote for measures which he knows are detrimental to the national welfare, but which, because of peculiar circumstances or special interests in his own legislative district, he must otherwise, because of political expediency, support."[29] At another time John E. Rankin gave the committee a "heat shield" role, "to protect the House and the country from a barrage of unwholesome, unnecessary, unreasonable, and unstable legislation at a time when every effort is being made by the enemies within our gates to take advantage of the opportunity to undermine and destroy this country and to discredit it abroad."[30]

The actual role that the Rules Committee has played has varied considerably over the years. In spite of the fact that the Cannon revolt made the committee a potentially important rival to the Speaker and the floor leader, it served largely as a protector of the party program in the House until 1937. Though party leaders rarely appeared before the committee, they maintained constant contact with the chairman. President Wilson received strong committee support for his program in the House. The committee supported Republican leaders in the 1920s, and continued to do so

28. Joseph Cooper, "Congress and Its Committees" (Ph.D. diss., Harvard University, 1961), p. 289.
29. *Congressional Record*, 81st Cong., 2nd sess., 1950, p. 571.
30. *Congressional Record*, 80th Cong., 1st sess., 1947, p. 407.

during the two Congresses that the Republicans have controlled since the Roosevelt victory of 1933. (Significantly, Republican Rules Committee members are ex officio members of the Republican policy committee.) Roosevelt's early legislative successes were achieved in large part by special rules devised by the committee to restrict the freedom of House members to amend the party program.

The formation of a southern Democratic-Republican conservative coalition dates from Roosevelt's attempt to pack the Supreme Court in 1937. It was strengthened as a result of his 1938 attempt to purge certain legislators in the name of party responsibility. Former Speaker Joseph W. Martin Jr. threw light on the operation of the coalition in both the House and the Rules Committee in his autobiography when he was describing his relations with Eugene E. Cox:

> Cox was the real leader of the southerners in the House. . . . He and I came to Congress in the same year, and we became friends while serving on the Rules Committee. After I was chosen leader, he and I were the principal points of contact between the northern Republicans and the southern Democratic conservatives. A bushy-haired Georgia lawyer, Cox was a typical, old-fashioned southern leader, who fought tirelessly for states' rights. His opposition to the New Deal was much more ingrown than mine, and he was ready to fight to any lengths to keep further power out of the hands of Franklin Roosevelt. In these circumstances, therefore, it was unnecessary for me to offer any *quid pro quo* for conservative southern support. It was simply a matter of finding issues on which we saw alike.[31]

Since the formation of the coalition, the Rules Committee has not been as closely tied to the Democratic leadership as previously; rather, it has acted with some independence in the complex field of scheduling.

31. Joseph Martin, *My First Fifty Years in Politics* (New York: McGraw-Hill, 1960), pp. 84–85.

There have been only four Democratic chairmen since the coalition was formed. John J. O'Connor of New York, who was chairman from 1935 through 1938, began to oppose the president in 1937. President Roosevelt backed a rival in the state primary, in his largely unsuccessful 1938 purge, commenting that O'Connor had worked "to pickle New Deal legislation."[32] O'Connor fought back, holding that "contrary to deliberately confounded public confusion, neither [the Rules Committee] nor any part of the legislative body is an instrument of the President."[33] When he was defeated in the primary, he ran on the Republican and Andrew Jackson tickets. "I knew what I was doing on the Reorganization Bill," he stated during the course of the campaign. "I knew the consequences, and before getting away from it, let me say that the Rules Committee has a pigeonhole and the bill is in it and the cobwebs are so thick over that pigeonhole that you can hardly see that it is a pigeonhole."[34] After O'Connor was defeated in the election, there were rumors that Roosevelt wanted a more aggressive chairman than Adolph J. Sabath, the next in line, but Speaker William B. Bankhead saw to it that the seniority rule was not interfered with.

Sabath, who served as chairman from 1939 until 1952, with the exception of the 80th Congress, was loyal to the party leadership, but he was often outmaneuvered by the coalition under the leadership of Eugene E. Cox.

Several members tell of the time when he pretended to faint in order to keep the committee from taking action on a resolution he opposed. In 1950 he adjourned a committee meeting to prevent it from reporting a proposal to abolish the 21-Day Rule, only to have the committee take action after he had left, reporting the proposal to the floor of the House.

Leo Allen, chairman during the Republican 80th and 83rd Congresses, was able to count on members of his own party, with some help from southern Democrats, to carry out Republican party policy.

32. *New York Times*, Aug. 21, 1938.
33. *Congressional Record*, 81st Cong., 1st sess., 1949, p. A 347.
34. *New York Times*, Oct. 25, 1938.

Howard W. Smith, whose chairmanship lasted from 1955 until 1966, was infinitely skillful as leader of the conservative coalition and of the Rules Committee. He maintained little more than an uneasy truce with the leadership during most of his years as chairman. During the 1957 session, Smith was out of town at a time when there was a great deal of pressure to bring out a civil rights bill. When it was announced that he was absent because one of his barns burned, Speaker Rayburn commented, "I knew he would do almost anything to block a Civil Rights Bill. But I never suspected he would resort to arson." When a majority of the members of the committee finally forced him to hold a hearing, he adjourned it as soon as he found out that a quorum was not present. "I felt like a well-fed missionary at a cannibals' convention," he commented. "They were really mad at me. I don't blame them a bit. I would have been mad had I been in their shoes."[35]

When Speaker Rayburn really needed Rules Committee support, he could win some Republican assistance through Minority Leader Martin. Democratic liberals, after the 1958 victory that gave their party a greater majority than at any time since the early New Deal, received a promise from Rayburn that "legislation which has been duly considered and reported by legislative committees will be brought before the House for consideration within a reasonable length of time."[36] Shortly after this, Martin was replaced by Halleck as minority leader and the Speaker found that he was unable to fulfill his promise. The coalition on the Rules Committee became more intransigent, with four conservative Republicans and two southern Democrats, Smith and William Colmer,[37] in a position to block action by the twelve-man committee. When Rayburn found himself unable to win Rules Committee backing, he gave consent to the use of such devices as discharge and Calendar Wednesday, which were originally de-

35. *Time*, Feb. 2, 1959, p. 14.
36. *Congressional Quarterly*, 1959, p. 214.
37. It is quite commonly believed that Rayburn had not intended to return Colmer to the committee in 1955, after he had been dropped because of the change in party control in the 83rd Congress, but that he was put back on because of a promise given by Majority Leader McCormack.

veloped to give bipartisan insurgent groups some means of opposing party leaders, as a means of overcoming bipartisan opposition to Democratic programs. A comment revealing the attitude of the leadership towards the Rules Committee was made by McCormack concerning a 1959 housing bill: "Of course, the leadership does not like to by-pass the Committee on Rules unless it is absolutely necessary. We have been very tolerant, although the Committee on Rules, outside the Housing Bill, has been very cooperative. But I think it is getting to the point where the leadership has the feeling that tolerance is being extended somewhat."[38]

At least six controversial measures were slowed down or blocked by the Rules Committee in the 86th Congress. One (minimum wage, HR 12677) was granted a special rule to reach the floor and another to go to conference but after such delay that action was not completed by the end of the Congress. The civil rights bill (HR 8601) was granted a special rule only when a discharge petition neared completion, and it was eventually enacted. Two were brought to the floor in spite of Rules Committee opposition—one by Calendar Wednesday procedure (depressed areas, S 723), and one by discharge petition (postal pay raise, HR 9883). Two were successfully blocked by the Rules Committee—omnibus housing (HR 12603), and federal aid to education (HR 1028). An initial rule was granted on the education bill but the committee refused a special rule to send the bill to conference.

As a result, Rayburn moved in 1961 to enlarge the Rules Committee by two Democrats and one Republican for the duration of the 87th Congress. He won one of the most hard-fought battles in recent years by a margin of five votes.[39] In 1963 this membership increase was made part of the standing rules by a vote of 235 to 196. The packing of the committee brought back more control to the Speaker. As Robert L. Peabody has put it, "when

38. *Congressional Record*, 85th Cong., 1st sess., 1959, p. 7226.
39. William R. MacKaye, *A New Coalition Takes Control: The House Rules Committee Right of 1961*, Bagleton Institute Case in Practical Politics (New York: McGraw-Hill, 1963); Milton C. Cummings Jr. and Robert L. Peabody, "The Decision to Enlarge the Committee on Rules," in Peabody and Polsby, *House of Representatives*, p. 167.

the eight votes were needed, they could almost always be counted on."[40] In the case of the civil rights bill of 1964, the committee voted not only to speed the hearings but also to deprive Chairman Smith of control of the measure on the floor, so that the bill could be signed by President Johnson on July 4.

Chairman Smith was able to "unpack" the committee from time to time, however, especially on measures involving civil rights and federal aid to public education. (On these controversial measures, religious and racial divisions have added an element of unpredictability to the traditional liberal-conservative division in the House.) In the press of legislative business at the end of a Congress, Howard Smith managed to regain much of his old control. He used his power mainly to block administration programs in 1962, but in 1964 he went further and reported out two measures aimed at nullifying the reapportionment decision of the Supreme Court, over the opposition of both the parent Judiciary Committee and the leadership.

Shortly before Chairman Smith was defeated in a primary race in the fall of 1966, he spoke as follows about his role as a member of Congress, "I am a conservative and I have been scrambling and scratching around for more than twenty years. I have always found that when you are doing that, you grasp any snickersnee you can get hold of and fight the best way you can."[41] In the 90th Congress, his full length portrait, hanging on the wall of the committee's hearing room, looked down on his successor, William M. Colmer of Mississippi, an equally conservative but less skillful legislator. One of the first things that the committee did under the new regime was to adopt its first set of special rules granting greater rights to the membership.

COMMITTEE MEMBERSHIP

Representative James W. Wadsworth Jr. has said, in commenting on the disadvantages of being a member of the Rules Committee,

40. Ibid., p. 152.
41. *Science*, July 29, 1966, p. 513.

"To be candid with you, service on the Committee on Rules is an utterly thankless job. . . . You are pulled and pushed, hauled and mauled, day after day, mostly by organized minority groups who flood our mails with demands that their pet projects be given preferential consideration by the House, and without the slightest regard for the future of the Country."[42] In spite of all this, however, membership is highly prized.

In the Cannon revolt, though George Norris was successful in taking away the Speaker's power to appoint members of the Rules Committee, he did not succeed in winning acceptance for his proposal that the members be chosen by congressmen meeting according to their geographical region. This method might have succeeded in severely cutting down party control over appointments. As has been noted in the chapter on committee assignments (chapter 4), however, majority and minority party leaders, working through their respective committees-on-committees, are in a position to designate the new members of this important committee.

Beyond this point, operation of the seniority principle serves to cut down much of the power struggle. Once on the committee a member stays unless he is thrown off by a change in party control which, in recent years, cuts the representation of his party in half. When an opening occurs again, he can reasonably expect to return, if he desires. An interesting exception occurred, however, at the beginning of the 86th Congress. J. Edgar Chenoweth of Colorado had been a Republican member in the 80th and 83rd Congresses. But he was not chosen when an opening occurred in 1959, partly because he came from a closely divided district and partly because his stand on a public power issue was unacceptable to the Republican leadership.

A Rules Committee member, according to the stereotype, is either a southern Democrat or a middle western Republican who is well along in years. He comes from a rural or small-town district where there is relatively little party competition. He is not a

42. *Congressional Record*, 81st Cong., 2nd sess., 1950, p. 709.

strong party man and, above all, he is a conservative. A statistical study of recent members bears out some of these characteristics and refutes others.

The statistics cover the postwar years from 1947 to 1968, including two Republican and nine Democratic Congresses. There have been 144 positions on the committee (12 for 7 Congresses, 15 for 4) that have been filled by 44 different people.

Table 9:2 shows the proportion of Rules Committee members coming from the various sections of the country. Comparing the first column, which gives the percentage of committee members from each region, with the fourth column, which gives the percentage of House members from each region, it can be seen that the West and East have been underrepresented and that the South and Midwest have been overrepresented. More than half of the Democratic members have come from the South, while 48.2 percent of the Republican members have come from the Midwest.

The average age of the Rules Committee members at the beginning of each Congress has been 57.9—6.3 years above the average age of House members. The oldest and youngest members to sit during this period have both been Democrats. Adolph Sabath was 85 at the beginning of the 82nd Congress and John E. Lyle Jr. was 38 at the start of the 81st Congress.

TABLE 9:2

*Percentage Distribution of House Rules Committee Members and All House Members by Geographical Region, 80th through 90th Congresses**

	Committee Members, D and R	Committee Democrats	Committee Republicans	All House Members
East	20.9	18.2	25.0	29.0
Midwest	33.3	23.9	48.2	30.0
South	34.7	51.1	8.9	28.0
West	11.1	6.8	17.9	13.0
	100.0	100.0	100.0	100.0

* The regional groupings are those used by *Congressional Quarterly*.

Table 9:3 shows the nature of the congressional districts from which each Rules Committee member has come (counting those who serve more than one term anew for each Congress). Surprisingly, more have come from districts characterized as metropolitan in nature than from any other type—39.6 percent. Nearly 43 percent of the Democrats have come from metropolitan districts, and the next highest percentage from rural districts, all of these being in the South. Republicans, on the other hand, have come from small-town, metropolitan, and mid-urban districts, in descending order. A comparison of the districts of the committee members with a classification of all House districts show remarkable similarity, though the committee does slightly overrepresent metropolitan and underrepresent rural districts.

Table 9:4 divides the districts according to degree of two-party competition. Nearly three-fourths of the members came from safe, essentially one-party districts, and 91.7 percent won by more than 55 percent of the vote. While there is a tendency to choose members for the Rules Committee from districts that are not closely divided politically, these percentages are not far out of line with those of all members of the House. In recent elections about 60 percent of all House seats have been safe and about 80 percent have been either fighting or safe.

TABLE 9:3
Percentage Distribution of Members from Districts Classified According to Degree of Urbanism, 80th through 87th Congresses*

	Committee Members, D and R	Committee Democrats	Committee Republicans	All House Members
Rural	15.7	25.0	2.2	20.0
Small-town	25.4	16.2	41.3	25.0
Mid-urban	19.3	16.2	23.3	22.0
Metropolitan	39.6	42.6	33.2	33.0
	100.0	100.0	100.0	100.0

* The classification of congressional districts found in *Congressional Quarterly*, 1956, pp. 790–91, is the basis for this table. This table stops with the 87th Congress since guidelines have been changed since that time and the new and the old classifications are not comparable.

TABLE 9:4

*Percentage Distribution of Committee Members from Districts Grouped According to Party Competition, 80th through 90th Congresses**

Margin of Electoral Victory	Democrats & Republicans	Democrats	Republicans
Safe (over 60%)	74.3	80.7	62.1
Fighting (55–59.9%)	17.4	12.5	24.1
Doubtful (under 55%)	8.3	6.8	13.8
	100.0	100.0	100.0

* Election percentages were taken from *Congressional Quarterly* for the appropriate years.

Table 9:5 notes the average performance of the members of the Committee on Rules in comparison with the voting of the average party member of the House, and with the floor leader. A party unity score is used that indicates the percentage of times that a member votes in agreement with a majority of his party, when a majority of the other party votes in opposition. There is a strong party difference here, as might be expected from the fact that the Republican Rules Committees have acted more in accord with their party than Democratic ones. Democratic Rules Committee members voted 3.2 percent less with their party than the average for all Democrats, and 19.6 percent less than Democratic floor leaders, during the eleven Congresses. Republican Rules Committee members voted 2.7 percent more with their party than Republican floor leaders, and 4.6 percent more than all Republicans.

Since much criticism of the House Rules Committee concerns its ability to block liberal legislation, a rough check of the degree of conservatism of the members is in order. Using material developed from table 6:4, 44.5 percent of the members could be ranked as conservatives, 41.8 percent as liberals, and 13.7 percent as moderates during the eleven Congresses under consideration.[43] There

43. Those voting between 30 and 69.9 percent conservative were classified as moderates, those with records falling below that were classified as liberals, and those with records falling above that were classified as conservatives.

TABLE 9:5

Average Party Unity Score for Committee Members Compared with that for All Party Members and the Floor Leader, 80th through 90th Congresses*

	Democrats	Republicans
Rules Committee	70.0%	80.1%
Party members	73.2%	75.5%
Floor leaders	89.6%	77.4%

* Data are taken from the appropriate volumes of the *Congressional Quarterly*.

were interesting party and regional variations. Democratic members were markedly more liberal than Republican members. Of the Democrats, five southern and all nine nonsouthern members voted liberal. Of the six remaining (all from the South), three voted conservative and three fell into the moderate category. Hugh Scott of Pennsylvania was the only Republican who fell into the liberal category. John B. Anderson, J. Edgar Chenoweth, and Katherine St. George voted in the moderate range during at least one of the Congresses in which they served, and the remaining eighteen were conservative in their voting record.

The stereotype of the member of the Rules Committee, then, is not far from wrong, on the basis of these statistical studies. It is true that the South and the Middle West are overrepresented, that the members tend to come from districts with little two-party competition, and that they support conservative causes. However, they appear to be somewhat younger than the stereotype and they come to a surprising degree from districts characterized as metropolitan and mid-urban. Also, Republican members make an above average showing in party support.

COMMITTEE PROCEDURE

This is a committee that can be—and generally is—dominated by its chairman. One of the earlier chairmen, Philip Campbell, is often quoted as having said to the committee in 1923: "It makes no difference what a majority of you decide. If it meets with my disapproval, it shall not be done; I am the Committee; in me reposes absolute obstructive powers."[44] Yet the chairman's obstructive powers have been trimmed somewhat since this statement was made. In 1924 members were given the right to call up matters on which a majority of the committee had taken favorable action. If a rule is not reported within three legislative days, it goes on the Calendar, and if it is not called up by the member assigned to make the report within the next seven days, any Rules Committee member may call it up and is guaranteed recognition by the Speaker.[45] While members are, quite naturally, hesitant to resort to this procedure, the mere fact that this power is written into the House rules is likely to force the hand of the chairman. In 1967, when Colmer succeeded to the chairmanship, the committee adopted its first set of rules calling for regular weekly meetings and a committee calendar.

Committee procedure varies greatly with different chairmen, though there is a consistent pattern of activity. After the House has gotten into full swing, the committee is likely to meet two or three times a week, working much of the time in cooperation with the floor leader in the interests of scheduling debate.

Nearly all hearings are open. While the Rules Committee members approach their task with some informality, members of Congress who appear before them are formal and respectful in their presentations, for they are there, after all, asking favors. Once when Chairman Graham Barden of the Education and Labor Committee was requesting a special rule, he was asked if he would care to sit down but replied, "in my business, it is safer to remain in a running position."[46] Occasionally, criticisms are voiced on the floor of the House. Representative A. S. Mike Monroney, during the debate over the repeal of the 21-Day Rule, suggested that the question was "Do we trust ourselves?" He went on to say:

44. Floyd M. Riddick, *The United States Congress: Organization and Procedure* (Manassas, Va.: National Capitol Publishers, 1949), p. 123.
45. House Rule XI, clause 23.
46. Hearing, August 24, 1960.

All of our committees in this Congress are coequal. No one created a supercommittee to veto the action of a coequal standing committee. Mr. Speaker, let me tell you that I have almost seen red as the great chairman of my own committee has gone before the Committee on Rules—and you members of other committees have seen this too—and has been treated far worse than any lobbyist would be treated in the standing committees.[47]

Chairman Emanuel Celler of the Judiciary Committee has commented that he did not want the Rules Committee "to act as a wet nurse for me."[48] And a statement made by Chairman Clarence Cannon of the Appropriations Committee must epitomize the reaction of many congressmen when they are frustrated by the Rules Committee:

The Committees of the House . . . spend weeks and months holding hearings, taking testimony, studying and investigating the many phases involved by competent staffs. Volumes of hearings are printed and great care is taken in sifting the issues, and finally a bill is drawn which represents the best judgment of the men versed in the subject with which they deal. Thereupon, the Committee on Rules—no member of which has heard a word of testimony or read a page of the hearings or consulted any authority—meet and throw the whole product of the Committee into the ashcan.[49]

Occasionally, committee chairman may attempt a little bargaining with the Rules Committee, but they do not lead from strength. In the 85th Congress the Judiciary Committee was holding a bill introduced by Rules Committee Chairman Smith, and the Rules Committee was holding a bill that had been reported to it by the Judiciary Committee. Chairman Celler, in testifying before the

47. *Congressional Record*, 81st Cong., 2nd sess., 1950, p. 710.
48. *New York Times*, Jan. 4, 1951.
49. *Congressional Record*, 84th Cong., 1st sess., 1955, p. 11059.

Rules Committee, commented, "I wonder whether or not I could get some action from the Rules Committee with reference to the pre-merger notification bill? Maybe then we could be placed in a better position to consider HR 3." Chairman Smith replied, "Now Mannie, I have got a bill before your committee that has been there for three years and your bill has been before my committee for only three weeks. Now, when we get down to the issue of time, why don't you drop around and see me?"[50] Chairman Celler's bill was not reported out in that session of Congress.

At a hearing the Rules Committee members show great interest in a brief summary of the proposed legislation—what need there is for it, what it will cost, what the leadership position is, and what opposition there was in the originating committee. They do not hesitate to ask how a particular bill is likely to affect their own constituents. On procedural matters, they ask for advice concerning the length of time for floor debate. They are less likely to ask whether amendments or points of order should be limited by a special rule, the chairman generally feeling that the originating committee should predict possible parliamentary difficulties without help from the Rules Committee.

Only members of Congress testify in these hearings, direct contact with pressure groups having thus been largely eliminated. Both proponents and opponents of proposed legislation may speak, and the discussion gives those present a preview of the way in which a measure will be presented and opposed on the floor, should a special rule be granted. Unlike most other committees, the Rules Committee rarely takes verbatim transcripts of testimony.

Following open hearings, the committee holds executive sessions attended only by the members and the staff. No proxy voting is allowed and the voting is secret, though it may sometimes be made public by committee members when reporting a rule.

50. *Congressional Quarterly*, 1958, p. 290.

COMMITTEE ACTION[51]

Most important measures are referred to the Rules Committee for a special rule—that is, a regulation of debate intended for a single piece of legislation for a single day. The members can act to block or modify the proposal, or they can speed it on its way. When acting in a negative manner, the committee can deny a requested hearing or deny a special rule, it can hold up action until a bill has little chance of clearing all the other legislative hurdles, and it can report a rule that makes emasculation of the original measure almost inevitable.

The committee refuses to hold hearings on a number of pieces of legislation in each Congress. Often as many as half of the bills denied a hearing have passed the House by unanimous consent or suspension of rules procedure, so that the committee can be said to have stood as a block at this stage to an average of fourteen measures in each Congress for which data is available. Most of the measures blocked by this means were not of great national importance, the most important being the Alaskan statehood bill in the 83rd Congress. They were often, however, directly concerned with the role that the government should play in relation to the national economy. For example, in the 85th Congress both a public housing measure and a proposal for self-financing of the Tennessee Valley Authority were blocked by this means.

The committee may grant a hearing but refuse to grant a special rule. This has occurred on a small number of bills in recent years —about the same number as are denied hearings. The subject matter of the proposals denied a rule has to do most frequently with public power, conservation, and veterans' affairs. The committee

51. Floyd M. Riddick's annual articles on Congress were particularly useful in the preparation of this section. They appeared in the *American Political Science Review* for the 80th Congress, vol. 42, p. 675; and vol. 43, p. 483. Since, they have appeared in the *Western Political Quarterly*, vol. 4, p. 48; vol. 5, pp. 94, 619; vol. 6, p. 766; vol. 7, p. 636; vol. 8, p. 612; vol. 10, p. 49; vol. 11, p. 86; vol. 12, p. 177; vol. 13, p. 113; vol. 14, p. 415; vol. 15, p. 254; vol. 16, p. 148; vol. 17, p. 235; vol. 18, p. 334; vol. 19, p. 354; vol. 20, p. 173; vol. 21, p. 206.

justifies its denial of rules on the grounds that it is a watchdog of the Treasury or, sometimes, at the end of a session of Congress, that there is a lack of time for proper consideration. Probably the most important pieces of legislation denied rules were the Hawaiian statehood bill in the 81st Congress, the omnibus housing bill in the 86th Congress, and a number of federal aid-to-education proposals as well as a measure calling for the creation of a department of urban affairs in the 87th Congress.

The Rules Committee members are in a good position to bring about changes in legislative proposals before they reach the floor. They may deny a rule until specific changes are made, or they may seek an agreement on the part of the originating committee that it will propose suggested amendments to its bill on the floor. It is common knowledge that this practice exists, although evidence is hard to track down. The following examples all show committee concern for the well-being of the Treasury, states' rights, or laissez faire capitalism. In the 82nd Congress the Rules Committee denied the Foreign Affairs Committee a rule on its bill (HR 3017) providing grain for India until the transaction was made a loan, not a gift. In the 84th Congress no rule was forthcoming on a bill (HR 3406) giving absentee voting rights to servicemen until antipoll tax provisions were deleted. In the 85th Congress it got the Banking and Currency Committee to offer amendments to its area redevelopment bill, eliminating authority to borrow directly from the Treasury without congressional appropriation, and also cutting out subsistence payments for unemployed workers taking retraining courses (HR 3683). Many less dramatic examples could be produced showing the Rules Committee bringing about changes in the interest of common sense or legislative consistency.

Occasionally, action on special rules is held up for a long time, perhaps to await committee modification of a proposal to suit the demands of the Rules Committee, but sometimes so that there will be little chance for successful action on the House floor and in the Senate before the end of a session. In the 84th Congress action was held up by the Rules Committee for thirteen months on a civil rights bill (HR 621)[52] and for eleven months on a federal aid-to-education measure (HR 7575). In the 85th Congress no action was taken on statehood bills for ten months, at which time they were brought to the floor under a little-used rule allowing direct reporting of statehood bills.

When the committee brings out a special rule, it is in effect creating conditions under which a particular piece of legislation can be handled, regardless of the standing rules of the House. It can, for example, specify the length of debate and the division of time, limit dilatory motions, and specify the method by which a vote will be taken. It may also limit or prohibit amendments and deny points of order. Rules Committee action can be contrary to that requested by the committee of original jurisdiction. In the 81st Congress, the committee refused to grant a closed rule (limiting amendments on the floor) on a bill (HR 2032) to repeal the Taft-Hartley Act. As a result, this measure, which had been aimed at repeal, merely became a vehicle for moderate revision. In the 84th Congress, the Interior Committee asked for an open rule on its bills for statehood for Alaska and Hawaii, but a closed rule was granted (HR 2535). This meant that the two proposals could not be separated on the floor and both went down to defeat.

Though the Appropriations Committee may report bills without clearance by the Rules Committee, it often asks for a special rule waiving point of order as a means of blocking claims from the floor that legislative matter has been included in an appropriations bill in violation of the rules of the House. Denial of this privilege by the Rules Committee may have dire effects upon appropriations proposals. In the 84th Congress, for example, the committee refused to waive points of order against HR 7278, an appropriations measure that included a ban on expenditures for the controversial Dixon-Yates proposal aimed at curbing expansion of the Tennes-

52. In the hearing on the civil rights bill in the next Congress, Chairman Howard Smith suggested that committee members might save up questions until it was their turn, saying, "I think it will save time, not that I am particularly interested in saving time" (U.S. Congress, House of Representatives, Committee on Rules, *Civil Rights*, Hearings, 81st Cong., 1st sess. [Washington, D.C.: Government Printing Office, 1957], p. 7).

see Valley Authority. Congressman Louis Rabaut of the Appropriations Committee raised thirty points of order against the bill in order to show, he said, how far Rules Committee inaction could go in frustrating Congress. In all, eighty points of order were raised and the total appropriation was cut by over one-and-one-half billion dollars.

The more controversial examples of House Rules Committee action are in opposition to committee and party desires. Much of its action, however, is helpful to the program of the committees and the party leaders. The Rules Committee reports out a high percentage of the bills referred to it. It can speed the process of getting to the floor, and it can create conditions of debate that help the committee of original jurisdiction by limiting dilatory action, by waiving points of order, and by limiting amendments.

Amendments may be limited in various ways. Generally, only committee amendments may be offered in a closed rule, though sometimes specific legislative proposals may be named as amendments or as substitutes. Closed rules are most commonly used on tax, appropriations, and tariff legislation, and other proposals of a highly complex nature. Closed, or if a member happens to be against it, "gag" rules, are controversial. Representative John Rankin once made the revealing comment that "the average member of the House does not want to be gagged on a measure he is against, but he does not mind being gagged on a measure he is for."[53] The issuance of a large number of closed rules in a given Congress is a fairly good indication that the Rules Committee is working closely with the party leadership.[54] The Republican 83rd Congress made by far the greatest use of this device during the period under consideration. The Democratic Rules Committees, less closely integrated with party leadership, have used closed rules more sparingly.

53. *Congressional Record*, 80th Cong., 1st sess., 1947, p. 11723.
54. Riddick notes that there were 15 closed rules in the 80th Congress, 24 in the 81st, 19 in the 82nd, 71 in the 83rd, 31 in the 84th, 11 in the 85th, 13 in the 86th, 20 in the 87th, 11 in the 88th, 16 in the 89th, and 8 in the 90th (*United States Congress*).

HOUSE ACTION ON SPECIAL RULES

Table 9:6 gives the quantitative picture of the acceptance by the House of the work of the Rules Committee. The committee's batting average is high. Between 76 (83rd Congress) and 93 percent (86th and 89th Congresses) of the special rules have been adopted, and on an average only two rules have been turned down per Congress. (The Republican controlled 80th and 83rd Congresses showed the least inclination to overrule their Rules Committees.)

After the Rules Committee has reported a rule, it is customary for the House leadership to make the decision as to when to call it up. (A special rule must have been reported on the day previous to its being called up, unless the rules are suspended by a two-thirds vote.) Light is brought to bear on the party leader–Rules Committee relationship in a comment made by John McCormack answering a question as to whether a post office bill was scheduled for the following week. He said, "I should very much regret if any Democratic member of the Committee on Rules would under-

TABLE 9:6
House Acceptance of Special Rules, 80th through 90th Congresses*

	80th	81st	82nd	83rd	84th	85th	86th	87th	88th	89th	90th
SPECIAL RULES											
Presented	143	181	100	176	176	160	136	167	169	214	231
Adopted	114	156	84	154	147	141	127	151	153	200	217
Tabled when bills passed under alternate procedures	17	14	10	19	17	9	5	3	2	5	2
On Calendar at end of Congress	12	8	3	2	10	6	3	11	13	9	10
Voted down	0	3	3	1	2	4	1	2	1	0	2

* The information in this table is gathered from the final edition of the *Calendars of the United States House of Representatives and History of Legislation* for the appropriate Congresses.

take to force the leadership to do it. If it is going to come, I hope it will come from the Republican side. After seven legislative days a member from the Committee can call it up. Before doing that I would expect him to confer with the leadership. If he did not, I would consider it very discourteous, to say the least."[55] Table 9:6 shows evidence that the leadership and the Rules Committee are not completely integrated. If they were, it is unlikely that so many rules would be left on the Calender at the end of the session or tabled when passage of legislation was brought about by other procedures. The measures concerned, though sometimes related to important issues, were never crucial in themselves.

At a time scheduled by the leadership, a member of the Rules Committee will rise and ask for immediate consideration of the special rule. One hour is allowed for debate on the rule, and it is usually divided evenly between a majority and a minority member of the committee. In Republican Congresses Chairman Leo E. Allen handled a great majority of the rules on the floor, while Democrats have tended to divide the responsibility for their presentation more evenly. The less senior members, quite naturally, tend to get the more routine measures and the senior conservative Democrats often reserve the handling of the more controversial measures for themselves, even when they are opposed to a rule reported out by their committee. When Congressman Colmer reported out a rule for civil rights legislation in the 84th Congress, for example, he commented "With complete frankness I reported this rule to the House some weeks ago for the simple reason that I desired to control its consideration and delay the proposed legislation as long as possible."[56]

It often happens that Democratic and Republican members who share the hour's presentation are in agreement. There is no evidence that those committee members who oppose a rule are discouraged from speaking, yet they generally show their disapproval, not by floor debate, but by voting against acceptance of a rule on the floor.

55. *Congressional Record*, 84th Cong., 2nd sess., 1956, p. 10417.
56. Ibid., p. 12922.

The debate during the hour more often than not relates to the subject matter of the bill to be brought up, not the rule itself, though complaints are sometimes made about closed rules, and questions are frequently asked as to the reasons for waiving points of order. James A. Robinson notes that, on an average, half of the rules are adopted with less than half a page of debate—that is, much less than the one hour allowed.[57] Voting on a rule is generally by voice, though roll calls are taken on more controversial matters.

A rule is rarely defeated simply because the members dislike the conditions of procedure set forth. The greatest controversy over the nature of a rule in the period since the 80th Congress took place in 1955. The Committee reported a closed rule on a reciprocal trade proposal. The House at first refused to accept the rule. Clarence Brown thereupon proposed an open rule. Speaker Rayburn commented from the floor at this point, "The House . . . has done a most unusual thing and under the circumstances a very dangerous thing. . . . Only once in the history of the House in 42 years of my memory has a bill of this kind . . . been considered except under a closed rule."[58] Thereupon the House in effect reversed itself, rejected the Brown proposal, and adopted the original closed rule by a vote of 193 to 192.

In only one instance since 1947 has the House amended a special rule. This was a 1950 rule to take a tax revision bill from the Speaker's Table, disagree with the Senate amendments, and send it to conference. The other rules were rejected because of general opposition to the legislation for which the rules provided.

The Rules Committee, which was fashioned as a vehicle of the majority party leadership, was cut loose from the party in 1910 when it became seniority dominated. While most Speakers and majority leaders since that time have managed to keep it in line, it played an increasingly independent role in the screening and

57. James A. Robinson, "The Role of the Rules Committee in Arranging the Program of the U.S. House of Representatives," *Western Political Quarterly* (Sept. 1959): 633.
58. *Congressional Record,* 84th Cong., 1st sess., 1955, p. 1068.

scheduling of legislation in the period from 1937 until the enlargement in 1961. Rules Committee member Richard Bolling has characterized that action as merely "the end of the beginning, a step towards making the Rules Committee an instrument of the majority party in the House."[59]

House Rules and Procedure

This section is concerned with the role that the standing rules and the customs of the House play in legislative scheduling. First to be described is the manner in which measures receiving committee support are brought to the floor for action. This will be followed by a discussion of the manner in which the House can bring up measures that have not received committee approval. Though the instances in which this is done are infrequent, they are important, and they give some insights into the degree of control the House exercises over its committees.

Bills are placed on the proper calendars in the order in which they are reported out of committees—public bills dealing with appropriations or revenues on the Union Calendar, other public bills on the House Calendar, and private bills (those granting relief to private persons or legal entities) on the Private Calendar (Rule XIII).

Before the enormous growth of the business of the House, bills were brought up during "the Morning Hour for the consideration of bills called up by committees," which is still listed as the sixth item in the order of business. However, with the gradual development of the concept that certain matters should be privileged, the order of business is rarely followed that far and this method of bringing up bills has fallen into disuse. The powers of the Speaker and the majority party were greatly increased at the expense of the freedom of the individual member under the Speakerships of Thomas B. Reed (1889–91, 1895–99) and Joseph G. Cannon

59. Bolling, *House Out of Order*, p. 220.

(1903–11). This was accomplished in large part by enhancement of the Speaker's power of recognition and by creating certain privileged committees. In 1909 and 1910 a bipartisan group of Republican insurgents and Democrats, whose main point of agreement was a desire to weaken the power of the Speaker, succeeded in gaining acceptance of a number of rules reforms. They took away the Speaker's power to appoint committee members; removed him from the Rules Committee; and established Calendar Wednesday, Consent Calendar, and Discharge Calendar procedures.

The pattern at present allows for certain types of bills to be brought up at any time and others to be brought up on certain days. According to Rule xi, clause 21, certain types of privileged bills can be reported at any time by the Appropriations, House Administration, Interior, Public Works, Rules, Veterans' Affairs, and Ways and Means committees, though only Appropriations, Rules, and Ways and Means use the practice at all frequently.[60] Despite the privilege, these committees often prefer a special rule from the Rules Committee, for it can create conditions favorable to successful passage. Further, the committees with the power to report at any time invariably consult with the majority leader on the matter of timing. The Appropriations Committee has a further limitation in that it cannot bring up a general appropriations measure until members of the House have had printed committee hearings and a report available to them for three calendar days (Rule xxi, clause 6).

Certain bills may also be brought up on special days set aside for their consideration. Private bills are taken up on the first and third Tuesday of each month. (According to Rule xxiv, clause 6, objections from two or more members can prevent action on such measures.) On the second and fourth Mondays, the District of

60. Lewis Froman Jr. points out that aside from appropriations and revenue bills, rules changes, and the admission of new states, the other kinds of privileged measures are strongly "constituency based": rivers and harbors bills from Public Works, bills affecting the use of public lands from Interior, and pension measures from Veterans' Affairs (*The Congressional Process* [Boston: Little, Brown & Co., 1967],p. 52).

Columbia Committee can bring up measures concerning government of the national capital (Rule xxv, clause 8). Bills on the Private and District Calendars are of a clearly specified type. There is also a variety of special procedures for the consideration of any legislative proposal on the Union or House Calendars— Consent Calendar, Suspension of the Rules, and Calendar Wednesday.

Measures that have lain on the Union and House Calendars for three days can be brought up on Consent Calendar days, the first and third Mondays. The Consent Calendar (Rule xiii, clause 4), established in 1909, expedites the passage of noncontroversial legislation and relieves the Speaker of the burden of entertaining individual motions for the consideration of bills by unanimous consent. No amendments are allowed. If there is one objection, the measure is passed over. When it is brought up at the next call of the calendar, three objections are necessary in order to block action, at which point it is removed from the Consent Calendar for the rest of the session. Both parties maintain groups of official objectors for both the Consent and Private Calendars, who are appointed by the floor leaders. They carefully scutinize all bills brought up and object to measures that would change national policy, that are not in accord with the president's program, that would cost over one million dollars, or that would affect the districts of a majority of the members.[61]

Bills that are likely to have some objectors but that can command the support of a two-thirds majority may also be brought up on the first and third Mondays of each month under suspension of rules. Here, the Speaker can exercise his discretion in recognition. In order to prevent a waste of time by forcing consideration of unpassable measures, a teller vote may be demanded.[62] If the motion receives less than a majority it is killed immediately. If it receives more than a majority, forty minutes of debate is al-

61. *Congressional Record*, 85th Cong., 1st sess., 1957, p. 1990.
62. If no teller vote is requested an immediate vote is taken, and, if the necessary two-thirds is reached, the rules are suspended and the bill is passed by the House simultaneously.

lowed before a final vote on passage is taken. No amendments are allowed and the vote must be by two-thirds (Rule XXVII, clauses 1–3). Before the growth of the Rules Committee's power to issue special rules, suspension of the rules was the most common means of bringing nonprivileged legislation to the floor, but it is not used with much frequency now. If a chairman can muster a two-thirds vote for suspension of the rules, he is likely to have so much sentiment behind him that he can get Rules Committee support. Party leaders, however, sometimes choose this procedure as a means of prohibiting amendments, as was done with the veterans' pension reform bill of 1956.

Calendar Wednesday, along with the Consent Calendar, was devised by Speaker Cannon in the face of growing insurgency in 1909. It was to make possible the consideration of bills of moderate importance that had been by-passed by the constant feeding of privileged matters to the House so that there was no longer any regular taking up of such bills from the calendars. It was not far-reaching enough to satisfy the insurgents, however, for George Norris referred to it as "a Trojan horse . . . and sticking out of the paunch of that horse I think I see several notable cold feet."[63]

On each Wednesday it is in order to call up business not otherwise privileged, which has been on a legislative calendar for at least one day. The committees are called alphabetically, and no committee may take up more than one day without a two-thirds vote of the House. Debate is limited to two hours, equally divided between proponents and opponents (Rule XXIV, clause 7). In spite of the fact that a two-thirds vote is necessary to dispense with Calendar Wednesday, it is nearly always dispensed with. The procedure is awkward and dilatory action is easy in the handling of controversial measures. Non-controversial measures have usually reached the floor by other means. From the 80th through the 90th Congresses, thirteen committees made use of this procedure on fourteen different Calendar Wednesdays. The most controversial

63. *Congressional Record*, 61st Cong., 1st sess., 1909, p. 3570, quoted in Kenneth Heckler, *Insurgency* (New York: Columbia University Press, 1940), p. 48.

pieces of legislation brought out were a fair employment practices bill in 1950, an area redevelopment bill in 1960, and a school construction measure in 1961. The other measures were of relatively little national importance. Some, such as the incorporation of the Girl Scouts in the District of Columbia, were brought up merely to delay the consideration of pending controversial measures. In all, only twelve measures have become law by this route in the period under consideration.

If a measure is not specially privileged as a result of its subject matter or the committee that has jurisdiction, and it cannot easily avail itself of unanimous consent or suspension or Calendar Wednesday procedure (no one of which provides a hopeful avenue for controversial legislation), its best chance of reaching the floor is by obtaining a special rule from the Rules Committee. If the committee of original jurisdiction is anxious for passage but the Rules Committee opposes it, there are a number of not very hopeful means of bringing a measure to the floor. Four main ways to get around the Rules Committee roadblock have been tried, one of which, the 21-Day Rule, was available only during the 81st and 89th Congresses. The others, devised in earlier periods, are by discharge petition, by Calendar Wednesday procedure, and by an almost unused procedure of taking a bill from the Speaker's Table.

First, according to the 21-Day Rule as it operated in the 81st Congress, a bill that had lain before the Rules Committee for twenty-one days could be called up on Discharge Calendar days (the second and fourth Mondays) by the chairman of the committee that first considered the bill.[64] Recognition by the Speaker was mandatory, though he could choose among chairmen competing for the floor. The rules change was devised by Representative Herman P. Eberharter and a group of liberal House Democrats seeking to prevent the bipartisan coalition in the Rules

64. Valuable background material on the rule may be found in Lewis J. Lapham, "Party Leadership," chaps. 8–10; and Legislative Reference Service, "Operation of the 21 Day Rule during the 81st Congress," *Congressional Record*, 86th Cong., 2nd sess., 1960, pp. A 7198–99.

Committee from blocking action on proposals embodying 1948 campaign promises. They won such support that the Speaker was presented with a *fait accompli* when he returned to Washington before the opening of the 81st Congress. The proposal received greater than a two-thirds vote in the Democratic caucus and was added to the rules of the House by floor action on the following day. An unsuccessful attempt at repeal was made in 1950, complicated by maneuvering over fair employment practices legislation. At this time, Speaker Rayburn defended the rule in one of his infrequent floor speeches:

> When a legislative committee of the House of Representatives has labored long and honestly, and by overwhelming majority brings in a bill and reports it to the House and asks for the privilege of being granted the right to try their case before the elected representatives of the people of the United States, there should be something in the rules of the House, regardless of one other committee, which is not a legislative committee, allowing the House to work its will on that bill.[65]

In spite of this statement, he was perhaps never entirely happy with the way in which the rule spotlighted his power to choose between competing chairmen, to the detriment of his role as party leader and representative of the people of the Fourth Texas Congressional District. He much preferred to operate less in the open and not to appear as the sole party member responsible for such decisions of legislative programming.

The experience under the 21-Day Rule was moderately impressive. Eight measures were taken from the Rules Committee. Of these, three became law (measures calling for contributions to international organizations, creating the National Science Foundation, and a traditional rivers and harbors bill), four passed the House but failed to pass the Senate (Hawaiian statehood, Alaskan statehood, an antipoll tax measure, and a bill for construction of veterans' hospitals), and one failed to pass the House (a bill call-

65. *Congressional Record*, 81st Cong., 2nd sess., 1950, p. 708.

ing for a mining subsidy). The measures were not the most basic in the Democratic program. They did not open the floodgates of government spending, an argument used to justify the role of the Rules Committee. Certainly other measures received Rules Committee approval (housing and minimum wage bills, for example) as a result of leverage gained by the threat of using the new rule.[66]

The 21-Day Rule was repealed at the end of the 81st Congress, after an election in which the Democrats lost twenty-nine seats. It was reinstituted, in slightly different form, at the beginning of the 89th Congress, the most heavily Democratic Congress in the postwar period. This time the Speaker was given discretion as to whether or not to recognize chairmen, whereas in the previous rule recognition had been mandatory.

As in the 81st Congress, the experience under the rule was moderately impressive. Eight measures were taken from the Rules Committee. Of these, five became law (measures calling for a federal pay raise, an increase in postal rates, a foundation for the arts and humanities, additional funds for public schools affected by national disaster, and amendment of the Bank Holding Company Act so that it would apply to the DuPont estate of Florida), two passed the House but failed to pass the Senate (the civil rights bill of 1966 and repeal of the right-to-work provision of the Taft-Hartley Act), and one failed to pass the House (a measure strengthening federal fair employment laws). A number of other measures gained Rules Committee approval after chairmen had filed 21-day resolutions (the demonstration cities bill and amendments to the elementary and secondary education acts, for example).

The measures helped by the rule were, on the whole, closer to the heart of the Democratic program than they had been in the 81st Congress. It must be remembered, however, that this Congress

---

66. Representative Eugene E. Cox of the Rules Committee justified his vote to report a rule on the housing bill by holding that "considering it under a special rule will afford better opportunity for resistance than would be the case if considered under the [21 Day] Rule" (*Congressional Record*, 81st Cong., 1st sess., 1949, p. 1648).

enjoyed a greater Democratic majority and had a somewhat more liberal Rules Committee than when the rule had been in effect previously, so that the rule was less necessary to the leadership than it had been. The 90th Congress, with forty-seven fewer Democrats, failed to reinstitute the 21-Day Rule. Some of those who voted against the rule claimed that it had been used unfairly in connection with legislative recesses and that its proponents were unwilling to accept amendments that would prevent such actions in the future.

Discharge is a second means of by-passing the House Rules Committee. Theoretically, the House controls its committees, and a motion to discharge a committee by majority vote is admissible. Such a motion, however, is not privileged and therefore practically impossible to bring up. Special discharge procedure is available, however. The first discharge rule was adopted in 1910 as part of the revolt against Cannon. In all, there have been six different rules and numerous changes in the required support for initiating discharge procedure.[67] The present rule (Rule xxvii, clause 4), adopted in 1931, may be summarized as follows: (1) a discharge petition is filed with the clerk of the House at least seven days after a bill has been referred to the Rules Committee (thirty days in the case of all other committees); (2) when the petition, which is kept secret from all but members of the House, receives the signatures of a majority of the House membership it is placed on the Calendar of Motions to Discharge Committees; (3) it may then be called up by any signer on the second and fourth Monday of the month, provided it has lain on the calendar for at least seven days; (4) debate lasts for twenty minutes, equally divided between the proponents and the opponents; and (5) if the vote is favorable, the committee is discharged of its jurisdiction and the bill comes up for immediate consideration.

There have been only three successful actions against the Rules Committee in the period under consideration. In the 83rd and 86th

67. For details see Riddick, *United States Congress*, pp. 236–53; P. D. Hasbrouck, *Party Government in the House of Representatives* (New York: Macmillan Co., 1927), chaps. 8, 10, 11.

Congresses, post office pay increases were reported favorably by the Post Office Committee and, as a result of skillful lobbying, resolutions making them special orders of business were discharged from the Rules Committee. In the 89th Congress, home rule for the District of Columbia reached the floor under this procedure. The success of the procedure should not be measured entirely by actual examples of discharge, however, for when a petition gains close to a majority of the members' signatures the Rules Committee may well decide to report the measure under its own conditions rather than lose control of it. Such leverage, for example, pried out bills rescinding a post office curtailment of services in the 81st Congress and a civil rights bill in the 86th Congress. The discharge petition on the latter bill was successful largely because liberals in the Democratic Study Group ascertained and made public the names of congressmen who had signed, thereby putting a number of vulnerable members on the spot and forcing them to sign also.

Calendar Wednesday procedure provides a third, not very hopeful, means of by-passing the Rules Committee. It is an awkward procedure, usually dispensed with, though it has been used successfully twice on controversial legislation when Democrats had a substantial majority and were able to impose some discipline on their members in connection with a single bill—the fair employment practices bill of 1950 and the depressed area bill of 1960. The legislative history of the latter bill, which passed the House on May 4, 1960, under Calendar Wednesday procedure, is a classic example of the difficulties of getting certain controversial proposals to the floor, even with the support of party leaders and a substantial majority of the members.[68]

The final means of by-passing the Rules Committee, taking a bill from the Speakers' Table, is extremely circumscribed and has been used only once in recent years. In the 81st Congress, the Commerce Committee was successful in getting around Rules Committee opposition to a union shop amendment to the Railway

68. *Congressional Record*, 86th Cong., 2nd sess., 1960, pp. 9417–73.

Labor Act under unique circumstances. A bill, nearly identical to the House committee measure, passed the Senate. It was sent to the House and brought out on the floor according to Rule xxiv, clause 2, which provides that "Senate bills substantially the same as House bills already favorably reported by a committee of the House" that do not involve an appropriation "may be at once disposed of as the House determines." This procedure is of limited usefulness. It cannot be used for bills involving the expenditure of money. Furthermore, the chances of a Senate bill, substantially the same as a House bill favorably reported but blocked by the Rules Committee, are limited. It does show, however, the ingenuity frequently exercised in making use of a complex system of rules.

Examples discussed so far have concerned the bringing up for floor action of legislative proposals that have been favorably reported by a committee of original jurisdiction. The statistical chances of bills being brought up that do not have the blessing of such a committee are extremely low, yet committees are so con-stituted that they may not express the will of the whole House. The rules make it difficult but not impossible for a disciplined (often bi-partisan) majority of the membership to force action on bills opposed by committee. Clarence Cannon lists five methods in his *Procedure of the House of Representatives:*[69] unanimous consent, suspension of the rules, change of reference, action by the House Rules Committee, and discharge. The first two are not likely to be fruitful, for no committee would attempt to block a measure that could command unanimous or two-thirds floor support. A motion to change reference to another committee is limited, partly by the rules (Rule xxii, clause 4), but more severely by the fact that it is not considered proper procedure. The latter two alternatives deserve somewhat fuller discussion.

In the 83rd Congress, the Rules Committee was influential in bringing to the floor President Eisenhower's bill extending the excess profits tax, which had been bottled up by Chairman Reed

69. 1959, p. 164.

of the Ways and Means Committee. The Rules Committee threatened to exercise an almost unused power developed by precedent in the late nineteenth century, that of reporting special rules on bills not referred to it by committees of original jurisdiction. Reed objected, claiming that in no case had this power been used in opposition to the committees involved,[70] but he finally reported out the measure rather than have it taken away from him. It is not surprising that this use of Rules Committee power to enhance the majority party occurred when the committee was controlled by Republicans. The only other time, in the period under consideration, it was used was in 1964 when a southern Democratic-Republican coalition on the committee exercised the power twice, in defiance of the leadership, by taking from the Judiciary Committee two measures designed to limit the Supreme Court's jurisdiction over state legislative reapportionment.

Discharge procedure, as it applies to committees of original jurisdiction, is the same as it applies to the Rules Committee, except that a petition may not be filed until a bill has been before a committee for thirty days (it is seven days in the case of the Rules Committee).

The argument for a discharge rule that is relatively easy to operate is usually made by those who feel that both party and committee leaders are likely to be too insensitive to the political demands of the nation as expressed by bipartisan groups of insurgents. The first discharge rule of 1909, for example, was welcomed as a means whereby insurgent Republicans and Democrats could force the Republican leadership to adapt to changing conditions. P. D. Hasbrouck, writing in 1927, favored a liberalized rule, for he felt that the House, with its scattering of power among seniority leaders and with the secrecy of its committee operations, was unwisely insulated from political change. A liberalized discharge rule, he felt, would force the House to overcome its "tendency towards lethargy" and allow members "to fulfill the expectations of the

70. *Congressional Record*, 83rd Cong., 1st sess., 1953, p. 7578.

country with regards to constructive legislation.[71]" At the time that Hasbrouck was writing, the bipartisan coalition of which he was thinking was made up of insurgents seeking to bring out constructive legislation over the opposition of conservative Republican party and seniority leaders. Discharge, he said, was, "clearly not necessary for use by party leaders, but is to be judged as a means whereby a nonpartisan majority may act. The responsible leaders may merely assume a policy of 'hands off' or they may throw the weight of their influence against action."[72]

A different situation has come to pass since 1937, however, where the dominant bipartisan coalition has been opposed to strong government action. The Democratic party leaders have been relatively liberal and they have lost the nearly absolute power over the Rules Committee that they enjoyed in earlier periods. Party leaders who have been critical of discharge procedure have been forced to make reluctant use of it and such other procedures as Calendar Wednesday in order to work their will against an unharnessed Rules Committee. In 1960, for example, Speaker Rayburn suggested that those wanting civil rights legislation should sign the discharge petition on the clerk's desk. He said that he was just pointing out this procedure, not advocating it, but Majority Leader McCormack passed around word that this was an invitation to sign. Frequent use of such tactics by party leaders is highly unlikely, however, for it points up the weakness of the majority leadership in too embarrassing a fashion.

One argument against a liberal discharge rule is that it lessens party responsibility by greatly weakening the power of the party leaders to control the legislative program. In 1931 Rules Chairman Bertrand H. Snell opposed lowering the required number of signatures, claiming, "You deliberately break down party control and responsibility and establish a block system which every one of you has openly condemned. When you advocate control of legislation by the 100 petition plan, you advocate the turning of

71. Hasbrouck, *Party Government*, pp. 195–99.
72. Ibid., p. 209.

the normal, logical, orderly procedure of the House into a town meeting."[73] Bertram Gross, in testimony before the Joint Committee on the Organization of Congress, held that a more liberal discharge procedure would be inadvisable until a generally more responsible party structure developed in the House.[74]

Another argument against frequent use of discharge against committees of original jurisdiction is that it deprives legislative proposals of the maturing effect of discussion and adjustment by committee specialists in the secrecy of executive session. Instead, the perfecting process takes place in the more haphazard, less thoughtful process of floor amendment.[75]

Experience has shown that it is exceedingly difficult to get the necessary number of signatures. Many members refuse to sign as a matter of principle, disliking to have legislation written on the floor and fearing that frequent usage will weaken all committees, including their own. Party leaders have generally encouraged members in this approach, suggesting that measures in which they are interested have a much better chance of passage if they keep their names off petitions. A total of only twenty-three bills have been discharged from House committees, eight of these in the period under consideration here. Only two bills discharged from either the Rules Committee or a committee of original jurisdiction have become law—the Fair Labor Standards Act of 1938, and the Postal Pay Act of 1960. Table 9:7 summarizes discharge experience in recent years.

To conclude, the House has solved the problem of getting floor action on measures to which there is virtually no opposition and measures that have overwhelming support. It has been less successful in gaining an outlet for measures that, probably, have majority support but that have strong, entrenched opposition. The Rules Committee has acted as an agency that could bring out such measures when desired by the majority leaders, but the development of the bipartisan block in the committee since 1937 weakened this

73. *Congressional Record*, 71st Cong., 3rd sess., 1931, p. 3701.
74. Joint Committee on the Organization of Congress, Hearings, 1945, p. 283.
75. Ibid., p. 332.

avenue for the Democratic party. Even the enlargement of the committee in 1961 and the retirement of Chairman Howard Smith in 1966 have not completely harnessed it as a vehicle of the majority party.

TABLE 9:7
Use of House Discharge Procedure, 80th through 90th Congresses

Congress	Number of Petitions Filed	Number of Bills Discharged	Number of Discharged Bills Passing House	Number of Discharged Bills Becoming Law
80th	20	1	1	0
81st	34	3	3	0
82nd	14	0	0	0
83rd	10	1	1	0
84th	6	0	0	0
85th	7	1	1	0
86th	5	1	1	1
87th	6	0	0	0
88th	5	0	0	0
89th	6	1	1	0
90th	4	0	0	0

10.

Committee to Floor: The Senate

SENATE RULES and customs are far more informal than those of the House. They grant greater freedom to the individual member, but at the same time they place fewer blocks in the way of a politically skillful party leader.

Party Leadership[1]

The Senate has never formally entrusted any person or group with as much power as the House did its Speaker under Cannon. In some ways, however, the Senate majority leader comes close to the Speaker of the House in his power to bridge the gap between committee and floor action. No one questions the fact that the Senate is run from the floor and not the chair, so there is less problem of division of power between the vice-president and the Senate majority leader than between the Speaker and the House majority leader. Further, the majority leader does not have to share his power with a bipartisan scheduling committee such as the House Rules Committee. In matters of scheduling, he may share power with the majority policy committee, but he has managed to harness this to his own needs with relative success. His powers are difficult to isolate. Custom guarantees that he will be recognized by the chair whenever he seeks to address the Senate. And the Democratic party has assigned its leader three important chair-

1. See Randall B. Ripley, *Power in the Senate* (New York: St. Martin's Press, 1969) for information on Senate party leadership.

manships: of the caucus, the policy committee, and the steering committee (though the Republicans have left these positions in separate hands). Beyond this, his power depends upon his skill at leadership. Mary McGrory of the *Washington Star* describes what went into the role as played by the Senate's most successful majority leader: "Being won over by [Lyndon B.] Johnson is a rather overwhelming experience. The full treatment is an incredibly potent mixture of persuasion, badgering, flattery, threats, reminders of past favors and future advantages."[2]

Because so much of his power is personal, the careless majority leader can become a general without troops. To a greater extent than in the House, individual members, even if they are not in strategic committee or party positions, are able to block what he wants to accomplish or to push him into action he would not otherwise take. The rules and the customs of this body, which put so much emphasis on the freedom of the individual member, account for the difference. Allen Drury, in *Advise and Consent*, said of the majority leader's role, "His world began and ended in ninety-nine minds whose endless surprises he could never entirely anticipate. No sooner had he got somebody pegged in one place than he turned up somewhere else; his plans for steering legislation had to be constantly revised to accommodate the human material with which he had to work."[3]

Even more than in the House, the rules necessitate the utmost of cooperation between the two floor leaders. Johnson described his relations with Minority Leader Everett M. Dirksen in the following manner:

> Well, after I evaluate the bills on the Calendar, I ask him to make his recommendations. When I walk into the cham-

2. Quoted in Booth Mooney, *The Lyndon Johnson Story* (New York: Avon Books, 1964), p. 153.
3. (Garden City, N.Y.: Doubleday & Co., 1959), p. 40. It is said that Senator Richard Russell could have had the majority leader position in the 81st Congress but that he turned it down because it involved too much coaxing of prima donnas. (It would also have forced him to moderate his role as spokesman for the South.)

ber every morning, he puts on my desk a memo stating what
he thinks about each bill and what his policy group thinks
and what his colleagues think—"this will be trouble," "This
will be long debate," "This will have relatively little opposition," and so forth. I evaluate them and mark my Calendar
in red pencil.[4]

There were seven Senate majority leaders during the period
under consideration. Wallace H. White Jr. (Maine) served during
the 80th Congress as the first Republican to hold the position since
1932. He clearly played second fiddle to Robert A. Taft and
Arthur H. Vandenberg, and his relations with the minority leaders
were poor. At one point he unsuccessfully offered his resignation
and, after an illness, he chose not to run for reelection for the
Senate in 1948. Scott W. Lucas (Democrat, Illinois) who served
during the 81st Congress, only to be defeated by Everett Dirksen
in 1950, is generally ranked as a good, but not a great party leader.
Ernest W. McFarland (Democrat, Arizona) was the choice of the
anti-Truman forces in the 82nd Congress. He lacked leadership
experience and was defeated in his Arizona reelection campaign
by Barry Goldwater in 1952. Up to this point in the postwar
period, the position of majority leader had not been marked with
greatness. Robert Taft (Republican, Ohio) brought intellectual
weight to the position in the 83rd Congress, after the Eisenhower
victory, but neither he nor his hand-picked successor, William F.
Knowland (Republican, California), had time to develop the position to the peak of power that Lyndon Johnson did in the 84th
through the 86th Congresses. While Taft was essentially aloof,
holding his power on the basis of the force of his personality and
his mastery of the legislative process, Johnson built his power in a
more divided party on a highly personal basis. He had served in
the House from 1937 to 1948, learning much from his fellow
Texan, Sam Rayburn. He spoke of his concept of the role of
leadership in the January 2, 1953, Democratic caucus. He em-

4. "Leadership: An Interview with Lyndon Johnson," *U. S. News and World
Report*, June 27, 1960, p. 89.

phasized the fact that "we all owe primary allegiance to our constituents" and that he as floor leader would respect the problems of his fellow Democrats and protect the rights of those with whom he disagreed, for he did not believe in suppressing party differences. However, he stated, "one of my deepest convictions is that there are more vital issues to hold Democrats together than there are issues to divide them." He showed the greatest skill in presenting issues in such a way that they would unite rather than divide the party.[5]

One senator commented that Johnson and his less commanding 1961 successor, Mike Mansfield, were "about as similar as Winston Churchill and St. Francis of Assissi,"[6] but the change apparently appealed to at least one senator. Joseph S. Clark commented:

> I for one have no desire to return to the days prior to 1961 when the Majority Leader spent his time, as described in *Newsweek* last week, in "back-slapping, chest jabbing and arm twisting." I do not share the nostalgia of the Senator from Connecticut [Thomas J. Dodd] for "an orchestra leader" who "it is alleged stood up and blended into a wonderful production all the discordant notes of the Senate." Those days are gone, I hope, forever. Let the past bury its dead.[7]

In the process of scheduling, the Senate party leaders make more use of policy committees than do the House leaders. If the system had greater party responsibility, these committees would undoubtedly assume even more important roles. Indeed, the Joint Committee on the Organization of Congress envisioned giving majority and minority policy committees in the House and Senate important party policy-making functions. Each of the four committees was to be composed of seven members appointed by their respective party conferences at the opening of each new Congress, and

5. Ralph K. Huitt, "Democratic Party Leadership in the Senate," *American Political Science Review* (June 1961): 333–34.
6. *Time*, March 20, 1964, p. 23.
7. *Congressional Record*, 88th Cong., 1st sess., 1963, p. 12618.

each was to be charged with the task of formulating legislative policy. The majority policy committees were to expedite "consideration and passage of matters pledged to the people by their party." Further, they were to meet regularly with the executive "to facilitate the formulation and carrying out of national policy, and to improve relationships between the executive and legislative branches of the Government."[8]

Provision for these committees was taken out of the Legislative Reorganization Act as part of the price of passage in the House. Senate policy committees were given a statutory basis, however, in the Legislative Appropriation Act of 1946 and they have received annual financial support. Senate leadership has been somewhat more receptive to sharing power with such committees than have been leaders of the House, partly because there was no existing agency such as the House Rules Committee that already played an important role in legislative scheduling. Yet these committees have not fulfilled the hopes of some of the framers of the original reorganization proposal. What Malcolm E. Jewell has said of the experience of the Senate Republican policy committee is applicable to the Democratic committee as well: "The roots of party disunity are too deep, the tradition of Senators' independence too strong, and the party leadership sanctions are too weak for the committee to play the unifying role some political scientists intended for it."[9]

The majority policy committee of the Senate has been held to be a distant parallel to the House Rules Committee and, indeed, it does perform some scheduling functions, though it has far less control over sequence and timing than the House committee. If the majority leader chooses to make use of it (and he is likely to, for it can strengthen his hand), it serves largely as a body that re-

8. Joint Committee on the Organization of Congress, *Organization of Congress,* Senate Report 1011, pursuant to H. Con. Res. 18, 79th Cong., 2nd sess., 1946, pp. 12–14.
9. Malcolm E. Jewell, "The Senate Republican Policy Committee and Foreign Policy," *Western Political Quarterly* (Dec. 1959): 980.

views the legislative proposals of the various committees and discusses which should be scheduled and which not. Traditionally, it has given the majority leader wide latitude to proceed in its name, working out details in conjunction with committee chairmen and other interested parties.

Democrats have created a small committee of nine members who have remained on the committee from the time of their initial appointment, leaving only when they leave the Senate. Three members serve ex officio: the floor leader (he is chairman of the policy committee, the steering committee, and the caucus), the whip, and the secretary of the conference. The remaining members were initially appointed by Floor Leader Alben W. Barkley and, since 1947, when vacancies have occurred, the incumbent floor leader has filled them.

Barkley appointed a number of less senior members, but he reportedly made little use of the committee. Lucas, in the 81st Congress, called weekly meetings at which problems of scheduling and strategy were discussed in an atmosphere of give-and-take. McFarland (82nd Congress) usually met weekly with his committee, but he used it more for discussion and less for decision-making. Johnson (83rd through 86th Congresses) tended to call meetings less frequently than did his predecessors, preferring to handle policy and strategy questions on a more personal and less institutional basis, though he did use it to help unify the party, believing that frequent meetings of the caucus would do nothing but raise party divisions.[10] In the 86th Congress, Johnson added the members of the Calendar Committee whose duty it is to prepare for the Call of the Calendar, a procedure for the expeditious handling of bills of minor importance. This served to broaden the base of the Democratic policy committee and made Calendar Committee work more desirable than previously, when it was considered

10. Hugh A. Bone, *Party Committees and National Politics* (Seattle: University of Washington Press, 1958), chap. 6; Huitt, "Democratic Party Leadership," pp. 331–344. Malcolm E. Jewell, "The Senate Republican Policy Committee and Foreign Policy," pp. 966–980.

little more than an onerous task imposed upon freshman senators. Mansfield relied heavily on his policy committee.

The Democratic policy committee has come under the criticism of liberal Democrats, especially since the 86th Congress, for not making policy and for acting as an arm of the leadership rather than of the Democratic membership of the Senate.[11] Further, charges have been made that the committee under-represents less senior, liberal, eastern Democrats. Proposals have been made that membership expire at the end of each Congress as the first Joint Committee on the Organization of Congress had suggested, and that the committee be enlarged and chosen by the caucus rather than by the leadership.

Republicans have created a somewhat different policy committee. Members are nominated by the chairman of the conference and ratified by the whole conference. Ex officio members include the floor leader, whip, chairman and secretary of the conference, chairman of the policy committee, and, since the 84th Congress, the chairman of the committee-on-committees, the campaign committee, and the personnel (patronage) committee. In the 83rd Congress Senator Homer E. Capehart suggested that the legislative committee chairmen be given ex officio membership. Nothing came of the proposal, however. Apparently party leaders regarded this as a challenge to their leadership and chairmen did not favor sharing their individual power with a collective body.

The size of the policy committee has ranged between nine and fourteen members, except during the 84th Congress, when all Republican senators up for reelection in 1956 were given the prestige of membership, thus bringing the total to twenty-three. There has been less criticism of the Republican than the Democratic committee, perhaps because Republicans are less likely to discuss their party squabbles in public, but also because meetings have been open to all Republicans, and deliberate attempts have been made

11. See Senator William Proxmire, *Congressional Record,* 86th Cong., 1st sess., 1959, pp. 2814–20, 3559–78, 3956–59; Senator Albert Gore, *Congressional Record,* 86th Cong., 2nd sess., 1960, pp. 192–202.

to include less senior members both as full members or as observers invited on a rotating basis. When Democrats were criticiz-
ing their committee in the 86th Congress, Republicans voiced satis-
faction with the representativeness of theirs and with the role it
has played in policy formulation.

The Republican policy committee has had a more formalized
role than that of the Democrats, though its activity has varied with
its chairman. According to Malcolm E. Jewell, Robert A. Taft
(80th through 82nd Congresses) made greater use of the committee than his successors, William F. Knowland (1953), Homer
Ferguson (1954), or Styles H. Bridges (84th through 86th Congresses). Its functions, according to a 1953 memorandum, include
consideration of party policy, legislative procedure, and legislative scheduling, as well as cooperation with the president, the
House of Representatives, Senate committees, and individual Republican senators.[12] It has been more concerned with research and
publication than its Democratic counterpart. Its remoteness from
floor operations is illustrated by the fact that the committee head-
quarters has always been in the Senate Office Building while the
Democratic committee has been housed in the Capitol. This is
partly the result of the fact that Republicans have been in control
of the Senate for only four of the twenty-two years under scru-
tiny here.

In summary, majority policy committees play a role in scheduling. They give general approval to an order of business but they
leave details to be worked out by the majority leader, in cooperation with the minority leader. The majority leader will be concerned with keeping an even flow of Senate work. He will try to
make sure that those with an unusual interest in a measure will
be able to be present. He may give priority to certain measures in
order to pick up necessary votes for other, more crucial measures.
In making his decisions, he will, of course, be governed by the
rules and customs of the Senate.

12. Bone, *Party Committees*, p. 175.

Senate Rules and Procedures

Bridging the gap between committee and floor is simpler in the Senate than in the House, from a procedural standpoint. There is no complex system of calendars and no elaborate system of special days. The process is less institutionalized and more informal.

Bills reported from committees are placed on the Calendar in the order in which they are received. Noncontroversial measures are often disposed of by the Call of the Calendar which is privileged business after the "morning hour" on Monday. Under this procedure, measures are read by the clerk in their Calendar order. In a manner somewhat similar to that used in the House for Consent and Private Calendar procedure, there are official party objectors, now known as Calendar Committees. A committee member will object to unanimous consent passage of a bill if his committee has received a request to do so from a senator of the same party, or if it considers the bill too important to pass without explanatory debate, in need of amendment, or lacking in merit. If objection is made, the bill is returned to its original position on the Calendar, to be brought up again the next time that the Senate reaches it in its periodic Call of the Calendar.

Most important legislation, however, is taken up out of order, by special action of the Senate. This may be done by majority vote or by unanimous consent. Any member may move to take up a measure that has been on the Calendar for one legislative day (three days for appropriations measures). If this is done during the "morning hour" of a new legislative day (in the first two hours of a Senate day unless it has been formally terminated earlier) the motion is not debatable under the rules.[13] After the morning hour such a motion is debatable; although cloture now applies to such a motion, the two-thirds vote necessary to limit debate is difficult

13. The "morning hour" takes place only at the start of a new legislative day, that is, after the Senate has adjourned rather than recessed.

to secure.[14] Such majority decisions to take up legislation are rarely successful, therefore, for measures that have determined opposition.

On more important measures, conditions for floor handling are frequently worked out by unanimous consent agreements. They have been developed largely as a vehicle for the shortening of debate because of the lack of limitations in the rules. These agreements have long been used but they have become increasingly important since World War II, especially under the leadership of Lyndon Johnson. They are somewhat similar to special orders issued by the House Rules Committee. They may be concerned with the division of time among the senators speaking on a measure, the amount of time allowed for debate, the time at which a vote will be taken, and a limitation on the amendments that may be made.[15] In working out these agreements, the majority leader "touches base" with those concerned with the prospective legislation. Except on highly controversial measures, it is generally accepted Senate etiquette to agree to these self-imposed limitations.[16]

The foregoing is concerned with measures that have been re-

14. In the 80th Congress, President Pro Tem Arthur H. Vandenberg interpreted Rule XXII as not being applicable to debate on a motion to bring up a measure. In the 81st Congress, Vice President Alben W. Barkley held that cloture did apply in such a situation but he was overruled by the Senate. Later in 1949 a new cloture rule was adopted which extended its application to debate on a motion to bring up a measure, but an absolute two-thirds vote was made necessary to invoke cloture rather than the previous two-thirds of those present and voting. In 1959 the rule was changed to two-thirds of those present and voting.

15. Such limits may take the form of allowing no amendments at all, only committee amendments, or only germane amendments. The Senate has no general rule that amendments must be germane except in connection with appropriations measures.

16. Some senators feel that too much consideration is given to the minority in order that agreements may be reached. Senator Wayne Morse has said, "How long, O Lord, how long must the Senate wait for majority rule?" For further comments by Senator Morse on unanimous consent agreements, see *Congressional Record*, 82nd Cong., 2nd sess., 1952, pp. 8827–32; 85th Cong., 2nd sess., 1958, p. 15431.

ported by Senate committees. What recourse does the Senate have if one of its committees fails to act? It can refer legislation to a committee for a limited time with directions that it must report by a certain date; it can discharge a committee of a measure before it; or it can by-pass the committee stage entirely, by suspension of the rules, by operating under Rule xiv, or by adding the measure as an amendment to a bill under floor consideration. Any one of these alternatives needs the acquiescence, if not the outright support, of the Senate leadership. These procedures are infrequently used. In recent years they have been resorted to largely in connection with civil rights measures when the Judiciary Committee has been hostile to action and the leadership has been favorable.[17]

The Civil Rights Act of 1960 is one of the very few measures to have been referred to a committee for a limited period of time, though occasionally a measure that has been referred to one committee and reported out may be referred to another committee under these conditions. Majority Leader Johnson was successful in referring HR 8601, the House-passed civil rights bill that was considered more acceptable than the Senate version, with instructions that the measure was to be reported back in five days, over the charge by Judiciary Chairman James O. Eastland that this was an example of "legislative lynching."

The second alternative, discharge procedure (Rule xxvi, clause 2), requires a simple majority vote in the Senate, as compared with the signatures of an absolute majority in the House, yet the procedure has been used with even less success here because of the tradition of "club fair play" and the possibility of blocking action by means of a filibuster.[18] Discharge is not generally favored by

17. For case studies of two civil rights measures, see Howard E. Shuman, "Senate Rules and the Civil Rights Bill," *American Political Science Review* (Dec. 1957): 955–75; Daniel M. Berman, *A Bill Becomes a Law: The Civil Rights Act of 1960* (New York: Macmillan Co., 1962).
18. A discharge motion must be introduced in the "morning hour" unless unanimous consent has been obtained. It must lie over one legislative day, and here action can be blocked by recessing rather than adjourning. Both

the leadership. As Lyndon Johnson said in 1960, "I know of no more disorderly procedure that the Senate could take than for it to begin to discharge its various committees from further consideration of bills under their consideration."[19] Resort to discharge procedure has been infrequent. There have been only fourteen motions to discharge a committee in the history of the Senate; only six have been successful; and only one has become law, a 1964 measure allowing the Treasury to strike medals for the state of Florida.[20]

A committee may be by-passed entirely. One means is by suspension of the rules, though this is used infrequently for this purpose. When a House bill is laid before the Senate for reference, a motion may be made to suspend the rules. This motion must lie over one legislative day, to be called up in the next morning hour. Such a motion is debatable and requires a two-thirds vote. If secured, the bill could be called up by a majority vote (again, subject to unlimited debate) in the next legislative day.

Another means of by-passing a committee is to operate under Rule XIV, clause 4, which provides that if objection is made to further proceedings on a measure after a first and second reading, it is to be placed on the Calendar instead of being referred to a committee. In 1948 a point of order concerning the precedence of Rule XIV and Rule XXV (which provides for reference of bills to committee) was decided in favor of mandatory reference to committees. In 1957, however, the Senate reversed its previous

---

the motions to proceed to consider and to pass the petition are subject to unlimited debate.

19. *Congressional Record,* 86th Cong., 2nd sess., 1960, p. 2625. In the 87th Congress, when Floor Leader Mike Mansfield proposed, unsuccessfully, to discharge the Government Operations Committee of the reorganization plan creating a Department of Urban Affairs, Chairman John L. McClellan spoke of the action as "a wanton attack on the committee system" (*Congressional Record,* 87th Cong., 2nd sess., 1962, p. 2540).

20. Lewis A. Froman Jr., *The Congressional Process* (Boston: Little, Brown & Co., 1967), p. 132.

position and successful use was made of this device as a means of by-passing the Judiciary Committee in connection with civil rights legislation.[21] This was done again in 1964 and 1965 for the civil rights bills.

A final means of by-passing a committee is to bring up a measure in the form of an amendment to a bill that is up for consideration. Senate general appropriations bills are subject to points of order as to germaneness (Rule xvi, clause 7), as are bills considered under the cloture rule (Rule xxii, clause 2). Further, unanimous consent agreements frequently provide that amendments must be germane. Beyond this there are no Senate restrictions as to the relevancy of amendments. An advantage is that there is no necessity for a motion to consider a nongermane amendment as there is with a measure that comes directly from the Calendar. There is one less point for a filibuster. Two examples of the use of this method to by-pass a committee occurred in the 86th Congress. Extension of the life of the Civil Rights Commission was brought to the floor as an amendment to the foreign aid appropriations bill (HR 8385), and in the following year the Civil Rights Act of 1960 was first brought to the floor as an amendment to HR 8315, a House passed measure to authorize the Secretary of the Army to lease a portion of Fort Crowder to the Stella, Missouri, school district. Towards the end of the 88th Congress, an amendment was attached to the foreign aid authorization bill limiting the effect of the Supreme Court's reapportionment decision. This method is sometimes used with success, for though the House has a strict rule governing the germaneness of amendments (Rule xvi, clause 7), precedent denies members of the House the right to raise points of order as to the germaneness of Senate amendments. Further, this procedure has the advantage of providing one less point of attack by filibuster, since there is no necessity for a motion to consider a nongermane amendment, as there is for a measure that comes from a committee via the Calendar.

21. Charles L. Watkins and Floyd M. Riddick, *Senate Procedure* (Washington, D.C.: Government Printing Office, 1958), p. 506.

Chamber Control of House and Senate

Which has the upper hand, the "little legislatures" or the full legislature? Theodore Lowi, in a provocative review article, suggests that the kind of issue being handled has a lot to do with the fact that some measures reach their essentially final form before they are even submitted to a committee, some mature in committee and are merely ratified by the full legislative, while others are molded on the legislative floor.[22]

In his explanation, Lowi distinguishes among domestic policies according to their impact upon society, categorizing them as distributive, regulatory, and redistributive. Distributive policies involve subsidies to private groups or to other levels of government with the goal of increasing the activities in a given area. Examples would be public works programs, the use of public lands, defense procurement, and the traditional services provided for agriculture, business, and labor. He suggests that relatively small units seek indulgences for themselves of the sort that do not interfere seriously with the desires of others. Nearly every party-in-interest with any strength at all can win something in the process that is often called logrolling. Treaties can be worked out among interest groups, administrative bureaus, and congressional committees, with a decision reached by the committee that usually receives little detailed review or revision by the full Congress.

Regulatory policies involve restrictions on the freedom of private groups. Examples would be the detailed restrictions that have been placed on public utilities, antitrust regulations on other types of businesses, and restraints placed on organized labor. These policies are more controversial, for government regulation of one group is often government indulgence of another, and the decision as to which group is to be indulged and which deprived is often hard-fought. Such policy proposals, Lowi suggests, are likely to be reviewed by the full Congress.

22. Theodore Lowi, "American Business, Public Policy, Case Studies and Political Theory," *World Politics* (July 1964): 677.

Redistributive policies alter the social, economic, and political reward structure for broad groups in such a way as to polarize the "money providers" and the "service demanders." Examples can be seen in our tax and monetary policies, welfare programs, and civil rights measures. These most controversial policies tend to be fought out in the national political arena. When "their time has come," measures are likely to be worked out by the executive and the major interests, and merely ratified by Congress and its committees.

Committees do not fall neatly into this helpful framework, for they frequently handle several different types of policies. Some generalizations can be made, however (see table 6:1, for example). Redistributive matters are frequently the concern of the Labor and Banking committees (both clientele oriented) and the Judiciary and Finance committees (both categorized as national issue). These committees can expect to receive from the executive a number of carefully worked out treaties that have been drawn up outside the legislature. They can do relatively little but ratify them and pass them on to the parent body for its stamp of approval.

Most of the clientele committees, except those primarily concerned with business and labor, tend to handle policies that are redistributive in nature, those concerned with agriculture, merchant marine, public lands, public works, and veterans. Committees on Appropriations, Armed Services, and Science (all classified as being concerned with national issues) and the housekeeping Post Office committees also handle a large number of distributive policies. These committees can be expected to have considerable autonomy when handling such matters.

Regulatory matters tend to be handled by clientele committees concerned with banking, commerce, and labor. These groups can expect considerable disagreement and amendment when they bring such measures to the floor, for interests that have felt themselves underrepresented on these particular committees will try to have a say in the final outcome.

Lowi helps explain the varying degrees of chamber review of positive committee action. What are the chamber's powers when a committee pigeonholes a measure it wants to act on? The fifteen measures cited in this and the previous chapter, which were forced to the floor and eventually became law, are listed in table 10:1. All ten House measures were pried from the Rules Committee during Congresses of considerable legislative energy and large Democratic majorities. Nearly all fall into the distributive category. The Rules Committee, evidently, was most likely to be overruled when it was attempting to block government largess of the sort that was spread widely throughout the country. All Senate examples, on the other hand, were directed against the Judiciary Committee under the chairmanship of Senator Eastland, all involved civil rights legislation, and all could be classified as redistributive in character. Evidently, the redoubtable Mississippian was unable to withstand the strong civil rights drive of the time.

Perhaps the Congress is not so far out of tune with the political tides as some critics claim. One gets the impression that committee and party leaders are in a fair amount of agreement and not immune to pressures from the outside political world. When party and committee leaders do differ, the party leaders, though they do not have the kind of partisan rawhide that Speaker Cannon once had, have been able to muster bipartisan majorities to do what committees thought ought not to be done and to redo what committees thought ought to be done.

TABLE 10:1
Measures Forced Out of Committee That Became Law, 80th through 90th Congresses

Congress	Measure	Procedure	Nature of Policy
HOUSE			
81 (1949–50)	National Science Foundation	21-Day Rule	Distributive
	Rivers & harbors	21-Day Rule	Distributive
	Contributions to international associations	21-Day Rule	Foreign affairs
86 (1959–60)	Postal pay increase	Discharge	Distributive
	Depressed areas	Calendar Wednesday	Distributive
89 (1965–66)	Federal pay raise	21-Day Rule	Distributive
	Increased postal rates	21-Day Rule	Distributive
	Foundation for Arts & Sciences	21-Day Rule	Distributive
	Public school funds	21-Day Rule	Distributive
	Bank Holding Company Act amendment	21-Day Rule	Regulatory
SENATE			
85 (1957–58)	Civil Rights Act of 1957	By-pass committee	Redistributive
86 (1959–60)	Extension of Civil Rights Commission	Nongermane amendment	Redistributive
	Civil Rights Act of 1960	Nongermane amendment and limited reference	Redistributive
88 (1963–64)	Civil Rights Act of 1964	By-pass committee	Redistributive
89 (1965–66)	Civil Rights Act of 1965	By-pass committee	Redistributive

11.

Committee Business: Postpartum

A COMMITTEE's work does not by any means stop when the legislation it has helped prepare reaches the floor. It continues by managing the debate on the floor, by participating in the conference that seeks to compromise House-Senate versions of a measure, and by supervising the administration of it once it becomes law. However much the full committee membership participated in the early stages, in these later stages of the committee process the senior members assume greatly increasing importance.

Committees and the Floor

When the legislative process is most visible it is often least interesting, as is inevitable in a system where major decisions are worked out by specialized committees. A committee that represents, however imperfectly, a range of partisan, ideological, and regional opinions, and that has an eye to the range of opinions in the full legislature and in the country, works out its compromises in executive session. Then it gives its senior members the task of managing the measure on the floor. In this they are helped by the customs of the body, which tend to discourage floor amendment and a challenge to the expertise of committee seniors. As a result, floor debate, which "is the distillate of thousands upon thousands of hours of talk that had preceded" is not very exciting nor is it generally likely to change many minds.[1]

1. Clem Miller, *Member of the House* (New York: Charles Scribner's Sons, 1962), pp. 114–15.

In more party-oriented legislatures, floor leaders play a major role in managing measures. In Congress, however, most special orders in the House and unanimous consent agreements in the Senate give the task to committee chairmen and ranking minority members. Their goal, generally, is to bring measures through successfully and as nearly intact as possible.

The degree of agreement among committee members concerning one of its measures has a marked effect upon the fate of that measure when it reaches the floor. Speaker Champ Clark once suggested that "a unanimous committee report generally, but not always, means the passage of the bill through the House; whereas, if there is a minority report, its passage is endangered, the danger increasing with the number of members who sign the minority report."[2] Donald R. Matthews, in a statistical survey made of the 84th Congress, found that in all cases when 80 percent or more of the members of a committee voted for a measure on a floor roll call, the measure passed. Ninety-one percent of the measures passed that had between 70 and 79 percent of their committee members supporting them. At the other end of the spectrum, only 16 percent of the measures passed that were supported by between 20 and 29 percent of their committee members, and none was successful when committee support fell below the 20 percent level.[3]

An interesting example of what can go on when a measure lacks necessary floor support was given in a House debate on the 1962 agriculture bill. Chairman Harold D. Cooley, when asked why he was willing to accept a certain amendment, said it was because "the membership probably might be softened up by it." Whereupon Congressman Frank Chelf explained further, "It's because he needs fellows like me to vote for the bill."[4]

2. Champ Clark, *My Quarter Century of American Politics*, 2 vols. (New York: Harpers, 1920), 1:229.
3. Donald R. Matthews, *U.S. Senators and Their World* (Chapel Hill: University of North Carolina Press, 1960), p. 170.
4. *Congressional Record*, 87th Cong., 2nd sess., 1962, p. 11345, cited in Neil MacNeil, *Forge of Democracy* (New York: David McKay, 1963), p. 346.

Ordinarily, there is a hesitancy to amend measures too freely, and in the House, the Rules Committee has been enpowered to allow only committee approved amendments or to prohibit all amendments. The reason for this hesitancy is described by Clem Miller:

> Unless the stakes are high and there is a good base of political support, it is not attempted. It is too vast a place for localized action; there are too many watchdogs. The traditional deference to the authority of one of its committees overwhelms the main body. The whole fabric of Congress is based on committee expertness, and the practice of "rewriting a bill on the floor" is thought of as a bad business.[5]

The strength of the committee system is reinforced by the fact that legislators, busy with constituency matters and the work of their own specialized committees, seek advice from members of other committees as to how to vote on matters beyond their immediate purview. One first-term member of the House has described the situation:

> I turn to committee members in whom I have confidence for their integrity and ability and rely on them especially when the legislation is not of paramount importance. The best I can do is to devote my time to the major pieces of legislation which come before the House, and rely on others for advice in connection with less major legislation. I admit there are many drawbacks to such a system, but I want to impress upon you that there is no alternative.[6]

---

5. Miller, *Member of the House*, p. 51.
6. Charles L. Clapp, *The Congressman: His Work as He Sees It* (Washington, D.C.: The Brookings Institution, 1963), p. 147.

Conference Committees[7]

Inevitably, most important measures pass the two houses in different form. Unanimity must be reached eventually if legislation is to be achieved. To do this there are two broad alternatives available to the two houses: the house that initiated a measure may agree to the changes made by the second house or the houses may agree to go to conference and seek to settle the differences by compromise.

A member of Congress has said that the conference is "the most interesting thing that happens on Capitol Hill." Much of what makes conferences fascinating for the insider—the fact that they are gatherings of powerful, senior committee specialists from both houses meeting in carefully guarded secrecy—makes them difficult for an outsider to describe, as a survey of the very limited literature on conferences will demonstrate.

Within a session of Congress there tends to be a pattern of few conferences during the first four of five months, followed by a slow increase in the number, and with roughly half being held in the last two months of the legislative year. The pattern of conference activity for the entire period under consideration is given in table 11:1. Since almost all conferences are held on measures that become public laws (as opposed to private laws that deal with individual matters such as claims against the government), it can be seen that roughly 15 percent pass through a conference committee. A survey of these measures shows them to include most of the important measures that pass. This is not true of all, however, for when there is very strong demand for a measure and a knowledge that either the conference would be opposed to it or that the process could not be completed before the end of a session, the two houses may do the unique thing and

7. For a detailed discussion of the history and procedures of conference committees, see Ada C. McCown, *The Congressional Conference Committee* (New York: Columbia University Press, 1927); Gilbert Y. Steiner, *The Congressional Conference Committee* (Urbana: University of Illinois Press, 1951); Lewis A. Froman Jr., *The Congressional Process* (Boston: Little, Brown & Co., 1967), chap. 9.

TABLE 11:1

A Summary of Conference Activity, 80th through 90th Congresses*

Congress	Total Public Laws Resolutions Enacted	Successful Conferences Held	Measures That Died In Conference
80th	906	130	1
81st	921	157	9
82nd	594	90	8
83rd	781	109	3
84th	1028	137	2
85th	936	109	11
86th	800	100	8
87th	885	123	17
88th	666	81	8
89th	810	144	5
90th	640	129	6
	8777	1381	78

* Information in this table was gathered from the appropriate final editions of the *Calendars of the United States House of Representatives.*

agree so that this stage can be by-passed. A relatively small number of measures, 5 percent over the entire period, died in conference. Some were of major importance, but a large portion were clearly minor matters. Of the 78 examples, failure of passage came from the fact that no conference report was agreed upon (34), that one of the houses failed to appoint its delegation (31), that one house failed to take action on a conference report (8), and that the conference report was rejected (5).

Everyone closely concerned with a piece of legislation takes into consideration the possibility of a conference. There are reasons for trying to avoid one if it is felt that a conference will mean weakening or defeating a measure. There are reasons to try to have one if it is felt that it will improve a measure. During committee mark-up sessions and on the floor, amendments may be accepted or deleted, with the idea that changes can be made later in the quiet of a conference. Roll-call votes may be requested, if there is a feeling that a provision has strong support, as a means of increasing its chances in conference later. Congressman Clem

Miller spoke perceptively of a chairman's approach to the conference:

> It is a rare House chairman who pilots his bill through the House without keeping at least one eye on the conference which will almost certainly result, for rarely does an important bill exactly conform to the companion bill in the Senate. When he so affably makes points with the Member by adopting his pet amendment, the chairman knows he can recede gracefully from it in conference. He may adopt a very weak or a very strong position on a certain issue to put himself at a better bargaining position at the conference. The larger the bag of tricks a chairman takes to a conference, the more free play he has in the negotiation.[8]

It is not always easy to reach an agreement to go to conference. Different procedures are used in the House and in the Senate. Prior to a 1965 rules change in the House, a Senate-amended measure could be sent to conference only by unanimous consent or by a special rule from the Committee on Rules. Obviously, a special rule was usually needed for controversial measures, and this increased the powers of the Rules Committee. It could instruct the conference committee as to how to handle Senate amendments; it could even refuse a rule, as it did in its controversial 1960 decison not to send to conference the first general aid-to-education bill ever passed by the two houses of Congress. In 1965, however, the liberal 89th Congress took an important step in the integration of the powers of the Speaker by increasing his control over conference procedure. He may now, in his discretion, recognize a member of the committee that originally handled a measure for the purpose of moving that it be sent to conference; the decision is made by a simple majority floor vote. In the Senate, a motion to send a House-amended measure to conference is made by the majority leader and determined likewise by a majority vote. The right of unlimited debate does give

8. Miller, *Member of the House*, pp. 113–14.

some chance for individual senators to attempt to block the establishment of a committee, but it is rarely exercised at this stage of Senate procedure.

Conference committee members are nominally appointed by the presiding officers of their respective bodies, according to House rules and Senate custom. Invariably, however, the leadership, making a basic accommodation to the committee system, accepts the nominations of committee chairmen. In drawing up the slate, the degree of cooperation between the chairman and the ranking committee member varies according to the way in which they have worked out their personal relations. Especially on important matters, the senior members of the majority and minority parties (including the chairman of the subcommittee that may have handled it) are designated. A check of the distribution of conference committee assignments in the 89th Congress (1965–66) showed Representative George Mahon, chairman of the House Appropriations Committee, and Senator Leverett Saltonstall, ranking member on both the Senate Armed Services and Appropriations committees, as having been involved in the greatest number of conferences (thirty and twenty-five respectively). The Senate, which is more likely than the House to designate subcommittee members than senior members of the full committee, spread its conference assignments more widely throughout the membership. Only three senators did not serve on at least one conference committee during thhe 89th Congress, while 44 percent of the House members received no assignments.

Senator Joseph S. Clark has long favored a rule providing that conferees must have shown, by their debate and their vote, their sympathy with the position of their house on a measure before they can be appointed to a conference committee that handles it. As an example of the problem, he has cited a 1959 conference that dropped a Senate amendment liberalizing an unemployment compensation bill and noted that four of the five Senate conferees had opposed the measure on the Senate floor.[9] Members of the

9. Joseph S. Clark, *Congress: The Sapless Branch* (New York: Harper and Row, 1964), p. 11.

House, in discussions at the Brookings Institution, agreed that conference committees were frequently not faithful to the intent of the House.[10] There is little hard evidence as to the number of times that this happens, however, except a study by *Congressional Quarterly* that found only four instances in the 1958 session of Congress when members who had been opposed to major provisions of a measure has served as conferees.[11]

Since each chamber's delegation on a conference committee votes as a unit, with a majority of its members controlling, there is no need to have delegations of equal size. The number of members on a delegation can be of great importance, however. Bertram Gross notes an occasion when Senator Alexander Wiley increased the number of his appointees to a conference committee on the displaced persons bill from three to five in order to create a majority that favored the Senate's (and his own) point of view.[12] In the 89th Congress, the delegations ranged from two to eighteen, though both houses chose more delegations of five than any other size. Delegations may be divided in relation to party strength on the committee, though this is not necessarily the case. Over-representation of the minority can serve the purpose of placing a dissident member of the majority party in a balance of power position. A survey of the party makeup of all conference committees in the 90th Congress showed that nearly half of each house's delegations had a 60 to 40 ratio in favor of the Democrats. The Democrats held 57 percent of the House seats and 64 percent of the Senate seats at the time. Eighty-six percent of all House delegations had a ratio equal to or greater than that prevailing in the parent chamber. This was true of only 28 percent of the Senate delegations, however. In four instances the Senate delegations even consisted of an equal number of members of the majority and minority parties. Two concerned minor measures, but one was the Legislative Appropriations Act of 1969 and the

10. Clapp, *The Congressman*, p. 246.
11. *Congressional Quarterly Weekly Report*, May 1, 1959, pp. 597–98.
12. Bertram M. Gross, *The Legislative Struggle* (New York: McGraw-Hill, 1953), p. 321.

other the armed forces appropriation authorization for that year.

Conference meetings are generally held on the Senate side of the Capitol, with the first named senator presiding. The secrecy with which conference activities are conducted makes it difficult to generalize about many aspects of the process. No written records are kept. The sessions are open to very few beyond the members themselves. There is generally a representative of the legislative counsel's office, to handle the drafting, and staff aides to the committees and the members involved may be allowed. Experts from the executive branch are sometimes invited, though it depends very much on the chairman whether they remain throughout the meetings. Whether or not proxies are allowed depends upon the chairman and the customs of the parent committees.

Conference committees are entitled to deal only with matters in disagreement, adding nothing that has not been adopted in one house and deleting nothing that has been agreed upon by both. If these rules are abrogated, as they often are, it may mean that some liberties were necessary to the process of compromise. The greatest conference freedom comes when the second chamber to consider a measure has passed an essentially different piece of legislation by having struck out all provisions after the enacting clause and inserted its own version. In such instances all provisions are considered to be technically in disagreement and the conference need only come up with a measure that is germane to the original versions.

One senator, quoted by Richard Fenno, describes what goes on in a conference with real insight, though what he says, of course, cannot encompass all the variety that exists in that institution:

> The conference is the most interesting thing that happens on Capitol Hill. The managers on the part of the two houses sit at the head of the table and the others straggle on down the sides. Most of the conversation goes on between these two—the chairman and the vice-chairman of the conference.

Each will poll their delegations. There's a lot of jockeying around—"I'll give you this if you'll give me that." . . . If you can't agree, you go back to your house for a vote. And that puts pressure on you. They'll say, "If you don't agree on this, we'll take it back to the House and get a vote insisting on our position. Then we won't be able to compromise with you—so you'd better take what we give you now." Then, of course, if both houses get votes insisting on their position, you have to hold another conference to see how you can compromise.[13]

Conferences can take minutes or weeks, depending upon the negotiability of the subject matter, the skills of the chairman and vice chairman, and the attitudes of the other members. Fenno noted in his interviews of Appropriations Committee members a strong desire to win for one's house. As one member described this to him: "It's psychology, being stubborn, being boisterous—even walking out if something is important."[14] An adamant position is most likely to be successful towards the end of a session, especially if the bargainers know their opponents want a measure badly. The senior member of the House in the 90th Congress, Emanuel Celler, described, with some relish, the problems of a particular conference:

> The attempt to get an agreement was difficult—as difficult as trying to shave an egg—and that is rather difficult.
>
> There was no lack of diligence and effort. We labored from June onward. We had eight conferences. Debate was vigorous and keen.
>
> We met frequently, and as frequently we found ourselves at loggerheads. There were as many points of view as a centipede has legs. We got nowhere. It was like walking up a descending escalator. The longer we debated, the deeper we plunged into the quicksands of frustration. It became

13. Richard F. Fenno, Jr., *The Power of the Purse* (Boston: Little, Brown & Co., 1966), p. 652.
14. Ibid., p. 625.

apparent that further discussion would be as useless as an empty bucket in an empty well.[15]

Stephen K. Bailey, in his case study of the passage of the Employment Act of 1946, gives an inside view of conference proceedings that points up the importance of staff, the psychological factors that go into the act of compromise, and the difficulty of weighing accurately which house wins in any given dispute:

> The deadlock was broken on the third and fourth days of the conference when [Bertram M.] Gross worked out for [Senator Alben W.] Barkley a series of alternate policy declarations, none of which contained the term "full employment," but all of which contained the phrase "conditions under which there will be afforded useful and remunerative employment opportunities, including self-employment, for all Americans who are willing to work and are seeking work." The nature of the first concession on the part of the Senate sponsors is important, for it illustrates the technique used by Gross all the way through the conference debate. If the House managers objected to a particular phrase, Gross went to a thesaurus and juggled words around until he hit on a verbal equivalent. The fact that both sides were ultimately satisfied with most of the compromises made during the conference struggle cannot be understood without an appreciation of this technique. The House managers believed that Senate concessions were being made with every change in language; the Senate sponsors were satisfied that a rose by any other name smells as sweet.[16]

Fenno notes, however, that along with the desire to win comes a desire to write a bill, an approach that does not come hard to a body that lives by compromise. As one conference manager described the prevailing attitude of most congressmen: "A con-

15. *Congressional Record*, 90th Cong., 1st sess., 1967, p. 30241.
16. Stephen K. Bailey, *Congress Makes a Law* (New York: Columbia University Press, 1950), pp. 223–24.

ference report is not expected to be completely satisfactory to both sides. If the report is a reasonable compromise, one which takes into account and properly weighs the judgments of both sides it is a good report. If it rides roughshod over the views of one or the other, it is a bad report."[17]

The mixture of pressures on conference decision-making differentiates it from any other congressional decision-making situation. Members are designated by their respective committees, generally from their senior membership, and often without too close regard for party ratios or whether they had supported the measure as it passed. The meetings are more secret than most, thus giving the members a near monopoly of information as to the decisions being worked out. Voting is by unit rule, a majority of the members of each delegation controlling. The final conference report, usually presented on short notice, must be accepted or rejected without amendment. These procedures all work to keep the pressures from constituents, interest groups, and political parties somewhat remote. They tend to give greater freedom to the expertise or prejudices (the difference may depend on one's attitude towards the legislation under consideration) of the senior committee specialists. Clem Miller spoke of the conference as "the ultimate flowering of the power of seniority" when "most of the partisanship has been wrung out, and what remains is the seniors versus the rest, the seniors in both parties who preside over the roiling mass below."[18]

A conference delegation does not operate in complete freedom from its chamber, however. It may receive instructions from the parent body, though this rarely happens unless a conference stalemate has developed. It pays close attention to the support its chamber gave various amendments and would rarely ignore a ringing roll-call vote. It knows that points of order may be raised if conferees delete agreed-upon provisions or add new ones, and that unsatisfactory agreements may be rejected. Beyond these informal controls, lie a number which are even more in-

17. Fenno, *Power of the Purse,* p. 620.
18. Miller, *Member of the House,* p. 113.

formal. Richard Fenno says, "An exhortation by chamber colleagues, a promise extracted from the conferees, a roll-call vote,
formal instructions, legislative committee interest, pressure from
the party leadership—all these forms of external influence, singly
or in combination, produce a dependent pattern of decision-making."[19]

Conference reports are privileged business and thus can be
taken up promptly, though House rules provide that they must
remain on the Calendar for one day and that they must be ac-
companied by a written explanation of the agreement reached.
In the House, one hour is provided for consideration; in the
Senate there is no time limit unless one is worked out by unanimous
consent. The time is controlled by the conference manager for
the house involved.

Reports must be accepted or rejected without change. If rejected, they may be returned to the same or a newly constituted
conference. In the period under consideration, forty measures
that were eventually passed, were rejected. On only eleven of
these were the conferees changed. A survey of the floor debate
that took place on conference reports during the 90th Congress
shows a strong tendency for a manager to claim that his delegation has won. Statistics demonstrating success in holding the
line on appropriations figures and disputed amendments were
frequently used to attempt to prove it. Emphasis on victory was
especially pronounced in the House and is, perhaps, a sign of that
body's inferiority complex.

Students of conferences have been interested in comparing the
relative success of the two branches. Gilbert Y. Steiner, in a
study that covered the actions of 56 conference proceedings
between the years of 1928 and 1948, generalized that the House
side had had a greater percentage of victories, especially with
appropriations, taxation, and agricultural measures.[20] Richard
Fenno, in an exhaustive study of the appropriations process
found general agreement that the conferees from the House

19. Fenno, *Power of the Purse*, p. 677.
20. Steiner, *Conference Committee*, p. 170–72.

Appropriations Committee were "better prepared, better organized, better informed, more single-minded in their interest, and
[employed] a more belligerent bargaining style."[21] Nevertheless,
he found that in some 331 conference committee contests in the
appropriations area, between 1947 and 1962, the Senate conferees
came closer to their goal more frequently than House conferees.
His generalization as to the reason, while it applies specifically to
the two Appropriations committees, has broader implications:

> The Senate is stronger in conference because the Senate
> Committee and its conferees draw more directly and more
> completely upon the support of their parent chamber than
> do the House Committee and its conferees. . . . When the
> Senate conferees go to the conference room, they not only
> represent the Senate—they are the Senate. The position
> they defend will have been worked out with a maximum of
> participation by Senate members and will enjoy a maximum
> of support within that body. The figures they defend may be
> higher because of the bargaining process, but they will be
> backed by a more durable consensus. And the bill will be
> defended in conference by men who are the leaders not just
> of the Committee, but of the Senate.[22]

A further hint that the Senate may have the upper hand can
be seen from the fact that during the Congresses under consideration, after conferences have been called for, the House has conceded to the Senate and made further proceedings unnecessary
twice as often as the Senate has conceded to the House. Relative
strength, of course, varies with the committee, the subject matter,
and the political mood of Congress. Because of the complexity
of these variations and the difficulties of determining which house

21. Fenno, *Power of the Purse*, p. 668.
22. Ibid., pp. 668–669. House-Senate rivalries reached dramatic proportions in
1963 when the two Appropriations chairmen, octogenarians Carl Hayden and
Clarence Cannon, refused to meet because they couldn't agree to rotate between the Senate and the House the chairmanship of the conference committee, the meeting rooms, or the right to originate measures (Jeffrey L. Press-
man, *House vs. Senate* [New Haven, Conn.: Yale University Press, 1966]).

actually has the advantage in conference bargaining, this study has not attempted to do what Steiner did for an earlier period.

Though often criticized in the literature on Congress, the two hearings conducted by the first and second Joint Committees on the Organization of Congress produced surprisingly little unfavorable comment on conferences. If not everyone agrees with the senator whom Fenno quoted as saying that it was a "knockdown, dragout legislative fight with a lot of wisdom in it,"[23] those who know Congress best tend to agree that it is a necessary means for negotiation and compromise in a bicameral system.

Supervision of the Executive[24]

Inevitably Congress keeps an eye on the policies it makes as they are being carried out by the executive branch. The legislature is concerned with the organization, the personnel, the finances, and the programs of the administration. Committees play a central role in this. Many are concerned with the work of the specific agencies over which they have jurisdiction. Others, like the committees on Appropriations, Civil Service, and Government Operations, have a jurisdiction that extends to all government agencies.

In a classic article on the subject, Arthur Macmahon describes the purpose of congressional oversight of the administration:

> In the theory of the matter, four types of objectives have been recognized. First, the objective of legislative oversight

23. Fenno, *Power of the Purse*, p. 625.
24. Surprisingly little systematic work has been published that throws light on this topic, though a seminar on Congressional Supervision of Public Policy and Administration, which has been conducted by Arthur Maass of Harvard for a number of years, has been developing data that should be made available in the near future. For perceptive comments, see Arthur Maass' testimony on the subject in two congressional hearings: *The Organization of Congress*, 1965, pp. 940–57; U.S. Senate, Subcommittee on Separation of Powers of the Judiciary Committee, Hearings, *Separation of Powers*, 90th Congress, 2nd sess., 1967, pp. 186–201. Arthur Maass has given helpful suggestions on this section.

may be to check dishonesty or waste. . . . Apart from checking malfeasance, moveover, legislators have opportunities to see the results of governmental programs; at times they can serve administration almost as a supplementary inspectorate. Second, the objective of legislative oversight may be to guard against unsympathetic or perhaps merely over-zealous attitudes among officials which produce harsh or callous administration. Third, the ideal of legislative oversight has assumed the the ideal of non-special minds of legislators, brought to bear upon the administrative routines, may challenge the means in terms of broad and realistic ends. It may freshen inventiveness as to the means themselves; at least it may rebuke stupidity. Fourth, the objective of legislative oversight may be to see that there is compliance with the legislative intent as embodied in law.[25]

The amount and quality of administrative review has been a subject of concern to those who would reform the legislature. The report of the Joint Committee on the Organization of Congress in 1945 noted that "Congress has long lacked adequate facilities for the continuous inspection and review of administrative performance." It called on the newly reorganized standing committees, "armed with the power of subpoena and staffed with qualified specialists," to give continuous review to the activities of the agencies administering laws originally reported by them.[26] The resulting Legislative Reorganization Act, as characterized by John Saloma, "organized, directed and staffed Congress for expansion of its control and investigative functions."[27]

Twenty-one years later, the second Joint Committee on the Organization of Congress suggested that the 1946 act had failed

25. Arthur W. Macmahon, "Congressional Oversight of Administration: The Power of the Purse," *Political Science Quarterly* (June 1943): 162–63.
26. Joint Committee on the Organization of Congress, *Organization of Congress*, Senate Report 1011, pursuant to H. Con. Res. 18, 79th Cong., 2nd sess., 1946, p. 6.
27. John S. Saloma III, *Congress and the New Politics* (Boston: Little, Brown & Co., 1969), p. 137.

to achieve its goal. This time the committee stressed specific means of implementation—the authorization of a professional staff member for each committee whose sole duty would be to carry on administrative review; the suggestion that committees hold hearings on agency reports; and the requirement of an annual committee report, including an evaluation of the programs under its jurisdiction.[28]

Evidently, Congress has not been consistently interested in this supervisory function. Three recent articles, attempting to discover why congressional interest has been spotty and incomplete, have reached similar conclusions. Seymour Scher, in a study of congressional supervision of regulatory agencies, found legislative review "a time expensive, low priority concern except when there was likely to be something 'big' in it."[29] Something big, he suggested, might be an attempt to initiate a broad change in policy, to respond to strongly expressed constituent or group interests, to block a president who is challenging traditional congressional primacy, or to embarrass an administration of the opposite party. Ira Sharkansky, in a study of the relations between a House Appropriations subcommittee and the agencies with which it is charged, found that supervision tended to be annual and not continuous, and that scarce subcommittee time tended to be given "to the agencies that spend the most money, whose requests have increased the most rapidly and whose behavior towards the subcommittee has deviated most frequently from subcommittee desires."[30] John F. Bibby, in a study of the oversight activities of the Senate Banking and Currency Committee, found that they varied in relation to the chairman's interest, concept of his role, and willingness to grant subcommittees fiscal and staff autonomy; the type of membership the committee has and whether it has available alternate outlets (such as the Joint Eco-

28. Joint Committee on the Organization of Congress, Senate Report 1414, 1966, pp. 23–24.
29. Seymour Scher, "Conditions for Legislative Control," *Journal of Politics* (Aug. 1963): 532.
30. Ira Sharkansky, "An Appropriations Subcommittee and Its Client Agencies," *American Political Science Review* (Sept. 1965): 628.

nomic Committee for members of Banking and Currency); and the size, specialization, and professionalism of the staff.[31] The generalization made by Senator John J. Sparkman during the 1965 hearings on the reorganization of Congress explains a good deal. "I wonder," he said, "if perhaps some of the laxity in providing oversight within the legislative committees may be due to the fact that it is that non-glamorous, nose-to-the-grindstone work"[32]

Committees have a wide variety of relation with executive agencies. The most important formal control is that of legislative authorization and appropriation. Other formal controls include the audit, which gives Congress a review of expenditures; the legislative veto, which gives an opportunity for detailed review of certain proposed administrative actions before they take place; and the investigation, which allows broad review of administrative programs. With such an array of formal checks, it is not surprising that administrators pay close attention to the informal directions that are given by means of committee hearings and reports, floor debates, and conversation with members of Congress.

Committee control of this sort is far from monolithic, however. Since there are few meaningful joint committees, most agencies report to committees in each of the houses of Congress. As Arthur Maass has pointed out, if an administrator "doesn't like what is in the House report [he] tries to get something different put into the Senate report, and then he has some freedom as between the two."[33] An agency is also responsible to the president, whose support will allow further freedom from committee domination.

Three specific types of legislative supervision have been used with greater frequency in the last decade as a means of increasing the control of Congress and its committees over the administration. They are the legislative veto, annual authorization legislation, and nonstatutory guidance by Appropriations committees.

31. John F. Bibby, "Committee Characteristics and Legislative Oversight of Administration," *Midwest Journal of Political Science* (Feb. 1966): 78–98.
32. Joint Committee on the Organization of Congress, Hearings, *The Organization of Congress*, pursuant to S. Con. Res. 2, 89th Cong., 1st sess., 1965, p. 782.
33. Ibid., p. 951.

The legislative veto, which was first used as a means of reviewing administrative reorganization proposals of the president, has been extended to give individual committees, and even individual committee chairmen, a veto power over administrative action. The earliest clear example of such committee power was a 1944 measure requiring the Navy Department to receive the approval of the two naval affairs committees when disposing of or acquiring real estate for military installations. The most extreme form of committee power found by Joseph P. Harris, in his study of congressional control of the administration, occurred in the Supplementary Appropriation Act for fiscal 1953, which required that revision of housing allowance regulations set by the Bureau of the Budget be approved by the chairman of the House Appropriations Committee.[34]

The most definitive list of permanent statutes that involve committee veto provisions was prepared by the Legislative Reference Service for the 1967 hearings of the Senate subcommittee on separation of powers.[35] Nineteen statutes are listed. They vary considerably in minor details. The time involved may not be specified at all or it may be as long as six months, though it is most frequently set at thirty days. About half the statutes do not specify that committees must take specific action but merely state that proposed administrative undertakings must lie before them for a period of time. In all cases, the statutes designate either committees or party leaders to act for the Congress, as may be seen from table 11:2.

There is wide variety in the subject matter of the nineteen statutes. Approximately half are concerned with public works and redevelopment activities so important in congressional constituencies: flood control, irrigation, reclamation, and public building projects. The remainder are concerned with broader policies where, clearly, certain groups in Congress wanted to keep a rein

34. Joseph P. Harris, *Congressional Control of Administration* (Washington, D.C.: The Brookings Institution, 1964), chap. 8.
35. Norman J. Small, "The Committee Veto," in Hearings, *Separation of Powers*, pp. 277–81.

TABLE 11:2

*The Committee Veto in Permanent Statutes**

Agencies Granted Veto Power	Number of Statutes Granting Veto Power
Armed Services committees	6
Public Works committees	3
Agriculture committees	2
Interior committees	2
Joint Committee on Atomic Energy	1
Joint Committee on Internal Revenue Taxation	1
Joint Committee on Printing	1
Senate Foreign Relations Committee	1
Speaker of the House	2
President of the Senate	1

* Based on the list of statutes prepared by the Legislative Reference Service in 1967 and printed in Hearings, *Separation of Powers*, pp. 277–81. The veto power over flood control projects is divided between two committees. The Public Works committees have the veto over flood control projects involving over 4,000 acres; the Agriculture committees over those involving less than 4,000 acres. The Atomic Energy Act and its amendments have given the Joint Committee on Atomic Energy veto power in six different instances.

on administrative action. In the area of domestic policies, these included such diversified activities as the cutting of federal grants to state and local agencies that discriminate on the basis of race, the disposal of nuclear materials by the Atomic Energy Commission, and the granting of income tax refunds of over $100,000 by the Internal Revenue Service. In the foreign policy area, they included cultural exchange programs and international agreements on atomic energy.

The veto has been widely criticized. It has been attacked by a number of presidents. In 1965 Lyndon Johnson ordered administrators responsible for carrying out rivers and harbors, flood prevention, reclamation, and public buildings legislation to halt all programs that had veto provisions attached. A subcommittee on separation of powers of the Senate Judiciary Committee, under the chairmanship of Sam J. Ervin Jr. of North Carolina, held inconclusive hearings on the subject in the same year that tended to support the use of the veto. In 1969 President Richard Nixon reversed the Johnson policy and reinstituted the halted programs. As is often the case in disputes between the two branches, little change has taken place as a result of these actions, but a full-scale showdown has been avoided.

Criticisms center on the constitutionality and the wisdom of the veto. The constitutional argument turns on the meaning of separation of powers. The difficulty of drawing a precise line between legislative and executive functions makes it doubtful that a definitive answer can be given.[36]

The wisdom of the veto was discussed by Arthur Maass in his testimony before the Joint Committee on the Organization of Congress. He spoke of the legislative process as the laying down of basic objectives and standards that are to govern, and of the administrative process as the refining of these into "performance criteria" and carrying them out. He praised the use of the veto in the Rubber Producing Facilities Act of 1953, for standards could not be clearly defined. On the one hand, Congress wanted the government to get its money's worth from the sale, while on the other, it did not want disposal to promote monopoly in the rubber industry. He was critical of the Water Resources Research Act of 1964, which required the approval by the Interior committees of every research contract that the Department of the Interior entered into, suggesting that a better way for Congress to oversee the program would be an annual hearing at which the year's activities were reviewed. Aside from the wisdom of going into so much administrative detail, Maass raised the question of whether it is wise for Congress to delegate so much power to its individual committees. He suggested that such checks as the original form of the legislative veto or more frequent legislative authorization were preferable, for they give the full Congress greater control.[37]

Annual authorization, in addition to annual appropriation, has

36. See Joseph Cooper and Ann Cooper, "The Legislative Veto and the Constitution," *George Washington Law Review* (March 1962): 467–516.
37. Joint Committee on the Organization of Congress, Hearings, 1965, pp. 945–48.

been used increasingly as a means of giving Congress added control over the executive branch. Richard Neustadt found that:

> More than a quarter of the federal budget now is subject every year not only to annual appropriations but to prior legislation authorizing a continuation of existing agencies and programs. Among these are the Agency for International Development with foreign aid, the National Aeronautics and Space Administration with space exploration, and the new Office of Economic Opportunity with its poverty program.[38]

Arguments against frequent authorization stress the extra time required of administrators who have to appear before twice as many committees, the loss of administrative efficiency, and the difficulty of long-term planning. Against these, arguments can be made as to the educational value for the entire Congress, as well as the public, when authorization debates take place. Recent meaningful congressional discussion of our military systems, for example, has taken place during the authorization and not the appropriation stage. Maass has suggested that the administrative agency may gain in the process, for functional committees are often more sympathetic with the needs of "their agencies" than are the appropriations committees. He proposes, by way of illustration, that "new programs may be authorized for one year twice in succession, and that thereafter authorization should be for at least three years, except where the program is expected to terminate before that time."[39]

Nonstatutory guidance by appropriations committees has increased greatly of late. Maass noted that, "Appropriations Committee reports are filled with words of guidance, advice, requests, warning, direction, so that a departmental budget officer may be as much or more concerned with the committee report than he is with the appropriations statute. Yet the report is extralegal.

38. David B. Truman, ed., *The Congress and America's Future* (Englewood Cliffs, N.J.: Prentice-Hall, 1965), p. 105.
39. Joint Committee on the Organization of Congress, Hearings, 1965, p. 944.

Neither house of Congress votes on it. The President neither signs it nor vetoes it."[40] He suggested that the reasons for this were the increase in performance type budgeting, which has fewer appropriations accounts on which to fix statutory limitations, and House rules that limit legislation in an appropriations measure. This sort of guidance does allow greater flexibility than statutory control. It has disadvantages as well, which are somewhat similar to those of the committee veto. It gives a committee wide latitude without much chance for congressional review. It also means that there can be serious encroachment by appropriations committees into the jurisdiction of the regular legislative committees.

Committee-agency relations do not receive much praise from commentators on Congress. The committee often cannot make up its mind as to whether its role is that of generalist or nit-picker. It is not organized to administer but rather to seek legislative agreement. Therefore, it is not fitted for extensive participation in the affairs of the executive branch. What it does is limited by the time and interests of its members. The whole legislature often fails to keep a check over the actions of its constituent committees and committee chairmen.

Legislative supervision does have its fruitful side, however. As one student of Congress has said, "it does not outlaw legislative-executive agreement so much as it increases the opportunities for interim disagreement and for the slow exploration of alternatives by a diverse society as it seeks consensus."[41] And it has its inevitability. John Saloma has said that "the American solution of separated institutions sharing powers guranteed the development of an open, politicized, executive bureaucracy subject to the competing directives of presidential and congressional executives."[42]

40. Ibid., p. 950. See also Michael Kirst, *Government Without Passing Laws* (Chapel Hill: University of North Carolina Press, 1969).

41. J. Leiper Freeman, *The Political Process: Executive Bureau–Legislative Committee Relations* (New York: Random House, 1965), p. 15.

42. Saloma, *Congress and the New Politics*, p. 131.

IV
Conclusion

12.

Reform of the Committee System

THE PREVIOUS chapters gave a picture of decision-making in the American Congress. Competition among political organizations and government institutions plays an extremely important role. Political parties, both parliamentary and national, are relatively weak participants in the struggle. Bipartisan, specialized standing committees, often acting as surrogates for the whole Congress, are strong—strong enough that they can on occasion stand as equals of the president. In making their decisions, they are responsive to pressures brought to bear on them by constituents, interest groups, the president, administrative agencies, and political parties. In spite of this fact, they do have some room in the process for the exercise of independent, rational judgment arrived at by bipartisan consensus.

In other words, the American Congress as we know it most resembles the presidential-pluralist model as discussed in the preface of this book, though it has some elements of the constitutional balance model as well. It is my belief that Congress will continue to resemble these two models that fall in the middle of the spectrum, and not move very far towards either of the more extreme models —the congressional supremacy model with its strong parliamentary parties, or the presidential-responsible party model with its strong national parties. My reasoning is that there are advantages to the system as it exists for a country such as ours and that there are serious obstacles to drastic change.

Obstacles to change are both constitutional and political. A model in which Congress is supreme seems least likely of achievement. The constitutional grants of power to the executive are too clearly drawn and too obviously reinforced by the facts of modern life to give any real hope to those who would subordinate the president. The fact that the fate of a member of Congress is ultimately determined by a bipartisan coalition of voters in his home district and not by his legislative party leaders leaves little room to believe that strengthened parliamentary parties could be the vehicle for such a reform.

Presidential supremacy has had far more appeal, to political scientists at least, ever since Woodrow Wilson wrote *Congressional Government* in 1885. Yet, to me, the obstacles are almost as formidable.

The constitutional provision of separation of powers guarantees a legislature that no president can completely tame. The president has gained great initiative in the domestic and foreign crises of the twentieth century, but resulting claims of the death of Congress have been greatly exaggerated. Because of its constitutional autonomy, Congress has great power to modify or even scrap presidential initiatives, and also to oversee the administration of its adopted policies. It is strengthened further by the constitutional provision of federalism that protects units of government and party systems that are more supportive of state-based members of Congress than of the nation-based president.

Further, our heterogeneous and widespread population has not been willing to put its trust in one controlling majority party. The reasons are not hard to find. The major political parties have not been able to present two sets of coherent and differing policies to Americans and to ask for a clear majority decision as to the direction the country should take. The Civil War, the Great Depression, and the Second World War, in particular, have left deep fault lines that do not coincide with the divisions between the two parties. More recently, the Vietnam war and the urban crisis have muddied party waters further. For the Democrats, the truly divisive issue is civil rights. Economic and foreign policy matters divide both Democrats and Republicans. When Senator Barry Goldwater attempted to unite economic conservatives, nationalists, and segregationists in one party in the 1964 presidential campaign, the people answered with a resounding "no!" In 1968 Americans hedged their party bets, as they had in 1956, by electing a Republican president and a Democratic Congress.

The advantages of the Congress as we know it and its committee system are that it developed quite naturally from American politics, that it brings differing authoritative views to bear on policy questions, and that it encourages government moderation.

It was natural that a widespread, heterogeneous country should have hit upon a system of government that never puts all its eggs in one basket. Congress made a basic decision early in its history when it established permanent, bipartisan, specialized committees and depended upon them as more important sources of information than either executive agencies or party institutions. The fact that the American legislature has remained strong and uniquely dependent upon its committees over a century and a half later is fair evidence that the American people have supported this decision. Congress, in the words of Ralph Huitt, "resembles the social system it serves."[1]

There is something to be said for allowing subject-matter specialists to play a major role in the maturing process through which legislative proposals pass. Douglass Cater notes that "nothing guarantees that the President has sufficiently considered each item in the vast portfolio that he transmits to Capitol Hill."[2] Dean Acheson makes a more positive case for legislative-executive collaboration:

> What then are the qualities in men and the posture of circumstances which make for this creative process, when policy is moved forward to a new phase? On the committee's side what is needed is a chairman or senior minority member who is widely respected and trusted in his own party. Such a man usually stands well with the opposition also. He must

1. Ralph K. Huitt, "Congressional Organization in the Field of Money and Credit," Commission on Money and Credit, *Fiscal and Debt Management Practices* (Englewood Cliffs, N.J.: Prentice-Hall, 1963), p. 494.
2. Douglass Cater, *Power in Washington* (New York: Random House, 1964), p. 172.

be able to think vigorously about new problems, though he need not have an original cast of mind. His great function is to bring suggestions within the realm of the possible, to use method as a means of moulding a proposal to make it politically feasible. He will, of course, be a politician. He will protect the interests of his party, and perhaps of himself, so that what he becomes convinced is in the national interest is not done so as to injure his party or aggrandize his opponent. But he will not be tricky. What he requires as a condition of support will be frankly stated. He will keep in touch with his colleagues, particularly his own party colleagues, and have a pretty sound idea that what he agrees to back will have the needed support when the time for voting comes.

On the executive side what is needed is a man who can speak for the administration because he knows it and is trusted by it. He, too, must keep in touch, be frank and not tricky, and must pursue the main objective without being deflected by the nonessential. These two men must have confidence in one another.[3]

Acheson cites as an example the collaboration between Senator Arthur Vandenberg and Under Secretary of State Robert Lovett in bringing about "what neither could have produced separately," the Vandenberg Resolution, which led to the North Atlantic Treaty.

The situation is not as unique as the critics of Congress would make it seem. Granted, members rise on committees on the basis of longevity and weak political competition in the home constituency. (Even this factor brings a freedom from interest group and party pressures that may enable them to take a view of political questions that fits in with the classical democratic view of rational decision-making.) Those who have won appointment to the more important House and Senate committees have had to dem-

3. Dean Acheson, *A Citizen Looks at Congress* (New York: Harper and Bros., 1957), pp. 72-73.

onstrate certain qualities that are highly regarded in most areas of American life—a willingness to work hard, to master one's specialties, and to show respect both for one's fellow workers and to the institution to which one belongs. During the preparation of this book the author has, time and again, been impressed by the combination of subject-matter knowledge and political wisdom demonstrated by most of the senior members of congressional committees. A move to deny these people an important role in the policy-making process, placing full responsibility in the executive branch or in a policy committee of the majority party, would serve to decrease our political vitality and to lessen popular acceptance of governmental decisions.

Further, there is something to be said for allowing sectional and subject-matter congressmen to play an important role in our relatively low boiling point, increasingly complex, continental democracy. In a speech in Atlanta in which President Lyndon B. Johnson tackled one of the nation's most divisive problems, civil rights, and asked help in healing "the last fading scars of old battles," he implied that genuine sectional differences could not be completely wiped out. "Of course," he said, "I do not want to go as far as the Georgia politician who shouted from the stump in the heat of debate, 'My fellow citizens, I know no North, I know no South, I know no East, I know no West.' A barefooted, frecklefaced boy shouted out from the audience, saying, 'Well, you better go back and study some geography!' "[4]

An objective reading of the annual summaries of congressional action shows that Congress has been responsive to the strongly expressed demands of the American people. At the same time, it has rarely taken action to oppose an intensely held minority position without attempting to come up with a compromise. It seems wise in a country of continuing strongly held sectional and ideological differences of opinion to move "as far as possible," in the words of Walter Lippmann, "by consensus rather than by paper-thin majorities."[5]

4. *Congressional Quarterly Weekly Report*, May 15, 1964, p. 980.
5. *Newsweek*, January 20, 1964, p. 18.

The American governmental system has been far from static, however, and there is no reason to believe that the committee system as we know it is immutable. Indeed, during the eleven Congresses under consideration in this volume a number of changes have already been made.

In the process, Congress, with the support of its party leaders and its more partisan members, took some small steps in the direction of the two stronger party models. The clearest step in the direction of the presidential-responsible party model was the development of new precedents for denying committee seniority to congressmen who supported a president of the opposite party. Other changes tended to strengthen the congressional party system without necessarily tying it more closely with the national parties. During the period, legislative policy committees were created, though they did not come to play a particularly important role in decision-making. Both Speaker Sam Rayburn and Majority Leader Johnson played unusually active roles in making initial committee assignments and transfers, and they even managed to talk some members out of committee chairmanships, though not so much because they were out of line with their party as that they were thought to be inefficient chairmen. On some of the more partisan committees, the addition of majority and minority professional staff helped strengthen party positions. A few House committees adopted rules that strengthened the position of the majority party membership. The 21-Day Rule, in its 89th Congress reincarnation, strengthened, rather than weakened, the powers of the Speaker. And the House Committee on Rules was somewhat tenuously made more responsive to the wishes of the majority leadership.

It is relevant to note that while the Joint Committee on the Organization of Congress in 1945 proposed a strengthening of party machinery, it made little headway on this front. Its greatest and most successful thrust was in the direction of the constitutional balance model, by seeking to give Congress the tools to meet the president on more equal terms and to improve the rationality of its decision-making processes. The 1965 Joint Committee on the Organization of Congress paid no attention whatsoever to the strengthening of party institutions; its concern was with continued improvement of the decision-making processes. In both instances, the Senate accepted the proposed reforms with relatively few changes. The House dragged its feet on both, a development that is not surprising when one considers the difference in size of the two houses. The Senate can operate more closely to the more in-dividualistic and rational constitutional balance model. House leaders, at least, believe that the larger chamber cannot afford to lessen leadership powers to the degree called for by some of the Joint Committees' proposals.

Congress has taken somewhat larger steps in the direction of constitutional balance than of Presidential-party responsibility. Committee jurisdictions were clearly defined, thus cutting out much of the leadership's freedom in assigning measures. Within many committees, subcommittee jurisdictions were almost as clearly drawn, thus limiting a chairman's freedom and encour-aging specialization. On such committees as House Agriculture, small attempts were made at balance by adding members from consuming, urban districts. Both houses adopted rules granting protections to minority party members and increasing the powers of bipartisan committee majorities; some individual committees developed these even further. In general, committee democracy increased, as the old committee dynasts died off and a new type of more aggressive member was elected. Some committees ex-perimented with improved information-gathering techniques, such as round-table discussions by experts. Professional staff members, almost all of whom have been added since 1946, greatly increased the possibility of rational decision-making. Especially in the Sen-ate, some new tools were developed to allow the leadership (gen-erally bipartisan), with the support of a bipartisan majority of the members, to pry measures from committee pigeonholes. Such new techniques as the legislative veto, annual authorizations, and non-statutory guidance by Appropriations committees allowed more sophisticated control of the executive branch.

If Congress were to move farther in the direction of the constitutional balance model, it would adopt much of the following agenda.[6] Congress should be organized so that "inconvenient facts" can be brought out and thoughtful deliberation encouraged. A committee with too narrow a jurisdiction or a subcommittee with too great autonomy may overlook important technical and/or political information. While committees cannot be microcosms of the full house, attempts should be made in the assignment process to place some devil's advocates on the most highly specialized committees and to get an ideological diversity on the most important committees. In making initial assignments, careful attention should be paid to a member's experience and ability. Specialization, made possible by the operation of the seniority system, should be encouraged, though it should be possible to allow some leeway in the choice of chairmen so as to get the benefits of special talents when they outweigh those of seniority. Professional staff members should be knowledgeable in their fields and available to all committee members. (On committees where ideological splits are most clear, minority staff members may be advisable to encourage the presentation of opposing points of view.)

Committee and chamber procedure should seek to allow free expression of minority views without allowing the minority to obstruct action by the majority. Hearings should be carefully prepared, fairly run, and open to the expression of differing points of view. They should result in a meaningful, published record. There should be adequate opportunity in mark-up sessions for informal discussion and detailed amendment. If a subcommittee has been handling a measure, the full committee should be free to make changes it finds necessary, while showing deference to the more specialized knowledge of the smaller body. The committee report should be thorough and reasoned. A majority of the mem-

6. These two paragraphs draw heavily on John S. Saloma III, *Congress and the New Politics* (Boston: Little, Brown & Co., 1969), pp. 112–17; as well as two books to which Saloma noted his indebtedness: Donald G. Morgan, *Congress and the Constitution: A Study of Responsibility* (Cambridge: Harvard University Press, 1966), pp. 344–60; and Ernest S. Griffith, *Congress: Its Contemporary Role*, 3rd ed. (New York: New York University Press, 1961), pp. 33–37.

bership of the parent chamber should be able to act on any measure it desires to consider (even if it is opposed by the party leadership, a standing committee or a minority), using a device such as the filibuster. Floor debate should be full and informative. The right of free amendment should be limited only on the most complex measures that have already received careful consideration by broad-based committees. A conference committee should seek to reach agreement as close to the desires of the majorities of the two houses as possible, and it should give a thorough explanation of its compromise to both houses. Finally, Congress, working largely through its committees, should give sustained and general supervision to the administration of its policies.

This is still a heterogeneous country, with intensely held, differing points of view, and it is hard to imagine that Congress will not linger on the pluralist side, barring a revolution. There is reason to believe, however, that a growing number of Americans —the educated, affluent, politically independent, managerial middle class—and the people they are electing in increasing numbers to Congress, approve of the greater emphasis on rational decision-making of the constitutional balance model. This type of reform seems to me, at least, to be more possible than any other—and, in an increasingly complex world, it seems a worthy goal as well.

Index

Index